FEUDS, FOR⅃
REBELLIONS

FEUDS, FORAYS AND REBELLIONS

History of the Highland Clans 1475–1625

John L. Roberts

EDINBURGH
University Press

© John L. Roberts, 1999

Transferred to Digital Print 2009

Edinburgh University Press
22 George Square, Edinburgh

Typeset in Bulmer
by Pioneer Associates, Perthshire, and
Printed and bound in Great Britain by
CPI Antony Rowe, Chippenham and Eastbourne

A CIP record for this book is available from the
British Library

ISBN 9780748662449

The right of John L. Roberts to be identified as
author of this work has been asserted in accordance
with the Copyright, Designs and Patents Act 1988.

CONTENTS

NOTES AND ACKNOWLEDGEMENTS

For the sake of consistency, I have adopted the convention of spelling all the Mac names as MacDonald, rather than Macdonald. Variants of other names such as MacDonnell, MacKintosh and MacLaine are likewise given as MacDonald, MacIntosh and MacLean.

I am grateful to Nicholas Maclean-Bristol for his help in sorting out the genealogical complexities of the MacLeans of Duart, and to Professor G. W. S. Barrow for reading an earlier version of the typescript. As always, I owe a debt of gratitude to my wife Jessica and daughter Rachel, who were unstinting in their encouragement and support.

FOREWORD

Known to Gaeldom as *Linn nan Creach*, or the Age of Feuds and Forays, the years stretching between the forfeiture of the Lordship of the Isles in 1493 and the death of King James VI of Scotland in 1625 were a turbulent period in Highland history. It is often depicted as sheer anarchy, amounting to little more than a 'dark and dismal period of strife and plunder, hatred and revenge'. The destruction of the Lordship meant the Highland chieftains lost their dependence upon the MacDonalds, Lords of the Isles, whose hereditary right to the 'Headship of the Gael' they had implicitly recognised. Instead, they often came to hold their estates as tenants of the Crown, and later under the feudal superiority of such great magnates as the Gordons, Earls of Huntly, and the Campbells, Earls of Argyll.

Moreover, the monarchy in Scotland was repeatedly weakened throughout the fifteenth and sixteenth centuries by recurrent periods of minority rule. Indeed, until James VI started upon his personal reign in 1587, Scotland was governed more by regents than the Stewart kings themselves. They often succeeded to the throne when quite young, long before they came of age. The only exception was James IV, who made a determined attempt to deal with the vacuum in political power and influence that existed after the forfeiture of the Lordship of the Isles in 1493, despite his bewildering changes of policy. After his death at the Battle of Flodden in 1513, little attempt was made by the Crown to control the political turmoil endemic to the Highlands and the Western Isles for much of the sixteenth century. Only after coming of age did the Stewart monarchs start to address the Highland problem. However, they were only able to act effectively against such disorder once they had asserted their own authority in the Lowlands of Scotland, which they often struggled to achieve. Effective action was only taken by James V during the last few years of his personal reign, before his premature death in 1542, and subsequently during the final years in the minority of Mary Stuart, Queen of Scots, dominated as it was by the Dowager Queen Mary of Guise, her strong-minded mother. Otherwise, the intervening periods of minority rule often triggered major disturbances in the Highlands and the Western Isles.

Many of the Highland feuds which arose during these years resulted from conflicting claims over land. Powerful claimants, backed by the paper rights of feudal charters, battled to gain possession of territory granted to them by the Crown, or which they had obtained by marriage with the heiresses of now-extinct families. Equally, other Highland clans, especially in the more remote districts, sought to keep possession of their ancestral lands by sheer force of arms, whenever they lacked charters giving them a legal right of occupation. Often they had lost any rights that they had once possessed, whenever their own rebellious conduct had caused the Crown to forfeit their lands.

Hardly any of these territorial feuds arose from what might be called sheer aggrandisement. There was nearly always a legal pretext to justify the action of one protagonist against another, or else extenuating circumstances, most often rooted in their past possession of the land under dispute. Only the internecine struggles for leadership within individual clans lacked any such justification. They arose largely from the peculiar customs of secular marriage then prevalent within Celtic society, which allowed for polygamy, concubinage and divorce outside the canon law of the Catholic Church. The ancient law tracts of Celtic Ireland recognised the legal rights of the *cetmuinter*, or a man's chief or first wife, but he could also take other wives of lesser status, known in later texts as *adaltrach*, literally 'adulteress', as well as concubines.

Later, it seems that chiefs would exchange their daughters for a year and a day in what became known erroneously as hand-fasting. The repudiation of such temporary liaisons often caused hostility between the two families, leading on occasion to actual feuds. There can be little doubt that Highland chiefs married one partner after another, or lived with them in concubinage, so that they could beget a great many sons, thus proving their virility and fitness to lead their clan. Yet the very existence of such an extended family was often a source of discord, causing fratricidal quarrels to break out within clans as natural brothers struggled with one another for supremacy.

It was also common in such a kin-based society for marriages to occur well within the seven degrees of consanguinity prohibited by the Catholic Church. Consequently, dispensations were often sought to legitimise such unions, long after the event, so allowing the eldest son of such a union to be recognised as the heir of his father under feudal law. Yet within the context of Gaelic society, such unions were always regarded as valid, and their offspring as legitimate, whether or not they were recognised by the Church. Equally, as divorce was forbidden under canon law, annulments were often sought to bring such marriages to an end, usually on the grounds they had taken place within the forbidden degrees of consanguinity.

It is difficult to know to what extent the feudal principle of primogeniture had replaced the Celtic system of kin-based succession in the Highlands and Western Isles by the late Middle Ages, whereby the great-grandsons of a common ancestor had an equal right of inheritance. Often, there is nothing in the historical record to tell us which son succeeded his father, so we really do not know if he was the eldest or just the fittest. Equally, it is not even certain if he was elected to such a position at the head of his kindred by his peers, and then ruled with the advice of a council of his elders, as asserted by George Buchanan around 1567. Only for the Council of the Isles under the Lordship is there any detailed information, and then only from traditional accounts, on how it functioned. Often, all we know from the historical record is that sons succeeded their fathers when they received a charter to their lands, apparently to the exclusion of all their other brothers and their cousins, their father's nephews.

Indeed, the feudal practice of granting out charters was well-established in the Highlands and the Western Isles by the mid-fourteenth century at the very latest, when several grants of land were made by David II. Such grants gave the recipients greater security of tenure. and often confirmed their eldest sons as their rightful heirs according to the feudal principle of primogeniture. Moreover, it seems likely that the Crown only acknowledged the existence of canonical marriages in making such charters, thus explaining the necessity for seeking dispensations from the Church in order to legitimise their sons and heirs. The Crown thus endorsed the right of the eldest son of such a marriage to succeed his father at the expense of all his other brothers and half-brothers, born of other unions not recognised by the Church. Often, however, the eldest son would grant land to his rivals, so reinforcing the bonds between them in what was still a kin-based society.

Yet the common practice of appointing Tutors to administer the family's affairs whenever the eldest son succeeded his father while still a child surely suggests that the feudal principle of primogeniture was paramount. Most commonly, the young heir's uncle was designated as his Tutor, acting in this capacity as his father's younger brother. But equally, the Tutor was heir-presumptive to his elder brother should his young charge not survive to manhood. Yet the kin-based system of inheritance once prevalent in Gaelic society would have given him a far better claim to succeed his elder brother while his own nephew still remained a minor. Apparently, such an archaic system did not take precedence over the feudal principle of primogeniture, since otherwise there would be no need to appoint a Tutor in the first place to administer the family's affairs until a young heir came of age.

Occasionally, eldest sons did not succeed their fathers if they were judged quite unfit to act as the chiefs of their clan. Under these circumstances, their position might well be challenged by other claimants, hoping to succeed through the kin-based system of Celtic inheritance. Where such internecine dissension broke out within clans, it was usually fomented by the rightful heir's half-brothers, born of non-canonical unions of their common-law father. Doubtless, the protagonists justified their actions according to the tenets of Gaelic society, but nevertheless such feuds were often the prelude to the destruction of their entire family, as happened with the MacLeods of Lewis in the late-sixteenth century.

The downfall of Clan Donald in 1493 occurred at a time when Donald Dubh, grandson of the last Lord of the Isles and the only rightful heir to the Lordship of the Isles, was still only a child, held captive by his mother's family, the Campbells, Earls of Argyll. By then, the cadet branches of Clan Donald, founded by the younger sons of the MacDonalds, Lords of the Isles, were eight in number, including the all-powerful MacDonalds of Dunivaig and the Glens. Nearly all of them came forward as the leaders of Clan Donald over the next fifty years, repeatedly attempting to restore the Lordship of the Isles, usually acting in their own name. Often lending their support by strength of arms to these rebellions against the Crown were the erstwhile vassals of Clan Donald, among whom the MacLeods of Lewis, the MacLeans of Duart and their cadets of Lochbuie, Coll and Ardgour, as well as the Camerons of Locheil, were the most loyal. Only the MacLeods of Harris and Dunvegan consistently opposed the pretensions of Clan Donald to regain its former glory under the Lordship of the Isles, driven by feuds with the MacDonalds of Sleat over the lands of Trotternish, and with the MacDonalds of Clan Ranald over lands in North Uist. But even they joined the great confederacy of Clan Donald which culminated in the Council of the Isles, held by Donald Dubh in 1545.

Only after the death of Donald Dubh in 1545 from a sudden fever, caught in Ireland while serving Henry VIII of England, did Clan Donald start to disintegrate into its different septs. Holding vast estates in the Glens of Antrim as well as their lands in Scotland, the MacDonalds of Dunivaig and the Glens were drawn into the struggles of the native Earls of Ulster against the English Crown, even if their own self-interest often dictated confusing shifts in their allegiance. But only when a bitter feud erupted with the MacLeans of Duart over the Rhinns of Islay during the last two decades of the sixteenth century did the MacDonalds of Dunivaig and the Glens start on the downward path of internecine conflict which eventually led to their destruction, as the Campbells, Earls of Argyll, rose to supremacy in their place.

Elsewhere, the MacKenzies of Kintail profited greatly from the downfall of

Clan Donald once they were granted charters to lands they had previously held under the earldom of Ross. Acting as the loyal servants of the Crown, they consistently pursued a policy of territorial aggrandisement. It eventually brought them lands in Wester Ross, once held by the MacDonalds of Lochalsh, before they passed by marriage to the MacDonalds of Glengarry, as well as the island of Lewis, which they purchased from the Fife Adventurers after they had failed in its plantation. Created the Earls of Seaforth in 1623, they thus displaced the MacLeods of Lewis, another Highland clan that destroyed itself by its own internecine conflicts, leaving only the MacLeods of Harris and Dunvegan in possession of their ancestral lands. Farther north, the history of Caithness and Sutherland during the sixteenth century was dominated by the three-sided struggle between the MacKays of Strathnaver, the Sinclairs, Earls of Caithness, and the Gordons, Earls of Sutherland, who eventually triumphed over their other two protagonists.

The way forward to power and influence during these years of conflict and turmoil in the Highlands and Western Isles was always through service to the Crown. Among the Highland families to benefit from such service were the MacKenzies of Kintail, afterwards created Earls of Seaforth, and the Gordons, Earls of Sutherland. However, among the greatest beneficiaries were the Gordons, Earls of Huntly, and the Campbells, Earls of Argyll. Already territorial magnates in their own right, the Gordons rose to pre-eminence as 'Cocks o'the North' during the sixteenth century, acting as King's Lieutenants within their own sphere of influence in the north-east of Scotland. Even so, after the Scottish reformation of 1560, they adhered to the Catholic faith and slowly their power and influence in the north waned in favour of the Gordons, Earls of Sutherland, descended from a younger son of the second Earl of Huntly.

But even the Gordons were eclipsed in power and influence by the Campbells, Earls of Argyll, along with their cadet families, the Campbells of Glenorchy, afterwards Earls of Breadalbane, and their north-eastern branch, the Campbells of Cawdor. Already appointed as Sheriffs and King's Lieutenants for their lands in Argyll during the late-fourteenth century, the Campbells of Lochawe established themselves as landed proprietors with widespread estates, gained by marriage or royal grant and later by outright purchase, making them among the most wealthy of all the Highland magnates. Then, after their elevation to the peerage as the Earls of Argyll in the mid-fifteenth century, they first acted as Justiciars of Scotland north of the Forth, and then hereditary Masters of the King's Household, before they were appointed Justice-Generals of Scotland. gaining a hereditary office which they held virtually without challenge until 1628.

Even before 1476, when the MacDonalds, Lords of the Isles, lost the earldom of Ross by their treasonable conduct, the Campbells had gained the lordship of Lorn by a complex exchange of lands which had passed by marriage from the Stewarts of Lorn. Suppressing the repeated rebellions of Clan Donald against the Crown gave the Campbells, Earls of Argyll, not only ample opportunities but also rich rewards in serving as King's Lieutenants in Argyll and the Western Isles. Then, after the death of Donald Dubh in 1545 and the ensuing collapse of his rebellion against the Crown, the fourth Earl of Argyll, and more especially his son Archibald, the fifth Earl, attempted by judicious marriages to restore the hegemony of Gaeldom under their leadership, binding together the MacDonalds of Dunivaig and the Glens and the MacLeans of Duart in a close alliance with their own family.

Although strained at times, this alliance lasted for more than forty years, until it was broken by the renewed outbreak of the long-lasting feud between the MacDonalds and the MacLeans over the Rhinns of Islay. Thereafter, as disorder spread in the Western Isles, the Campbells became 'masters of aggressive feudalism' under the leadership of Archibald Campbell, eighth Earl of Argyll, known to history as Gruamach, or Grim-Faced. Profiting from his close connection with the Crown, he pursued with ruthless ferocity the policies of James VI in proscribing the MacGregors, now among the most lawless of Highland clans. Equally it is likely that he adopted the old Campbell tactic of fomenting disorder and rebellion among the western clans so justifying his intervention on behalf of the Crown. Eventually, by exploiting the internecine divisions among the MacDonalds of Dunivaig and the Glens, his machinations caused them to forfeit Kintyre and the island of Islay, which then passed into Campbell hands. A similar fate later befell the MacIains of Ardnamurchan around 1625. By then, the stage was set for the bitter quarrel between the Campbells, Earls of Argyll, and the various septs and erstwhile allies of Clan Donald that so divided Gaeldom in its support of the Stuart kings, which eventually ended with the defeat of the Jacobite army upon Culloden Moor in 1746.

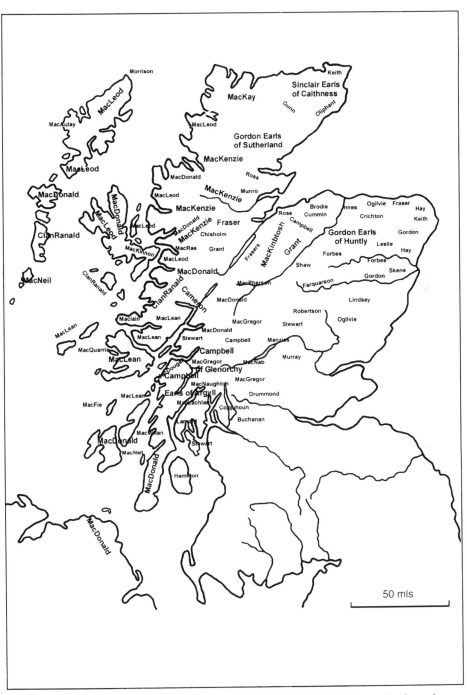

Distribution of the Highland clans and neighbouring families towards the end of the 16th century.

Chapter One

'WYLD, WYKKYD HELAND-MEN'

The manners and customs of the Scots vary with the diversity of their speech. For two languages are spoken among them, the Scottish [Gaelic] and the Teutonic [English or Lowland Scots]; the latter which is the language of those who occupy the seaboard and the plains, while the race of Scottish speech inhabits the Highlands and the outlying islands. The people of the coast are of domestic and civilized habits, trusty, patient, and urbane, decent in their attire, affable and peaceful, devout in Divine worship, yet always ready to resist a wrong at the hands of their enemies. The Highlanders and people of the islands, on the other hand, are a savage and untamed race, rude and independent, given to rapine, ease-loving, clever and quick to learn, comely in person, but unsightly in dress, hostile to the English people and language, and owing to diversity of speech, even to their own nation, and exceedingly cruel.

This well-known and much-quoted passage comes from *Chronicle of the Scottish Nation*. Written in Latin in the early 1380s, its author was John of Fordun. Although little is known of him, he doubtless took his name from Fordoun in Angus, and it seems likely that he was a minor cleric in the diocese of Aberdeen. He lived close to the Highlands, and his comments epitomise the deep rift that he then perceived to exist between the Highlands and the Lowlands of Scotland. Its very existence was echoed by other chroniclers down the centuries, such as John Major who wrote in 1521:

One half of Scotland speaks Irish [Gaelic], and all these as well as the Islanders we reckon to belong to the Wild Scots. In dress, in the manner of their outward life and in good morals, for example, these come far behind the householding Scots [Lowlanders] – yet they are not less, but rather more prompt to fight; and this . . . because born as they are in the mountains, and dwellers in forests, their very nature is more combative . . . One part of the Wild Scots have a wealth of cattle,

1

sheep, and horses, and these, with a thought for the possible loss of their possessions, yield more willing obedience to the courts of law and the king. The other part of these people delight in the chase and a life of indolence; their chiefs eagerly follow bad men if only they may not have the need of labour; taking no pains to earn their own livelihood, they live upon others, and follow their own worthless savage chiefs in all evil courses sooner than they will pursue honest industry. They are full of mutual dissensions, and war rather than peace is their normal condition.

Such a rift may well have arisen once the Scots tongue came to supplant Gaelic as the vernacular language spoken throughout much of the Lowlands of Scotland and especially in the towns and burghs. Gaelic was itself the language of the Scottish kingdom of Alba, established by the Scots of Dalriada under Kenneth macAlpine many centuries earlier, long after they had crossed the North Channel from Ireland to settle in Argyll. However, after it had come to be spoken throughout nearly all of Scotland apart from the very south-east of Lothian, Gaelic began to lose ground to a northern dialect of English during the twelfth century. By 1500, if not rather earlier, Gaelic was spoken only in the upland districts beyond the 'Highland Line', and it had become known derogatively as 'Irish'. The only exception was Galloway and parts of Ayrshire which remained Gaelic-speaking until the sixteenth century. By then, however, English had long replaced aristocratic French and bureau-cratic Latin as the establishment language of the Court, Church, and Parliament, after its use was first sanctioned in 1398. Indeed, even the MacDonalds, Lords of the Isles, began to abandon the use of Latin during the latter years of the fifteenth century, writing their charters instead in English.

Yet it was more the lawless nature of the Highlands and the difficulty of exercising any effective control over the Gaelic-speaking districts beyond the Highland Line which came to epitomise the utter dichotomy then perceived to exist between the Lowlands and the Highlands of Scotland. Indeed, the Highlands eventually came to be regarded almost as a foreign country with quite alien customs and way of life, inhabited by a people with their own sense of identity. Indeed, the bloody feuds which so disturbed the king's peace in the Highlands and the Western Isles during the course of the six-teenth century only reinforced the sense among the Lowland Scots that these wild and remote regions were a 'kingdom within a kingdom'. The antagonism first expressed by the chronicler Fordun towards the end of the fourteenth century slowly deepened into outright hostility over the next two centuries. Nobody came to hold such sentiments with more feeling than James VI, who wrote of his Gaelic-speaking subjects in the *Basilikon Doron*, advising his young son and heir:

As for the Hielands, I shortly comprehend them all in two sorts of people: the one, that dwelleth in our main land that are barbarous for the most part, and yet mixed with some show of civility; the other that dwelleth in the Isles and are all utterly barbarous, without any sort or show of civility. For the first sort, put straitly in execution the laws made already by me against their overlords and the chiefs of their clans, and it will be no difficulty in danton [daunting, subduing or suppressing] them. As for the other sort, think no other of them all than of wolves or wild boars; and therefore follow the course that I have begun, in planting colonies among them of answerable inlands [lowland] subjects, that within short time may reform and civilise the best inclined among them, rooting out or transporting the barbarous or stubborn sort and planting civility in the room.

His harsh opinions were echoed by yet another writer from around the same time:

True it is, that the Islemen are of nature very proud, suspicious, avaricious, full of deceit and evil intentions, each against his neighbour . . . Besides all this, they are so cruel in taking revenge that neither have they regard to person, age, time or cause . . . They [are] generally all so far addicted to their own tyrannical opinions, that, in all respects, they exceed in cruelty the most barbarous peoples that have ever been seen since the beginning of the world.

A Troubled Kingdom

It was only during the fourteenth century that the Highlands and the Western Isles came to be viewed as a wild and inhospitable region inhabited by 'wyld, wykkyd Heland-men', intent upon quarrelling among themselves and prone to raiding the Lowlands of Scotland, where 'all men take their prey'. Such a cultural and indeed racial division within Scotland was not even apparent before the Wars of Scottish Independence, as Professor Barrow has emphasised in discussing *The Highlands in the Lifetime of Robert the Bruce*. Indeed, the contemporary record from the twelfth and thirteenth centuries lacks any evidence for dividing the country into two parts by what later became known as the 'Highland Line'. It is striking that the copious body of written evidence from these two centuries never even mentions the 'Highlands' or the 'Lowlands' by name. Echoing the well-known ballad, Professor Barrow asks: 'Ye Hielans and ye Lawlans, oh whaur hae ye been?' He replies that the plain answer is nowhere, since such a distinction 'simply had not entered the minds of men'. Only after the fourteenth century did such a division, perhaps exaggerated at first by Fordun, become ever more striking.

Such a sense of national unity was largely a legacy of the twelfth and thirteenth centuries, which had seen Scotland established as a feudal kingdom ruled over until 1286 by the descendants of Malcolm Canmore (1057–93). But then the Wars of Scottish Independence intervened against the English and a civil war broke out after Robert the Bruce (1306–29) had seized the throne in 1306. His rule was followed by the broken reign of his son David II (1325–71), only four years of age at his accession, and the outbreak of further hostilities with England. When David II (1329–71) eventually returned in 1357 from long years of captivity in England, he found his kingdom wracked by more than sixty years of conflict, afflicted by natural disaster and suffering from recurrent outbreaks of the plague. Although he ruled with authority, he died suddenly in 1371 at the early age of forty-seven. Childless, he was succeeded by his nephew Robert the High Steward, who thus came to the throne as Robert II (1371–90) at the age of fifty-three.

Robert II and indeed his son Robert III (1390–1406) were both elderly when they first started to rule, while Robert III was already a cripple and later suffered from ill-health brought on by a debilitating disease. Moreover, both had to contend with the machiavellian ambitions of Robert Stewart, Earl of Fife and Menteith and the first Duke of Albany, a younger son of Robert II. He was the most capable and politically astute of all Robert II's children, even if he was devious, cynical and utterly ruthless. Appointed in 1388 as governor of Scotland in place of his elder brother, the future Robert III, Robert Stewart, first Duke of Albany, held this office with occasional setbacks until his own death in 1420. Meanwhile, James I (1406–37), who had succeeded Robert III in 1406, was held captive in England. He only returned to Scotland in 1424, almost a decade after he had come of age. He started his personal reign with the utmost vigour, destroying Murdach Stewart, second Duke of Albany, and attempting to bring the recalcitrant Highland chieftains to heel. However, his autocratic rule made him enemies and he was assassinated in 1437. His death ushered in a long period of minority rule, setting a pattern for nearly all the other Stewart monarchs until the reign of Charles I (1625–49).

Alexander Stewart, Lord of Badenoch

But long before the death of James I in 1437, the highest levels of feudal lordship had disintegrated in the north. Several of the northern earldoms had already come to be held by Lowlanders, and indeed David II in 1359 had even attempted to grant the earldom of Moray to Henry, Duke of Lancaster. Lacking any basis of power in the north, they were often more concerned with their affairs in the south of the country or even abroad. Among those to benefit from such a vacuum of political power in the central Highlands was Alexander Stewart, younger son of Robert II. He was first made King's Lieutenant in the north of Scotland in 1372. He thus gained far-reaching powers over the earldoms of Caithness, Sutherland and Ross and the Gaelic lordships farther west. Administering justice throughout the sheriffdom of Inverness, which then extended as far north as the Pentland Firth, only the regality of Moray was excluded from his jurisdiction. Farther south in Perthshire, he was Justiciar in the Appin of Dull, which covered Strath Tay, Fortingall and Glen Lyon, forming the western half of the earldom of Atholl.

Then, after amassing further territories in the north of Scotland, he greatly added to them in 1382, when he married Euphemia, Countess of Ross in her own right, after the death of her first husband Sir Walter Leslie, lord of the earldom of Ross. As well as her other territories, she brought him the barony of Kingedward, which was erected for her husband into the earldom of Buchan. Five years later in 1387, or possibly earlier, Alexander Stewart, by then Earl of Buchan, Lord of Badenoch and Ross and King's Lieutenant in the north, was appointed Justiciar of Scotland north of the Forth. It made him without question the most powerful man throughout the north of Scotland.

Caterans and Galloglasses

Alexander Stewart gained such a powerful position in the north even though Parliament had already censured him in 1385, at least implicitly, for allowing wandering bands of lawless 'caterans' to disturb the king's peace. Indeed, he was charged with doing nothing to stop their depredations against the clergy and other inhabitants of the Highlands, making them destititute. The word itself comes from the medieval Latin 'cateranus' or 'kethernus', a word most likely derived from 'caternava' in classical Latin, meaning a barbarian foot-soldier. Evidently adopted as a loan-word, it becomes *ceithearn* in Irish Gaelic, meaning a 'band', specifically of native Irish mercenary foot-soldiers or *ceatharnaigh*. The equivalent in Anglo-Irish is 'kerne', applied both to the individual foot-soldiers and to the bands formed by such soldiers.

Caterans were often depicted in later chronicles as marauding bands of Highland outlaws or freebooters, much like Border reivers. Responsible for devastating cattle-raids upon the Lowlands, they were often thought to be lawless bandits, acting quite independently of any regional authority. However, the contemporary record from the fourteenth century leaves little doubt that they were often mercenary soldiers employed by the great territorial magnates in the central Highlands, among whom was the renowned 'Wolf of Badenoch', namely Alexander Stewart, Earl of Buchan. Indeed, as Stephen Boardman has argued in his recent account of the 'Wolf of Badenoch', his lack of any territory in the Lowlands to supply him with armoured knights and feudal levies perhaps forced him to use such mercenaries in exercising power as the King's Lieutenant of the North.

Quite possibly, Alexander Stewart was only following the example of his father Robert the High Steward, who according to Stephen Boardman almost certainly employed troops of mercenary soldiers to impose his authority within Atholl in the 1340s and 1350s. Such practices were then more typical of the Gaelic west and especially Ireland. It is therefore significant that Robert the High Steward had close contacts with the western Highlands, and especially Kintyre, granted to him by King Robert the Bruce around 1318. Indeed, shortly after Robert the High Steward had received the lordship of the earldom of Atholl from David II in 1342, he granted the thanage of Glen Tilt to Ewen of the Isles. Although often thought to be a MacDonald, Stephen Boardman has suggested recently that Ewen was actually the brother of Ranald MacRuairi of Garmoran.

Ewen MacRuairi, if that indeed was his name, came from a family that had already established for themselves a formidable reputation as galloglasses, as the mercenary soldiers who settled in Ireland were known. The name itself comes from the Gaelic *gall-oglaich*, meaning literally 'foreign youths or servants' but more often translated as 'foreign warriors'. They first appeared in Ireland around the middle of the thirteenth century. Among the earliest to arrive were 160 fighting men who accompanied the daughter of Dugall mac Ruairi as a dowry for her marriage with Aodh O'Conchobhair of Connaught in 1259. Two other marriages are known to have taken place in the years before 1281, when the MacSweens of Knapdale and the MacDonalds of Islay gave their daughters in marriage to O'Donnell of Tyrconnell, bringing yet more galloglasses to Ireland.

However, the traffic was not all one way. Angus Og mac Donald of Islay married Aine Ni Cathan, daughter of Cu-mairge na nGal O'Cathan, chief of an important family from Limvady in what is now County Derry. Her dowry was 140 armed retainers. Among them were once said to be the ancestors of the Munros of Foulis. However, sustained by no evidence whatsoever, this dubious tradition most likely arose when MacDonald lords of the Isles first became the Earls of Ross in the fifteenth century and the Munros of Foulis became their vassals. Incidentally, several other Highland families have also claimed such an ancestry, including the Roses of Kilvarock, despite their Anglo-Norman origins.

By the end of the thirteenth century, the employment of Highland gallo-glasses by native Irish chieftains had become quite widespread in the north of Ireland, and especially in Ulster. Afterwards. they spread to Munster and then to Leinster. At first, they were not connected with any particular family. acting simply as free agents. However, hereditary links had started to develop by the mid-fourteenth century, especially between the MacSweeneys and the O'Donnells of Tyrconnell, as described below. Before the Tudors challenged their own supremacy in the sixteenth century, galloglasses were mostly recruited by the major Irish chieftains as an elite force to subdue their less powerful neighbours into submission, and then to keep them subjugated to their own authority as their vassals. It seems they were mostly employed as well-armed foot-soldiers to augment the native Irish cavalry, itself consisting of the high-born members of the chieftains' families. Well-armed and clad in chain-mail, they were much superior to the native foot-soldiers or 'kernes' who formed the bulk of any Irish army. The latter wore no armour and indeed ran barefoot, protected only by a round shield of wood or leather. while they were armed with only short swords and javelins.

Galloglasses in Ireland

Among the first galloglasses to establish a hereditary connection with a particular Irish kindred were the MacSweeneys, or Sweeneys, descendants of Suibhne. Their name is still commemorated by Castle Sween on the shores of Loch Sween. However, their hold on Knapdale and North Kintyre was finally brought to an end when they supported Edward II of England in his struggle against King Robert the Bruce after 1306. Now landless, they first settled in Tyrconnel in Ulster, now known as Donegal, where they played an important role in the prolonged struggle for power among the O'Donnells of Tyrconnel during the fourteenth century. They were first rewarded with lands in Fanad and later came to hold these lands as vassals to the O'Donnells of Tyrconnel. Eventually, they came to hold at one time a quarter of all the lands of Tyrconnel, or so it was said.

As the MacSweeneys prospered, cadet-branches established themselves elsewhere in Munster and Connaught. Typically, as Katherine Simms has shown in her study *From Kings to Warlords*, they held these lands as territo-rial lordships by virtue of the military service they rendered the O'Donnells. Moreover, as the captains of galloglasses, they were allowed to conscript their own tenants as mercenary soldiers who could then be quartered as a right throughout the O'Donnell lordship. Elsewhere in Ireland, galloglasses did not have such a close relationship with the lordships they served, receiving instead scattered estates together with the right of quartering their troops. However, they still made marriages with even the most aristocratic of the Irish kindreds, and their noble ancestry was recognised formally by native Irish historians.

The MacSweeneys were followed by the MacDougalls of Lorn. They had mostly lost their lands in Argyll to the Campbells of Lochawe after their defeat by King Robert the Bruce at the Pass of Brander in the years before 1314. They too settled in the north of Ireland, where they took the name of MacDowell, Doyle or Coyle. Never as numerous in Ireland as the Mac-Sweeneys, it seems likely the MacDougalls managed to keep hold of their ancestral lands in Scotland by sheer force of arms. Indeed, they were granted Coll and part of Tiree by royal charter in 1354, and only a few years later John MacDougall of Lorn appears as a powerful member of the 'Highland' party opposed to David II of Scotland under the leadership of Robert the High Steward.

Closely related to the MacDougalls as the descendants of Somerled, who reigned over Argyll and the Western Isles until his death in 1164, were the MacDonnells, as the MacDonalds came to spell their name in Ireland. While Angus Og MacDonald was a loyal supporter of King Robert the Bruce after 1306, his elder brother Alexander of Islay had adhered to the English cause. When he died in 1309, his lands were granted to Angus Og MacDonald, so disinheriting Alexander's six sons. After finding their way to Ireland, their descendants were among the most numerous of all the galloglasses, and were scattered across the whole country but especially in Ulster, Connaught and Leinster. They were later joined by the powerful family of the MacDonalds of Dunivaig and the Glens. However, they had gained their lands in the Glens of Antrim by marriage with a Bisset heiress towards the end of the fourteenth century. Another family of galloglasses who perhaps shared the same ancestry as the MacDonalds was the MacSheehys, in that they claimed descent from Sithech, great-grandson of Donald, progenitor of Clan Donald.

Apart from the MacCabes, whose origins are obscure, the only other galloglasses of note were the MacRuairis. They mostly settled in Tyrone and Connaught in the mid-fourteenth century, after their lands had passed by marriage to John MacDonald, first Lord of the Isles. Curiously enough, however, while the MacRuairis came to hold these territories of Garmoran and the Isles from a very early date, their name is often linked with the island of Bute. It was supposedly held by their eponymous progenitor Ruairi, grandson of Somerled, before it came into the hands of the High Stewards of Scotland in 1204, if not even earlier.

Fighting Qualities of the Galloglasses

Little is known of galloglasses in the fourteenth century, since most descriptions date from the sixteenth century. By then, however, 'redshanks' from Argyll and the Western Isles had taken the place of galloglasses in the armies hired by the native Irish chieftains. Their employment was seasonal since they came over to fight only during the summer months. But like the galloglasses of earlier times, they were portrayed as men of great strength and stature, distinctive in their dress and weaponry and widely regarded as the backbone of the Irish army. For example, the English poet Edmund Spenser wrote of them as foot-soldiers, heavily 'armed in a long sheet of mail down to the calf of the leg, with a long, broad sword in his hand . . . yet sure they are valiant and hardy, for the most part great endurers of cold, labour, and all hardness, very active and strong of hand, very swift of foot, very diligent and circumspect in their endeavours.' However, rather than the two-handed broadsword or claymore, which came into use only later, their favoured weapon was the double-headed battleaxe, 'like the Axe of the Tower'. It could be used to deadly effect even against cavalry if wielded with sufficient skill and strength. It was a Viking weapon, like the bow and arrow and the short heavy spears to be hurled at the enemy.

Another writer commented: 'these sort of men . . . do not lightly abandon the field, but bide the brunt to the death'. Indeed, they each took an oath not to turn their backs upon the enemy. They fought hand to hand with a single opponent, whom the galloglass either killed outright or was himself killed, in what was in effect a single-handed duel between two champions. It is reminiscent of the Battle of the Clans on the North Inch of Perth in 1396, when a territorial dispute between two Highland kindreds was settled by judicial combat between thirty combatants on each side, fighting man to man until one side was virtually annihilated.

Such descriptions tally with the rare depiction of galloglasses in a Dürer engraving of 1521. It shows two captains or constables, together with their armour-bearers. One of the principal figures is clad in a long quilted and pleated surcoat known as an aketon. The other figure is wearing a coat of chain-mail, reaching nearly to his knees, along with a gorget or collar of chain-mail around his shoulders, and a helmet. Dressed for battle, they greatly resemble the effigies of medieval warriors carved on the gravestones of Argyll and the Western Isles during the two centuries after 1350. Such monumental sculptures represent the dead chiefs of the Gaelic-speaking kindreds who then held sway over Gaeldom, or their kinsmen. Typically, they too wear a quilted surcoat, thickly padded and reaching to their knees, while their heads are protected by a smooth conical helmet known as a bascinet, along with a covering of chain-mail around their shoulders. They are usually shown armed with a large cross-hilted sword which is sometimes carved separately on their tombstones, and they often carry a shield.

Galloglasses in the Highlands

It is perhaps a moot point whether galloglasses were ever employed as such by Robert the High Steward in the central Highlands during the fourteenth century. There is little evidence that they ever settled as mercenary soldiers in Atholl, except perhaps for the grant of Glen Tilt to Ewen of the Isles. Subsequently, however, Parliament heard complaints in 1366 regarding the presence of lawless rebels in Atholl, Argyll, Badenoch, Lochaber and Ross. These districts were all under the control of Robert the High Steward, or his sons and allies, including his son-in-law John MacDonald, first Lord of the Isles, and his brother-in-law William, fifth Earl of Ross. Indeed, according to a later chronicle, the first Lord of the Isles was said to maintain 'a strong party of standing forces, under the command of Hector More Macillechoan [MacGille-Chomgain in Gaelic], for defending Lochaber and the frontiers of the country from robbery and incursions of the rest of the Scots'.

Then in June 1368, Robert the High Steward and two of his sons were forced to swear an oath for the good behaviour of all the inhabitants of their lordships. They gave a promise that they would not harbour malefactors or evil-doers, as 'caterans' were often known in the official record, or allow them to cross their territories. Hardly a month later, the Steward and his son Alexander Stewart, the future 'Wolf of Badenoch', were warded in Lochleven Castle, and Alexander was only released in March 1369. They were again urged on their release to enforce justice against malefactors in their earldoms of Strathearn, Atholl and Menteith and in all their other territories within the Highlands.

Not long afterwards, Alexander Stewart undertook to protect the men and lands of Alexander Bur, Bishop of Moray, especially in Badenoch and Strathspey, even before his father ascended the throne as Robert II in 1371 and made him Lord of Badenoch. Such protection often amounted to little more than blackmail. When the Bishop of Moray leased the lands of Rothiemurchus to Alexander Stewart of Badenoch in 1383, he promised in return to protect the bishop and his lands, and to keep them free of male-factors. But there is hardly any doubt these very malefactors were employed and maintained as galloglasses by the Lord of Badenoch himself, who was now the Earl of Buchan. Even so, the real basis of Alexander's power and authority was only fully revealed after the death of his father Robert II in 1390.

Downfall of the Lord of Badenoch

By then, power and authority had first passed in 1384 from the ageing Robert II to his eldest son John Stewart, Earl of Carrick, the future King Robert III. Then, four years later in 1388, he was removed in turn from this office in favour of his younger brother Robert Stewart, Earl of Fife and Menteith and afterwards Duke of Albany. Even before Robert Stewart was officially made Guardian of Scotland, Alexander Stewart of Badenoch was stripped of his office as Justiciar north of the Forth, judged to be 'useless to the community' in administering justice. Soon afterwards, the new Guardian appointed his own son Murdach Stewart in his place. Then in 1389, Alexander was prosecuted in the ecclesiastical court of the Bishops of Moray and Ross after he had abandoned his lawful wife Euphemia, Countess of Ross, in favour of Mairead, daughter of Eachainn.

Seemingly, all of Alexander's natural sons were born of this liaison which had probably existed ever since he became Lord of Badenoch in 1371, if not even earlier. By 1392, he had two sons old enough to lead the notorious raid upon Angus which ended with the death of its sheriff, Sir Walter Ogilvie, along with several other knights-at-arms and sixty of their retainers. Moreover, all his natural sons were born into a Gaelic-speaking milieu, since his eldest son and namesake Alexander Stewart, afterwards Earl of Mar, was said to be proficient in the composition of Gaelic poetry. Indeed, a Highland chronicler later portrayed him as a 'noble and generous person', evidently quite at home in Gaelic society with its distinctive culture and customs. Even his father was known to Gaelic-speaking society as Alasdair Mor Mac an Righ, or Great Alexander, the King's Son, rather than the 'Wolf of Badenoch'. It was a title only bestowed upon him later by Lowland chroniclers.

The ecclesiastical court in 1389 threatened to excommunicate Alexander Stewart, Earl of Buchan, if he did not return to his lawful wife Euphemia, Countess of Ross, with all her possessions. Forbidden to use any of his men illegally against her, it was a humiliating blow to his pride. But worse followed when Alexander Bur, Bishop of Moray, made an agreement early in 1390 with Thomas Dunbar, eldest son and heir of his great rival John Dunbar, Earl of Moray. Thomas Dunbar had already taken Alexander's place as sheriff of Inverness, and he now undertook to defend all the bishop's possessions and men for the rest of the bishop's life against all malefactors, caterans and everyone else apart from the king.

Reaction of the Wolf of Badenoch

Exactly what the Bishop of Moray had to fear materialised soon after Robert

II had died in 1390, even before his body was buried and his eldest son crowned as Robert III (1390–1406). Alexander Stewart, Lord of Badenoch and Earl of Buchan, first attacked Forres in early June with a cateran force of 'wyld, wykkyd, Heland-men'. They destroyed the town, the choir of St Lawrence's Church and the archdeacon's house. A fortnight later, he put Elgin to the flames, 'burning the whole town, and the Church of St Giles in it, the hospice beside Elgin, eighteen noble and beautiful mansions of canons and chaplains, and, what gives most bitter pain, the noble and beautiful church of Moray, the beacon of the countryside and ornament of the kingdom'. Such lawless actions earned Alexander Stewart, Earl of Buchan, lasting opprobrium at least among the Lowlanders of Scotland as the 'Wolf of Badenoch'.

Indeed, it was the most dramatic act of violence in the history of Moray. Most likely, it was perpetrated by Alexander Stewart of Badenoch simply to demonstrate that his territorial rival Thomas Dunbar was quite unable to protect the Bishop of Moray. But equally it displays the likely foundations of his power and influence in the north, as Stephen Boardman has argued. All the complaints raised against his lordship focus on its overtly aggressive nature. Even Hector Boecce, writing of the Bishops of Aberdeen more than a century later, charged Alexander Stewart with being a man 'whose wickedness had earned him universal hatred'. But his bitter accusations were levelled more at 'certain vile creatures, [who] drove off all the bishop's cattle, and carried away his property, killing at the same time in the most high-handed way the peasants . . . He [Alexander Stewart] divided as he pleased the lands stolen from the church, and gave them to be cultivated by certain wicked men who had no regard for God or man.' It can hardly be doubted that they were mercenary troops of galloglasses under his own control rather than lawless 'caterans' quartered upon the lands of the bishop.

Quartering of Galloglasses

Indeed, as already mentioned, the mercenary troops or galloglasses who served the great chieftains in fourteenth-century Ireland had the right to be quartered upon their employer's own tenantry, and especially upon the lesser chieftains who were his vassals. As Katherine Simms has shown, they were forced to provide such mercenaries with food and shelter according to the medieval Irish practice known as *buannacht*. It meant in effect that galloglasses exacted their own wages in kind from his tenants and vassals, rather than being paid directly by the chieftain they served. But if Alexander Stewart of Badenoch had resorted to using mercenary troops drawn from the Highland clans to impose his authority as King's Lieutenant and Justiciar north of the Forth, it is just as likely that he had adopted the same expedient in maintaining them. Indeed, the pledge given by Alexander Stewart of Badenoch to the Bishop of Moray in 1370 suggests that it was a practice adopted as well throughout the Highlands and Western Isles. Together with his 'friends and men', he agreed not to exact money or cattle from the bishop's tenants within his lordship of Badenoch.

The Irish practice of *buannacht* was later adopted in maintaining the military strength of the Highland clans, if indeed it was not customary during earlier centuries. Well over two centuries later, it was reported from Islay: 'Each merkland man sustain daily and yearly one gentleman in meat and cloth, who does no labour . . . as one of their master's household men, and [who] must be sustained and furnished in all necessities by the tenant, and he must be ready to his master's service and advice.' Even in the seventeenth century, it was reported that more than a hundred MacLean gentry were billeted for the winter upon the lands of Tiree. It is hardly surprising that Parliament heard many complaints during these years of 'caterans' and other malefactors, who occupied and exploited lands in the central Highlands to which they had no legal title.

By imposing such exactions on the churchlands of Badenoch and Strathspey, over which he claimed powers of regality, Alexander Stewart of Badenoch may well have aggravated his territorial disputes with Alexander Bur, Bishop of Moray. But other magnates evidently adopted the same practice. In 1389, John Dunbar, Earl of Moray, cleared himself on oath of having introduced 'caterans' into his lordship against the interests of the very same bishop. Even so, he was ordered to appoint officers to bring the malefactors to justice so that the bishop might be indemnified for the losses suffered by his tenants.

Likewise, Alexander MacDonald, Lord of Lochaber, promised in 1394 to protect the earldom and bishopric of Moray, while agreeing not to permit 'his men, nor other caterans he is able to [control], of whatever rank they shall be, to beg through the lands of Moray, nor to consume or ruin them'. Yet only four years later, he was assigning churchlands to his own adherents. His lawless activities culminated in his seizing Urquhart Castle in the years after 1395 when he displaced Thomas Chisholm as its custodian, and then by his expedition against Elgin in 1402 when he sacked the town in the manner of Alexander Stewart, Wolf of Badenoch. By then, Alexander MacDonald of Lochaber was firmly ensconced in the Great Glen, offering protection to Thomas Dunbar, now the Earl of Moray, in return for occupying the lordship of Dochfour.

'Another Kind of Man'

The political career of Alexander Stewart, Lord of Badenoch and Earl of Buchan, came effectively to an end in 1390 when he was forced to do penance for his wanton acts of sacrilege. His marriage with Euphemia, Countess of Ross, was dissolved in 1392, although he managed to keep his title of Earl of Buchan. He briefly regained some of his former glory after 1402, when the ranks of the Scottish nobility were depleted at the Battle of Homildon Hill. Moreover, the sentence of excommunication imposed on him was evidently lifted by the Church, since he was buried behind the high altar of Dunkeld Cathedral after his death in 1405, where his tomb can still be seen. But by then, authority in the central Highlands had passed to Sir Alexander Stewart, his natural son and namesake. Described as 'very head-strong and wild, and the oustanding leader of a band of caterans', he made himself Earl of Mar in 1404 by abducting Isabel, Countess of Mar in her own right, and forcing her into marriage.

It was effectively a coup against the power and influence of Robert Stewart, Duke of Albany, then acting as the Regent of Scotland. It evidently had the support of the Aberdeen burgesses, and the landowning families of Mar. Indeed, it was evidently his ability, so lacking in his father as the Lord of Badenoch, to control the 'caterans' who so threatened their lands and other possessions which appealed to the landowners around the fringes of the Highlands in north-east Scotland. Subsequently, he earned a reputation among Lowlanders as 'another kind of man' for his chivalric exploits and heroic defence of Aberdeen at the Battle of Harlaw in 1411 against the forces of Donald MacDonald, second Lord of the Isles.

Claim to the Earldom of Ross

Celebrated in a popular ballad, the Battle of Harlaw was remembered for the next two centuries as a momentous encounter between the Highlands and the Lowlands, Celts and Saxons, at least by the Lowlanders. Whatever its origins in a dispute over feudal rights of inheritance, the battle itself marked the deep division which then existed between the Gaelic-speaking Highlands and the English-speaking Lowlands of Scotland. Even though Alexander Stewart, Earl of Mar, owed his strength to his lordship of Badenoch, inherited from his father, the 'Wolf of Badenoch', it was ultimately a clash between two different cultures. Feudalism still held sway throughout the Lowlands of Scotland. However, its very existence was evidently threatened north of the Highland line by an even older tradition of military overlordship. It would be repeatedly wielded over the next two centuries as Clan Donald fought at first to gain the earldom of Ross, and then sought to reclaim their possessions by sheer force of arms after its loss in 1476 and the forfeiture of the lordship of the Isles in 1493.

Origins of Clan Donald

Ever since the time of Somerled, who made himself 'King of Argyll, and Lord of the Isles' before his death in 1164, the Western Isles of Scotland had been ruled over by his descendants, among whom were the MacDonalds, the MacDougalls and the MacRuairis. Then, during the struggle for Scottish independence, the MacDonalds of Islay as the descendants of Somerled's grandson Donald triumphed over the MacDougalls of Lorn, who were themselves descended from Somerled's eldest son Dugall. Fighting alongside the Campbells of Lochawe against the Comyns, Earls of Buchan, and their MacDougall allies, the MacDonalds of Islay were greatly rewarded in the person of Angus Og MacDonald, to whom King Robert the Bruce granted vast territories in Argyll and the Western Isles, forfeited from his enemies.

Then, his eldest son John married Amie MacRuairi, heiress to the territories of Garmoran and the Isles, taking for himself the proud title of 'Lord of the Isles' held by his forebears. By now a territorial magnate of the first order, John MacDonald, first Lord of the Isles, then allied himself to Robert the High Steward by marrying his daughter Margaret in 1350 after he had divorced his first wife. Then, when his father-in-law unexpectedly succeeded David II in 1371, the first Lord of the Isles found himself favoured as a royal son-in-law. He received grants confirming him in possession of all his territories. They now extended throughout the Western Isles, excluding only the island of Skye and perhaps Lewis, together with much of the western seaboard of the Highlands stretching from Glenelg as far south as Duror, as well as Knapdale and Kintyre.

Seemingly in return, John MacDonald, first Lord of the Isles, agreed that his son Donald, who was Robert II's grandson by his second marriage, should succeed him in his territories as Lord of the Isles. But by the time the first Lord of the Isles died in 1387, after a long life marked by a commendable sense of opportunism, power had already passed to Robert Stewart, Earl of Fife and Menteith and later Duke of Albany. Two years later, his son Murdach Stewart was appointed as Justiciar of Scotland north of the Forth. The Albany Stewarts, acting together as father and son, now pursued a relentless course of territorial aggrandisement in the north.

Claim to the Earldom of Ross

Inevitably, this brought conflict with Donald MacDonald, second Lord of the Isles, who was married to Mary Leslie, daughter of Euphemia, Countess of Ross. After Euphemia's death in 1394, the earldom of Ross was held by her son Sir Alexander Leslie. He married Isabel Stewart, elder daughter of Robert Stewart, now Duke of Albany and the Regent of Scotland. Their only issue was a sickly daughter, named Euphemia in honour of her grandmother, who was still a minor when Sir Alexander Stewart died at his castle of Dingwall in 1402. His death was a grievous blow to the northern interests of the Albany Stewarts.

Robert Stewart, Duke of Albany, now obtained the wardship of Euphemia Leslie, but her inheritance to the earldom of Ross was challenged by Donald MacDonald, second Lord of the Isles, acting on behalf of his wife Mary Leslie. It reached a climax near Inverurie at the Battle of Harlaw in 1411, when an Highland army of ten thousand men fighting under the banner of Clan Donald engaged the mounted cavalry of Alexander Stewart, Earl of Mar and the eldest son of the 'Wolf of Badenoch'. Known as 'Red Harlaw', the bloody engagement ended indecisively when Donald, second Lord of the Isles, withdrew from the field under the cover of darkness leaving the Earl of Mar to claim a dubious victory.

Aftermath of Harlaw

After the battle of Harlaw, it is said that Alexander Stewart, Earl of Mar, 'ruled with acceptance nearly all the north of the country beyond the Mounth'. He entered at first into an uneasy alliance with Robert Stewart, Duke of Albany, who was now Guardian of Scotland. However, when James I returned in 1424 from captivity in England, almost his first act was the destruction of the Albany Stewarts. It left Alexander Stewart pre-eminent in the north. However, he suffered a devastating defeat at the hands of Clan Donald at the Battle of Inverlochy in 1431, when a royal army under his command was routed by Donald Balloch of Dunivaig and the Glens. It forced James I to reach an accommodation with Alexander MacDonald, now acting as the third Lord of the Isles after his father's death in 1423. Even so, the powerful role that Alexander Stewart had played as the 'Guard-dog of the North', to paraphrase Stephen Boardman, was revealed only after his death in 1435. It left a vacuum of political power beyond the Mounth. Even before James I was assassinated early in 1437, the third Lord of the Isles had occupied Inverness and was perhaps even then acting as the Earl of Ross.

Even so, it was only under the regency of Archibald, fifth Earl of Douglas and a close ally, that the third Lord of the Isles was finally created Earl of Ross later in 1437. Soon afterwards, he was made Justiciar of Scotland north of the Forth. He was now among the most powerful magnates in the kingdom, along with the Earls of Douglas and the Lindsays, Earls of Crawford. Indeed, when he died twelve years later in 1449 he was buried not on Iona like his ancestors, but at the Chanonry of Ross on the Black Isle, suggesting in the words of Jean Munro in her article on 'The Lordship of the Isles': 'It seems that he had died as he had lived, as Earl of Ross, rather than . . . Lord of the Isles.'

Treasonable 'Band' with Douglas and Crawford

Alexander MacDonald, third Lord of the Isles and Earl of Ross, had witnessed the rise of Clan Donald to its peak of territorial power and political influence under his leadership. All would be lost by his son and heir John, fourth Lord of the Isles and Earl of Ross. But the seeds of destruction were perhaps already sown by John's father Alexander. It is said that he had entered, most likely in 1446, into an infamous 'band' with William, eighth Earl of Douglas, then Governor of Scotland, and Alexander Lindsay, the 'Tiger' Earl of Crawford, or his father. It was later described as 'an offensive and defensive league and combination against all men, none excepted, not [even] the King himself'. It brought all three parties into violent conflict with the Crown after James II had started upon his personal rule in 1449, causing the virtual destruction of the Black Douglases when they would not acknowledge his authority. Moreover, it saw the rise to power of the Gordons, Earls of Huntly, who would increasingly challenge Clan Donald in their future role as the King's Lieutenants in the North.

Rise of the Gordons, Earls of Huntly

The foundations of Gordon power in the north-east of Scotland were laid around 1320, when King Robert the Bruce rewarded Sir Adam Gordon with the lordship of Strathbogie (now Huntly). However, although loyal servants of the Crown, they remained among the lesser gentry until 1380 when marriage brought them the barony of Aboyne with its vast estates once held by the Frasers. Even so, the Gordons died out in the male line around 1408, leaving Elizabeth Gordon as sole heiress. She married Sir Alexander Seton who was among the most loyal of James I's courtiers. Their eldest son was also called Alexander, and he married Elizabeth Crichton, daughter of Sir William Crichton, Lord Chancellor of Scotland during the minority of James II. It was perhaps under his father-in-law's patronage that Alexander Seton was made the first Earl of Huntly, most likely when the Lord Chancellor became reconciled in July 1455 to William, eighth Earl of Douglas, then acting as the Lieutenant-General of Scotland. The newly-created earl afterwards took his mother's name of Gordon by which his descendants are known.

Two other earls were created at the same time as Alexander Gordon, first Earl of Huntly. Both were the younger brothers of William, eighth Earl of Douglas. Hugh Douglas was made Earl of Ormond, while Archibald Douglas was recognised as the Earl of Moray by virtue of his marriage with Elizabeth Dunbar, younger daughter of James Dunbar, Earl of Moray, thus setting aside her elder sister Janet. Moreover, the northern possessions once held by the Morays, Lords of Bothwell, had also come into the hands of William, eighth Earl of Douglas, long after his grandfather Archibald the 'Grim, third Earl of Douglas, had gained control of them by his marriage to Joanna Moray in 1362. She was the widow of Sir Thomas Moray of Bothwell, who had died in 1361 without any issue. Such a concentration of Douglas power in the north meant that Sir Alexander Gordon's status as the first Earl of Huntly was eclipsed at first by the Black Douglases.

However, even before William, eighth Earl of Douglas, was murdered by James II in 1452, the first Earl of Huntly was granted the lordship of Badenoch with its castle at Ruthven. He was most likely charged with containing the rebellion of John MacDonald, fourth Lord of the Isles and Earl of Ross, which had apparently broken out only a month earlier. Then, after the final downfall of the Black Douglases in 1455, and the forfeiture of all their lands in the north, Alexander Gordon was left to profit from their downfall. By then, he was acting as the Lieutenant-General of the North, and after his defeat of Alexander Lindsay, fourth Earl of Crawford, at the Battle of Brechin in 1452, he was evidently rewarded with further grants of land, including the lordship of Enzie.

The fate of William, eighth Earl of Douglas, evidently alerted John MacDonald, fourth Lord of the Isles and Earl of Ross, to the dangers of allying himself too closely with the Black Douglases. Indeed, after James II had reinstated his father-in-law Sir James Livingston to his former position as Lord Chamberlain of Scotland, John MacDonald evidently sought to reconcile himself with the king. James II later rewarded him for his new-found loyalty by granting him the castle and lands of Urquhart, together with the lands of Glen Moriston, Abertarff and Stratherrick and the sheriffdom of Inverness. By then, however, Alexander Gordon, first Earl of Huntly, had consolidated his powerful position in the north-east. His descendants would establish a pre-eminent position for themselves as the 'Cocks o' the North' by acting as the loyal servants of the Crown over the next hundred years.

Challenge of the Campbells, Earls of Argyll

The favour shown by James II to John MacDonald, fourth Lord of the Isles and Earl of Ross, was offset in 1457 when Colin Campbell, Lord of Lochawe, was created the first Earl of Argyll. As John Bannerman has commented in discussing the historical background to the *Late Medieval Sculpture in the Western Highlands*, the Lords of the Isles were preoccupied during the early fifteenth century with their claim to the earldom of Ross, and then with exerting their authority over its lands. Indeed, nearly all the charters granted by them in the years after 1437 were issued at Dingwall or Inverness and dealt with the lands of the earldom. It meant that they neglected their affairs in Argyll and the Western Isles during these years to the ultimate benefit of the Campbells, Earls of Argyll.

Unlike the Gordon earls of Huntly, the Campbells were a family long established in the Gaelic-speaking Highlands. Most likely of British ancestry, as W. D. H. Sellar has argued in his article 'The Earliest Campbells – Norman, Briton or Gael?', their origins can perhaps be traced to the district of Lennox in the ancient kingdom of Strathclyde. It was probably marriage with a Celtic heiress that brought them their ancestral lands around Lochawe in Argyll. Several generations later, their lands were erected into a free barony in 1315 after Sir Neil Campbell had supported King Robert the Bruce in his struggle for Scottish independence. Thereafter, his descendants embarked on a highly successful course of territorial aggrandisement, mostly by settling their younger sons on lands gained by marriage. Their services to the Crown also brought them forfeited estates, while their own marriages apparently brought them other lands, especially in Knapdale and Cowal, bestowed upon them by the Menteith family. By the late fourteenth century, they were probably acting as the King's Lieutenant and Justiciar of Argyll, since they were afterwards confirmed in these local offices of power and influence under the Crown.

Thus, their elevation to the peerage in 1457 merely served to confirm that the Campbells had established a position of strength in Argyll, bringing increased security and prosperity to their lands through their own power and influence. But equally, as John Bannerman has argued, the Campbells could now claim to be recognised by the Gaelic-speaking society of the Western Highlands by the title of Ri Airir Goidel once held by Somerled, King of Argyll. Yet the Campbells never turned their backs on central authority. Indeed, Colin Campbell, first Earl of Argyll, soon obtained the office of Master of the King's Household which afterwards became hereditary to his family, and later became the Lord Chancellor of Scotland. Eventually his grandson Colin Campbell, third Earl of Argyll. gained the hereditary office of Justice-General of Scotland in 1514, which his descendants held until 1628. Meanwhile, the Campbells had consolidated their territorial position under the first Earl of Argyll, who received the lordship of Lorn, once held by the MacDougalls, in exchange for their lands of Innermeath.

Treaty of Ardtornish-Westminster

James II was killed accidently by the bursting of a cannon at the siege of Roxburgh Castle in 1460, leaving his eldest son to be crowned as James III (1460–88), then aged only eight. Chaos reigned in Scotland immediately after the king's death, but matters were even worse in England where the Wars of the Roses were raging. However, by 1461, Edward IV of the House of York had triumphed over the Lancastrian dynasty of Henry VI. The defeated king sought refuge in Scotland with his queen and other notables. There the exiles gained the support of the Scots by offering to surrender Berwick, held by the English almost continuously since 1333. Intent on undermining the Lancastrians' influence in Scotland, Edward IV now dispatched the exiled Earl of Douglas on an embassy to the Western Isles. There he negotiated the notorious Treaty of Ardtornish-Westminster of 1462 with John MacDonald, fourth Lord of the Isles and Earl of Ross, and his chief lieutenant Donald Balloch of Dunivaig and the Glens. They had foolishly embarked on a course which would ultimately bring down Clan Donald from its pre-eminent position within Gaeldom.

Both John MacDonald, fourth Lord of the Isles, and Donald Balloch of Dunivaig and the Glens agreed to become the loyal adherents of the English king, along with all their subjects. They promised to aid him to their 'uttermost might and power' in his wars in Scotland and Ireland in return for an annuity from the English exchequer. But they were also encouraged to hope for territorial spoils as well, since it was further agreed: 'If it so be hereafter the said realm of Scotland . . . be conquered, subdued, and brought to the obeisance of the said most high and Christian prince [Edward IV] . . . the same earls [of Ross and Douglas] and Donald [Balloch] shall have . . . all the possession of the said realm beyond Scottish Sea [the Firth of Forth].'

Forfeiture of the Earldom of Ross

The treasonable actions of John MacDonald, fourth Lord of the Isles and Earl of Ross, remained unknown to the Scots for more than a decade. Indeed, they were only revealed in 1475 after an Anglo-Scottish treaty of friendship was agreed upon the betrothal of James III's son and heir James, Duke of Rothesay, and Edward IV's youngest daughter Cecilia. James III reacted immediately by summoning John MacDonald to appear before Parliament in December 1475. He was charged with treason for entering into the Treaty of Ardtornish-Westminister with Edward IV, King of England, against the Scottish Crown, along with various other treasons and crimes. When he failed to appear, Parliament unanimously judged him guilty and the dempster pronounced sentence upon him, forfeiture of his life along with all his lands, rents, superiorities and offices to the king.

It was undoubtedly the military strength of the Lordship of the Isles that now allowed John MacDonald to come to terms with the Crown. The sentence against him was put aside the following July when John MacDonald 'humbled himself and came to the King's will upon certain conditions'. He resigned to the Crown his earldom of Ross with all its lands, his lands of Knapdale and Kintyre and his offices as Sheriff of Inverness and Nairn. In return, his remaining territories in the Western Isles, now including the island of Skye, and his mainland territories of Garmoran, Morvern, Lochaber, Glencoe and Duror were restored to him. He was to hold them merely as baron and lord of Parliament, even if he retained his once-proud title of Lord of the Isles. He agreed to render all due rights and services to the Crown, including the collection of Crown revenues. Together with his tenants and the other inhabitants of his lands, he accepted the laws and customs of the realm like the other barons, freeholders and lieges of Scotland.

Internecine Quarrels of Clan Donald

In accepting such humiliating terms in 1476, John MacDonald of the Isles split apart Clan Donald and its vassal kindreds, including the MacLeods and the MacLeans. He had already sought to strengthen his own position by granting out lands to his own adherents, rewarding his elder half-brother Celestine of Lochalsh with the lands of Lochbroom, Lochalsh, Torridon, Lochcarron and Kishorn in the earldom of Ross, and his other half-brother Hugh of Sleat with the lands of Sleat on the island of Skye and the islands of North Uist, Benbecula and parts of South Uist in the Outer Hebrides. He also granted Alexander Ionraic MacKenzie of Kintail the lands of Killin, Garve and Kinlochluichart in the Braes of Ross, and Duncan MacIntosh, Captain of Clan Chattan, the lands of Lochaber. But it was the grant of widespread lands in Islay at the heart of the Lordship to Lachlan Og MacLean of Duart which infuriated John MacDonald's natural son Angus Og. He became fearful that his father was intent on depriving him completely of his patrimony.

The animosity between father and son reached its climax in the sea-battle of Bloody Bay, fought off Tobermory at some unknown date, most likely between 1481 and 1485. According to MacDonald traditions, John MacDonald, fourth Lord of the Isles, had the support of the MacLeans of Duart, Lochbuie and Ardgour, the MacNeills of Barra, the MacLeods of Lewis and the MacLeods of Harris and Dunvegan. Against them were ranged the clansmen of Clan Donald under Angus Og MacDonald, along with his own allies, the MacDonalds of Sleat and the MacDonalds of Clan Ranald. The victory of Angus Og MacDonald at Bloody Bay forced his father to recognise his natural son as Master of the Isles and the Captain of Clan Donald. It seems likely that they afterwards divided the territories of the Lordship between themselves.

Aftermath of Bloody Bay

It was perhaps after his victory at Bloody Bay that Angus Og MacDonald reacted to the loss of the earldom of Ross in time-honoured fashion by rebelling in 1481. He first captured the burgh of Inverness and its castle with a large force of his clansmen drawn from the districts of Lochaber, Moidart, Knoydart and Glengarry. He then installed himself in Dingwall Castle for the next two years, defeating an army sent north by James III under John Stewart, Earl of Atholl. He was perhaps only dislodged from Easter Ross by another army under the command of David Lindsay, fifth Earl of Crawford, and George Gordon, second Earl of Huntly, who had acted since 1479 as Justiciar of Scotland north of the Forth. But Angus Og MacDonald had evidently returned to occupy Inverness in the years before 1490 when he was assassinated by an Irish harper in his retinue while staying there.

The death of Angus Og MacDonald deprived Clan Donald of its natural leader. His place at the head of Clan Donald was taken by Alexander MacDonald of Lochalsh, nephew of the last Lord of the Isles. He mounted yet another attack against the earldom of Ross in 1491, advancing from Lochaber through Badenoch and Strathspey to attack Inverness. After destroying Inverness Castle and plundering the Black Isle, Alexander MacDonald of Lochalsh was defeated when his forces were surprised at night by the MacKenzies of Kintail. This further outbreak of violence in the north occurred three years after James III was killed at the Battle of Sauchieburn in 1488. He was succeeded by his young son James IV. He appointed a commission early in his reign to inquire into 'the matter of the Isles . . . and to provide so that the King's lieges may live in quiet and peace'.

Forfeiture of the Lordship

The final denouement came in 1493, when James IV lost patience with John MacDonald, fourth Lord of the Isles, who seemed quite unable to control the lawless behaviour of Clan Donald and its vassal kindreds. Parliament forfeited all his lands in the Lordship of the Isles, which was annexed to the Crown. Perhaps he had connived at the violent unrest that followed his resignation of the earldom of Ross in 1476, or perhaps he was simply unable to restrain his kinsmen from rebelling against the Crown. But either way, he was merely seen as an obstacle to the 'daunting of the Isles', which James IV was now determined to undertake. Deprived of all his lands and a pensioner of the Crown, John MacDonald, fourth Lord of the Isles, lived for another ten years. He died a broken man in 1503 while staying in an obscure lodging-house in Dundee. But he left an heir to the Lordship in his grandson Donald Dubh, born of Angus Og's marriage with Isabella Campbell, daughter of Colin, first Earl of Argyll. Although held captive in the Campbell stronghold of Innis Chonnel on Loch Awe, his very existence was sufficient to rally the forces of Clan Donald into rebellion against the Crown. Time and again for the next fifty years, they attempted to restore the Lordship of the Isles in his name and perhaps even hoped to regain the lost lands in the earldom of Ross.

Chapter Two

CLAN DONALD IN REBELLION

After the forfeiture of the Lordship of the Isles by the Crown in 1493, James IV lost little time in attempting to impose his own authority over the territories that he had so recently acquired. He acted with moderation at first, prepared to pardon any rebels in return for their submission and even to grant out their lands again. Late in the summer of 1493, he travelled to Dunstaffnage Castle, now held for the Crown by the Campbells, Earls of Argyll, and he may have toured the Western Isles as well. Soon afterwards, he visited Inverness and its surrounding districts, which only two years previously had been invaded by the MacDonalds in pursuit of their claim to the earldom of Ross. Now, however, Alexander MacDonald of Lochalsh as the leader of this insurrection submitted to the king's authority, along with John Mor MacDonald of Dunivaig and the Glens. They were both knighted as a sign of royal favour.

John MacLean of Lochbuie, John MacIain of Ardnamurchan and Duncan MacIntosh, Captain of Clan Chattan, were among the other Highlands chiefs who submitted around this time. No doubt, they were persuaded to do so after James IV had promised Sir Alexander MacDonald of Lochalsh that they would receive charters to nearly all the lands that they had previously held under the Lordship of the Isles. But apparently James IV only honoured this commitment by granting a charter to Ewen Cameron at this time, whose lands were later erected into the barony of Lochiel.

Many other Highland chiefs delayed their submission, even after the King had paid a second visit to Argyll and the Western Isles in the spring of 1494. Indeed, James IV may well have had serious doubts about the loyalty of Sir John Mor MacDonald of Dunivaig and the Glens. The Irish annals refer to him as Ri Innse Gall after his death, suggesting that he was now recognised by Clan Donald as the Lord of the Isles in the wake of the forfeiture. A military expedition was therefore mounted in July 1494, when the royal castle at Tarbert was rebuilt and fortified and a naval force established in the Firth of Clyde.

But although James IV granted Sir John MacDonald a charter to his lands in Islay and Kintyre, it excluded his castle of Dunaverty, which had long been in the possession of his family. Occupying a strategic position on the Mull of Kintyre, Dunaverty guarded the sea lanes between his territories in Scotland and his lands in the Glens of Antrim, the stronghold of the family. James IV now installed his own garrison in the castle with a force of artillery. This act so incensed Sir John Mor MacDonald of Dunivaig and the Glens, who regarded the castle as his own, that he stormed and recaptured the castle as soon as the royal fleet set sail. Reputedly, the governor of the royal garrison was even hanged from its battlements in sight of the king and his fleet.

MacIains of Ardnamurchan

Angered by such a flagrant affront to his own authority and dignity, James IV determined upon revenge. He found a willing ally in John MacIain of Ardnamurchan, who was married to a sister of Colin Campbell, third Earl of Argyll. The MacIain family was itself descended from John Sprangach the 'Bold or Imperious', younger brother of Angus Og MacDonald, compatriot of King Robert the Bruce. They had benefited greatly over the years from their steadfast loyalty to succeeding Lords of the Isles, gaining lands in Islay, Kintyre and Jura in addition to their original territories of Ardnamurchan and Sunart. However, this expansion had brought them into conflict with the MacDonalds of Dunivaig and the Glens, who also laid claim to the MacIain lands of Sunart. After the downfall of the Lordship of the Isles, John MacIain of Ardnamurchan evidently decided to support James IV, no doubt hoping to profit at the expense of the other branches of Clan Donald and their erstwhile vassals. Indeed, he was almost immediately rewarded with a grant to lands in Islay previously held under the Lordship, and further grants would follow.

John MacIain of Ardnamurchan may have first served the Scottish crown by slaying Sir Alexander MacDonald of Lochalsh, whom he took by surprise at the Isle of Oronsay on 14 October 1494, or so it was recorded in the Annals of Ulster. Although knighted by James IV in 1493, it seems Alexander MacDonald of Lochalsh became frustrated when the promise of a royal charter to his territories failed to materialise. Taking matters into his own hands, he afterwards tried once again to seize the earldom of Ross to avenge his earlier defeat of 1491. But once again, he was defeated in a battle fought at Drumchatt by the combined forces of the MacKenzies and the Munros. Retiring to Colonsay, he then attempted to rally the other chieftains of Clan Donald to his banner, but without success. It was there that he was surprised and killed by John MacIain of Ardnamurchan, aided it seems by John

Cathanach, eldest son of Sir John Mor MacDonald of Dunivaig and the Glens.

Afterwards, John MacIain of Ardnamurchan may well have used John Cathanach to gain access to Finlaggan, where it is said that he apprehended Sir John Mor MacDonald of Dunivaig and the Glens and two of his grandsons, as well as John Cathanach himself, in what was surely another act of treachery. The captives were brought to Edinburgh where they were tried for high treason and found guilty. But they were not executed until 1499 when they were 'justified' by hanging on the Boroughmuir near Edinburgh. Indeed, given the long delay, it may well be doubted that John MacIain of Ardnamurchan captured them in 1495. It is difficult to see how he could have seized them on Islay, which was the stronghold of their clan. It is perhaps more likely that they were later persuaded by him to visit James IV in Edinburgh, hoping to obtain a royal pardon for their earlier insurrection, only to be arrested. Their execution horrified the Irish annalist who recognised Sir John Mor MacDonald of Dunivaig and the Glens as Ri Innse Gall in recording his death.

Only the two grandsons of Sir John Mor MacDonald of Dunivaig and the Glens escaped the destruction of their family, since they were then living in Ireland. The elder was Alexander MacDonald of Dunivaig and the Glens. He gained the chiefship of the clan, and indeed founded its later fortunes with a formidable reputation as a leader of the Highland mercenaries or galloglasses who flocked to fight in Ireland in the early sixteenth century. There can be little doubt that he was regarded throughout the Western Isles as the rightful successor to his grandfather as Ri Innse Gall, Lord of the Isles.

John MacIain of Ardnamurchan duly received his reward for his act of treachery, as it was doubtless seen in the eyes of Clan Donald, when James IV granted him twenty merklands in Sunart, ten merklands in Jura and other lands in Islay. Not long afterwards, it is said that he mounted an expedition against the Glens of Antrim, commanded by his two sons who, however, were killed when their attack was repulsed by the MacDonald clansmen.

Oddly enough, Alexander MacDonald, now the chief of Dunivaig and the Glens, married John MacIain's daughter Catherine, so cementing an alliance between the two families. Even so, doubt may be cast on the romantic story that Alexander MacDonald took advantage of his victory over MacIain's sons by sailing post-haste to Islay where he captured his future father-in-law who was forced to agree to their marriage. Indeed, John MacIain continued to administer his estates on Islay until his death in 1518, which perhaps even occurred at the hands of his son-in-law. However, according to a contemporary report, MacIain was himself married to a kinswoman of Colin Campbell, third Earl of Argyll, most likely his sister, and it seems almost certain that Catherine herself was born of this union.

There can be little doubt that Catherine's marriage was itself arranged as a means of allying Alexander MacDonald of Dunivaig and the Glens with the Campbells, Earls of Argyll, rather than with the MacIains of Ardnamurchan. It was probably around this time that Lachlan Cattanach MacLean of Duart married Catherine, sister to Colin Campbell, third Earl of Argyll. Evidently, the Campbells had embarked on a policy of allying themselves by marriage with the septs and erstwhile vassals of Clan Donald once the lordship was forfeited in 1493, so strengthening their own position in what was now a vacuum of political and military power.

Policy of Reconciliation under James IV

Meanwhile, James IV had responded to the lawless state of the Western Isles by mounting yet another expedition in May 1495. He visited Mingary Castle for the second time in two years, now held in his name by John MacIain of Ardnamurchan as its keeper. There he received the submission of John MacDonald of Sleat, Donald MacDonald of Keppoch, Alan MacDonald of Moidart, chief of Clan Ranald, Hector Odhar MacLean of Duart, Ewen Allanson of Locheil, Captain of Clan Cameron, and Gilleonan MacNeill of Barra. They later entered into a 'band' with Archibald Campbell who had succeeded his father as the second Earl of Argyll after his death the previous year. They all agreed to abstain from hostile acts against one another, or else be liable to a penalty of 500 pounds. In return for their submission, these chieftains and erstwhile vassals of Clan Donald were given royal charters to their lands. It was apparently in the same year that Farquhar MacIntosh, Captain of Clan Chattan, and Kenneth MacKenzie of Kintail were both imprisoned in Edinburgh Castle so that they might keep the peace. A year later, the Lords in Council passed an act requiring every chieftain of a Highland clan to execute any summons issued against his clansmen, failing which he was himself to be prosecuted as if he were the principal defendant in the case.

It now seemed as if the king's policy of reconciliation might succeed. Next year, the king paid three hurried visits to the Western Isles, using as his base the newly-constructed castle at Loch Kilkerran, or Campbeltown as it is now known. During one visit, he took the submissions of Alasdair Crotach MacLeod of Harris and Dunvegan and Torquil MacLeod of Lewis among others, granting them royal charters to their lands. Ranald Ban MacDonald of Clan Ranald was likewise granted lands in Uist, Eigg and Arisaig, while his distant kinsman Angus 'Reochson' also received lands in Benbecula, Eigg, Arisaig and Morar, which had all been resigned to the king by John MacDonald, son of Hugh MacDonald of Sleat. This effectively restored to

Clan Ranald its ancient patrimony, since these lands had originally been granted to Ranald, son of John MacDonald of Islay, first Lord of the Isles, by his marriage with Amie MacRuairi, heiress of Garmoran and the Uists.

Revocation of Charters by James IV

What now persuaded James IV to embark on a much more divisive, ill-advised and dangerous course remains a mystery. Even before he had come of age, he had issued a sweeping and symbolic act of revocation throughout the Lowlands in 1493 intended to mark the end of his minority. Now 25 years of age, he was entitled to make a formal revocation of all the grants issued during his minority. By revoking their charters, this act in effect allowed James IV to extract blackmail from his nobility over the possession of their lands. They were made to pay handsomely for the renewal of their charters, which the act had forced them to surrender into the king's hands in the first place. It was a tactic that James IV determined to enforce upon the chieftains and erstwhile vassals of Clan Donald. No sooner had he returned from Argyll and the Western Isles in 1498 than James IV revoked all their charters apart from the ones he had just issued. The chiefs thus affected regarded this act as a flagrant insult to their pride. It broke what they regarded as a solemn promise by James IV to recognise their inalienable rights to their own territories.

Worse followed in 1500 when James IV appointed Archibald Campbell, second Earl of Argyll, as his Lieutenant-General for Argyll and the Western Isles. He was granted a commission to let out three-year tacks or leases of all the lands throughout the entire Lordship of the Isles except for Islay and Kintyre. Argyll had already been made Keeper of Tarbert Castle in 1499, when he was also appointed baillie of the Crown lands in Knapdale. A similar policy was pursued by James IV elsewhere in the Highlands, since in 1501 he appointed Alexander Gordon, third Earl of Huntly, to act as his Lieutenant-General beyond the Mounth. He was granted very wide powers to compel the earls, lords, barons, and chief kinsmen to keep the peace. At the same time, he also received grants of numerous lands in Lochaber, previously held under the Lordship of the Isles. Duncan Stewart of Appin was likewise granted the lands of Glencoe and Duror, and it seems likely that John MacIain of Ardnamurchan was suitably rewarded at the same time. However, nearly all the other families that had once acted as the vassals of Clan Donald under the Lordship were faced with the imminent prospect of being expelled from their lands.

Escape of Donald Dubh

The threat of losing their lands to Duncan Stewart of Appin may well have prompted the MacIains of Glencoe to spring Donald Dubh from the castle of Innis Chonnel on Loch Awe, where he was held captive by Archibald Campbell, second Earl of Argyll. He was taken on his release to Lewis, where he came under the protection of his uncle Torquil MacLeod, despite Torquil's marriage to Catherine, daughter of the first Earl of Argyll. Donald Dubh had already been recognised by Clan Donald as the grandson and rightful heir of John MacDonald, fourth Lord of the Isles, after the murder of his father Angus Og MacDonald, and thus the natural successor to the Lordship itself.

Whether Donald Dubh was three years of age when his father was killed by his Irish harper in 1490 or whether he was born posthumously after his father's death as he later stated in a letter to Henry VIII of England remains uncertain. However, his mother was Isabella Campbell, daughter of the first Earl of Argyll, whom Angus Og had married perhaps in 1478. It is often said that Donald Dubh was kidnapped from Finlaggan by John Stewart, second Earl of Atholl, immediately after the Battle of Bloody Bay, acting with the connivance of his father-in-law, the first Earl of Argyll. But the Battle of Bloody Bay was fought in the years before 1485, making the dates difficult to reconcile. Perhaps more likely, if less romantic, is the view that he was born posthumously after his father's death once his Campbell mother had returned to her father's house.

Once at liberty, Donald Dubh was proclaimed Lord of the Isles by many of the families who had once followed Clan Donald as its vassals. As well as the MacLeods of Lewis, he was supported by the Camerons of Locheil and the MacLeans of Duart, together with the MacLeans of Lochbuie, the MacQuarries of Ulva, the MacNeills of Barra and the MacDonalds of Largie, all of whom forfeited their lands as a consequence of their treasonable actions. Only the MacLeods of Harris and Dunvegan and the MacIains of Ardnamurchan remained loyal to the Crown. The insurrection itself broke out late in 1503, perhaps triggered by the death of Donald Dubh's grandfather John MacDonald, fourth and last Lord of the Isles, at least in the eyes of the Crown. It was first directed against Badenoch, where the forces of Clan Donald under Donald Dubh plundered and laid waste with fire and sword the lands of Clan Chattan who were by now the vassals of the Earl of Huntly.

Rebellion by Donald Dubh

We know very little about the subsequent course of events apart from the actions taken by the government to contain the rebellion which was not quelled until 1505. Indeed, it was judged so formidable a threat that all of Scotland north of the Forth was called out under the leadership of the Earls of Argyll, Huntly, Crawford and Marischal, as well as Thomas Fraser, second Lord Lovat. Huntly undertook to seize and garrison the castles of Strome and Eilean Donan, provided that artillery and ammunition were supplied by sea at the king's expense, while the castles at Kilkerran (now Campbeltown), Dunaverty and Inverlochy were to be repaired. A naval expedition set sail from Dumbarton in May 1504 under the command of James Hamilton, Earl of Arran, charged with laying siege to the almost inaccessible Castle of Cairnaburgh in the Treshnish Isles, held by Lachlan Cattanach MacLean of Duart. It was evidently captured since Archibald Campbell, second Earl of Argyll, acted as its Constable for the next four years.

It is not recorded if Alexander Gordon, third Earl of Huntly, was equally successful farther north against the castles of Strome and Eilean Donan. However, two more naval expeditions were needed in 1505 before nearly all the rebels were brought into submission, overawed by the display of sea-power that the Scottish navy could now exercise under the rule of James IV. Only Torquil MacLeod of Lewis remained defiant until 1506 when the Earl of Huntly launched yet another expedition against the Outer Hebrides from Dumbarton. The MacLeod stronghold of Stornoway Castle was finally captured by October 1506, after it was attacked with artillery brought by sea from Edinburgh Castle. Torquil MacLeod apparently took refuge in Antrim, although there is an oral tradition that he was killed near Kilchrist on Skye. His name disappears from the historical record, while he forfeited his mainland territories of Assynt and Coigeach. They were given in life-rent to Iye Roy MacKay of Strathnaver in return for the services he had rendered to the Crown. It was left to Torquil's son John MacLeod to take forcible possession of Lewis, even though Torquil's brother Malcolm MacLeod received a charter to these lands in 1511. They eventually passed to Malcolm's son Ruairi MacLeod, who received charters from the Crown in 1538 and 1541 giving him a legal title to Lewis and Waternish.

Donald Dubh was evidently recaptured during the course of these campaigns, since he is found imprisoned in Stirling Castle by August 1507. He was then held captive in Edinburgh Castle for almost the next forty years, presumably acting as a hostage for the good behaviour of his own followers in the Western Isles, such was the threat that he posed to the central government.

Aftermath of Donald Dubh's Rebellion

The rebellion of Clan Donald under the leadership of Donald Dubh had only been suppressed with the greatest difficulty by the Crown after three arduous years of naval expeditions. Its sudden outbreak in 1504 had forced the central government to attend once more to the administration of justice in the Highlands and Western Isles, where 'the people are almost gone wild'. Convinced that the lack of justice was the prime cause of the rebellion, James IV first divided the Western Isles into two separate sheriffdoms, based at Tarbert or Kilkerran (now known as Campbeltown) for the southern Isles, and at Inverness or Dingwall for the northern Isles. Districts on the mainland were to come under the jurisdiction of circuit courts, held as appropriate at Inverness, Perth, Dumbarton or Ayr. These arrangements were further strengthened after the insurrection was successfully brought to an end in 1507.

Alexander Gordon, third Earl of Huntly, as the hereditary Sheriff of Inverness as well as Aberdeen, was now given jurisdiction over the latter-day counties of Inverness, Ross and Caithness. He was empowered to appoint deputy-sheriffs for Badenoch based at Kingussie, Lochaber based at Inverlochy, Ross based at Tain or Dingwall and Caithness based at Wick. The royal castles of Inverlochy and Inverness were to be fortified and put under his command. Archibald Campbell, second Earl of Argyll, was given equally sweeping powers as Sheriff of Kintyre and the southern Isles. Other actions were evidently taken by James IV to bring the rule of law to the Highlands and Western Isles, since it was decreed that 'all the Isles be ruled by our sovereign lord's own laws and the common laws of the realm, and by no other laws'. Evidently, the practice of Celtic law was still widespread. James IV even gave a grant of land in the Isle of Skye to a certain Kenneth Williamson to support him in becoming a master of Scots law, which he was then to practise within the bounds of the Western Isles. As John Bannerman has demonstrated, he was the contemporary head of the legal dynasty which had served the Lords of the Isles. No doubt, James IV hoped that he would turn his hand instead to practising the king's law.

Death of James IV at Flodden

Such measures brought a brief period of peace and calm to the Western Isles after 1507, which it was argued had been 'daunted' by the king's strength of purpose. It was perhaps bolstered by the evident rapport that James IV was able to establish with his Gaelic-speaking subjects. They even shared a common language, since he was an accomplished linguist, able to converse in Gaelic as well as Latin and several other languages. He patronised Gaelic music and poetry, rewarding harpists for their playing of the clarsach and commending bards for their work. Indeed, it is said that nearly all the

Highland clans rallied to his banner when James IV raised an army in 1513 to attack England, drawn by the 'Auld Alliance' into a distant conflict between England and France.

The battle fought at Flodden turned into an utter defeat for the Scots, and James IV himself was killed 'fighting like a common soldier' along with many of his nobility. Among the dead were Archibald Campbell, second Earl of Argyll, and Matthew Stewart, Earl of Lennox, who had together commanded the Highlanders on the right wing of the Scots army. Several of Argyll's kinsmen, including Sir Duncan Campbell of Glenorchy, also lost their lives. Alexander Gordon, third Earl of Huntly, survived the battle, as did many Highland chieftains often said to have died on Flodden field. However, their presence at the battle in such large numbers may well be doubted. Certainly, apart from the losses among the Campbell kinsmen, there is no evidence that any Highland chieftain of note fell at Flodden, since Lachlan Cattanach MacLean of Duart, Thomas Fraser of Lovat, Ewen Cameron of Lochiel and John MacIain of Ardnamurchan all survived the battle, despite the later claims of Pitscottie to the contrary.

Rebellion by Donald Gallda of Lochalsh

The death of James IV at the Battle of Flodden ushered in another long minority, for his eldest son was barely a year old in 1513 when he succeeded his father as James V of Scotland. Almost immediately, the banner of rebellion was raised in the north by the MacDonalds of Lochalsh, acting on behalf of Donald Dubh as the true heir to the Lordship of the Isles, or so they claimed. As we have seen, Alexander MacDonald of Lochalsh had attempted an earlier revolt in 1491, and again in 1494, before his murder by John MacIain of Ardnamurchan. After falling into the king's hands, his three sons were taken south to be educated in Edinburgh and his eldest son was later knighted by James IV as Sir Donald Gallda MacDonald upon the field of Flodden.

Known in the Highlands as Donald Gallda, 'the Stranger', from his lowland upbringing, Sir Donald MacDonald of Lochalsh took advantage of the confused state of the country immediately after Flodden by launching an armed invasion of Ross in November 1513. Backed by a large following, he seized Urquhart Castle and expelled its royal garrison. The surrounding lands of Glen Moriston, belonging to John Grant of Freuchie, were plundered. Among his allies were Lachlan Cattanach MacLean of Duart, who now seized back the Castle of Cairnaburgh in the Treshnish Islands, and Alastair Crotach MacLeod of Harris and Dunvegan, who captured the MacDonald Castle of Dunscaith in Sleat.

Such a powerful challenge to central authority was resisted by Colin Campbell, now third Earl of Argyll after the death of his father at Flodden, who was soon afterwards made Justice-General of Scotland in July 1514. An act of Council under the regency of Margaret Tudor, the dowager queen, directed him to attack Lachlan Cattanach MacLean of Duart and the other rebels in the southern Isles. Prominent among them was Alexander MacDonald of Dunivaig and the Glens. He had returned from his territories in the Glens of Antrim to reclaim the lands on Islay, forfeited in 1494 after the rebellion and subsequent execution of his father John Cathanach and his grandfather Sir John Mor MacDonald. The royal Council further charged Ewen Cameron of Locheil and William MacIntosh of Clan Chattan despite the feud that existed between these two families, to guard Lochaber against the rebels, while John MacKenzie of Kintail and William Munro of Foulis were to harass the forces of Donald Gallda in the north.

Such actions against him forced Donald Gallda to enter into negotiations with John Stewart, Duke of Albany, who by then had returned to Scotland to take charge of the country as its Governor. Donald Gallda was given a safe-conduct to come to Edinburgh. Once there, it seems he became involved in a lawsuit against the Earl of Argyll, while his various disputes with John MacIain of Ardnamurchan were apparently settled to the satisfaction of both parties. However, despite the success of these negotiations and the leniency shown by the government to Donald Gallda in accepting his submission, it was not long before he again rebelled against the Crown.

Attack on Ardnamurchan

Donald Gallda now attacked John MacIain of Ardnamurchan, suggesting that the quarrel between them still had not been settled to his satisfaction. He first deceived his followers by implying that he had been appointed as Lieutentant of the Western Isles by the royal council under the Duke of Albany. This stratagem gave him sufficient authority to raise a large body of men, expelling John MacIain from his lands of Ardnamurchan where he took possession of Mingary Castle. The government reacted by insisting that he return Mingary Castle to its rightful owner while restoring his lands to him as well. Donald Gallda refused contemptuously, put the castle to the flames and ravaged Ardnamurchan with fire and sword. His followers now realised they had been deceived and turned against him. Alarmed by the reckless nature of his behaviour which threatened to destroy them all, they plotted his capture. However, forewarned, Donald Gallda managed to escape, but his two brothers fell into the hands of Lachlan Cattanach MacLean of Duart and Alasdair Crotach MacLeod of Dunvegan. After their captors had surrendered them to the government, they were taken to Edinburgh, tried for treason and executed in 1518.

Alliance with Colin Campbell, Third Earl of Argyll

Meanwhile, in 1517, Lachlan Cattanach MacLean of Duart and Alasdair Crotach MacLeod of Harris and Dunvegan had entered into an alliance with Colin Campbell, third Earl of Argyll, which was intended to bring the rebellion of Donald Gallda finally to an end. MacLean of Duart petitioned the Regent Albany to pardon the treasonable behaviour of himself and his followers, among whom were named: his uncle Donald MacLean, Gilleonan MacNeill of Barra, Neil MacKinnon of Mishnish, Donnsleibhe MacQuarrie of Ulva and Lachlan MacLean of Ardgour. He urged that Donald Gallda and his adherents should all be treated as traitors and their lands forfeited to show that the government was serious in 'destroying the wicked blood of the Isles; for, as long as that blood reigns, the King shall never have the Isles in peace.' Indeed, Lachlan Cattanach MacLean of Duart proposed in future to act zealously on behalf of the Crown, but only if he was granted lands in Tiree and Mull for his good services.

Alasdair Crotach MacLeod of Harris and Dunvegan and John MacLean of Lochbuie made similar demands of the government, which were likewise agreed by the Regent and his royal Council. Colin Campbell, third Earl of Argyll, successfully petitioned the Regent to make him King's Lieutenant over the Western Isles and the adjacent districts of the mainland, but he was only granted the office for three years. He was given wide powers to receive submissions from all who would accept his own authority. It allowed him to pardon all their previous offences against the Crown and restore them to their lands on lease. For their part, they had to agree to pay all their rents and other duties, while surrendering hostages for their own good behaviour. Only Donald Gallda and his followers were to be excluded from such a reconciliation. Even so, Colin Campbell, third Earl of Argyll, argued that Alexander MacDonald of Dunivaig and the Glens should be given a lease to his estates on Islay, so enabling him to live off his own lands without any need for plunder provided that he was willing to submit to the king's peace.

Death of Donald Gallda of Lochalsh

Alexander MacDonald of Dunivaig and the Glens evidently refused this far-sighted offer of clemency, at least for the time being. He came to the aid of Donald Gallda when he launched his final attack upon John MacIain of Ardnamurchan in 1518, assisted by the MacLeods of Lewis who were still among his adherents. The climax of their campaign came at the Battle of Creag-an-Airgid, when John MacIain and his two sons were killed. Their deaths marked the beginning of a slow decline in the fortunes of their family, which came increasingly under the influence of the Earl of Argyll and his Campbell kinsmen. Indeed, the Earl benefited from MacIain's death since he was granted the wardship of MacIain's young son Alexander. It brought him control of his estates in Islay for the first time: he granted them out to his brother, Sir John Campbell of Cawdor. Donald Gallda greatly strengthened his own claim to the Lordship of the Isles by his victory, much to the dismay of the Regent and the royal council. However, his rebellion came to a sudden end in 1519, when Donald Gallda of Lochalsh died of natural causes, possibly while seeking refuge at Cairnaburg Castle in the Treshnish Isles. He left no male heirs to carry on his line which became extinct, while his sister carried what remained of his estates to the MacDonalds of Glengarry by her marriage to their chief.

Feuds among Clan Chattan

The death of Sir Donald Gallda MacDonald of Lochalsh and the continued captivity of Donald Dubh in Edinburgh Castle brought several years of peace to the Western Isles. But elsewhere, it was a different matter since struggles over the Captaincy of Clan Chattan reached such a pitch during these years that it required the intervention of central authority. James IV had imprisoned Farquhar MacIntosh in 1495, after he had supported the earlier rebellion of Alexander MacDonald of Lochalsh in 1491. He was finally released in 1514 after the death of James IV at Flodden, but he died only a year later. His cousin William succeeded him, but he was murdered the very next year by his second cousin who was himself slain in revenge. William's younger brother Lachlan MacIntosh then become the Captain of Clan Chattan until 1524, when he too was killed out hunting near Inverness.

He left only a young son William, then aged three years, who was given in ward to James Stewart, Earl of Moray, himself a natural son of James IV and the feudal superior of Clan Chattan. Hector MacIntosh, natural brother of Farquhar MacIntosh, took control of Clan Chattan during the young chief's minority. William himself was given in custody by the Earl of Moray to the Ogilivies, who also received some lands once held by Clan Chattan. Angered by this turn of events, Hector MacIntosh invaded their lands in Moray and massacred twenty-four gentlemen of the name of Ogilvie.

These events occurred while George Gordon, fourth Earl of Huntly, was still only a minor. It was therefore James Stewart, Earl of Moray, who was given a commission in 1528 against Clan Chattan: 'to their utter destruction, by slaughter, burning, drowning and other means, and leave no creature living of that clan, except priests, women and bairns' who were to be transported to Shetland and Norway. This was evidently sufficient to deter Hector MacIntosh, who ceased his depredations until 1531. He then invaded the Earl of Moray's territories, laying siege to Darnaway Castle, only to suffer a serious reverse when three hundred of his clansmen were captured and executed. Hector MacIntosh himself escaped and his lawless ways must have continued, since George Gordon, fourth Earl of Huntly, was given a Commission of Fire and Sword against Clan Chattan in 1534. Eventually, after receiving a royal pardon, Hector MacIntosh was assassinated, supposedly by a monk from St Andrews, and William MacIntosh became Captain of Clan Chattan after coming of age in 1540.

James Stewart, Earl of Moray and an illegitimate son of James IV of Scotland, was his feudal superior as well as being his uncle by marriage, but he died in 1544. George Gordon, fourth Earl of Huntly, was then appointed Lieutenant-General in the north. Five years later in 1549, he was granted the gift of the lands and earldom of Moray. He thus became the feudal superior of William MacIntosh, Captain of Clan Chattan, whose destruction he eventually accomplished as recounted later.

Feuds in the Western Isles

The troubled year of 1528 also witnessed the climax of yet another feud in the Western Isles, when Donald Gruamach MacDonald of Sleat seized the lands of Trotternish from the MacLeods of Harris and Dunvegan, supported by his half-brother John MacLeod of Lewis. Donald Gruamach was the grandson of Hugh MacDonald of Sleat, who was himself a half-brother of John MacDonald, fourth Lord of the Isles. His territories in the south of Skye first came into the possession of his family in 1469 when Hugh MacDonald received a grant of twenty-eight merklands in Sleat from his half-brother, together with a large grant of lands in South Uist, Benbecula and North Uist. Later, after receiving a charter in 1495 from the Crown to these lands, he also laid claim to the lands of Trotternish in the north of Skye as the heir of Angus Og MacDonald, who had styled himself 'Master of the Isles and Lord of Trotternish' before his death in 1490.

Hugh MacDonald of Sleat died three years later in 1498, and he was succeeded by his eldest son John. He in turn lacked any male heirs at his death in 1505 although he had five half-brothers, each born of a different mother. Indeed, his father had entered into liaisons with the daughters of the Crowner of Caithness, MacLeod of Harris, MacLeod of Lewis, MacLean of Coll and the vicar of South Uist, as well as with John's own mother Finvola, who was the daughter of MacIain of Ardnamurchan. He was succeeded by his half-brother Donald Gallach, but he was murdered in 1506 along with his half-brother Donald Hearach. The assassin was yet another half-brother, known as Gilleasbuig Dubh, or Archibald the Black, acting in concert with his two remaining half-brothers. After this fratricidal bout of bloodletting, the succession eventually passed around 1518 to Donald Gallach's son, known as Donald Gruamach, meaning the 'Grim-Looking'.

Battle of Glendale

According to MacLeod traditions, it was during the chiefship of Donald Gruamach MacDonald of Sleat that the Battle of Glendale was fought in the north-west of Skye. It took place against the MacLeods of Harris and Dunvegan under their long-lived chief Alastair Crotach, the 'Hump-Backed'. A large party of MacDonalds had landed at Loch Eynort on the west coast of Skye, and then marched north towards Dunvegan, laying waste to Minginish, Bracadale and much of Duirinish on the way. Alasdair Crotach of Harris and Dunvegan was absent in Harris, but on hearing the news, he returned in force with his own clansmen. They landed at the head of Loch Pooltiel where the valley of Glendale reaches the sea.

Battle was then joined between the two clans, and the MacDonalds were winning when the MacLeods unfurled the Fairy Flag with its miraculous powers. The tide of battle immediately turned in favour of the MacLeods and the MacDonalds were routed with heavy losses. Donald Gruamach was supposedly killed in this battle, but he was certainly alive in 1530, dying perhaps four years later in 1534. Indeed, if this battle occurred around 1490, as the MacLeods maintain, it must have taken place long before Donald Gruamach became chief of the MacDonalds of Sleat, but during the lifetime of Alan MacDonald of Clan Ranald, who it is said was another of the combatants.

However, it may well be that two separate encounters have been confused in the MacLeod traditions. The fratricidal strife among the MacDonalds of Sleat during the early years of the sixteenth century must surely have made it difficult for them to pursue feuds with other clans. It therefore seems more likely that the Battle of Glendale occurred somewhat later. Possibly, the MacDonalds invaded the north-west of Skye after Alasdair Crotach MacLeod of Harris and Dunvegan had captured the MacDonald stronghold of Dunscaith during the rebellion of Donald Gallda after 1513, only to be defended at the Battle of Glendale.

Alasdair Crotach afterwards received a lease from the Crown to the lands of Trotternish as a reward for his services. These lands had previously been held at various times by Torquil MacLeod of Lewis and by Ranald Ban MacDonald of Clan Ranald. Even later, the chief of Harris and Dunvegan received a heritable grant to the MacDonald lands of Sleat and North Uist, but there is little evidence that he was ever able to gain their possession. Indeed, Donald Gruamach joined forces in 1528 with his half-brother John MacLeod, who was the eldest son of Torquil MacLeod of Lewis. Together, they drove Alasdair Crotach MacLeod of Harris and Dunvegan from Trotternish. John MacLeod was then assisted by Donald Gruamach in regaining his ancestral lands in Lewis, which his father Torquil MacLeod had earlier forfeited to the Crown in 1505 for his support of the rebellion of Donald Dubh in the years after 1504. As already mentioned, they passed ten years later in 1538 into the hands of his cousin Ruairi MacLeod. It was the internecine quarrels among Ruairi's sons that eventually destroyed the MacLeods of Lewis, leaving no survivors.

Aggrandisement of the Campbells

After the death of Donald Gallda in 1519, and the collapse of his rebellion against the Crown, the Campbells were active in pursuing their own territorial interests. Already they had entered into marriage alliances with their neighbours. Now, Colin Campbell, third Earl of Argyll, used his office of King's Lieutenant to extract a bond of manrent from Lachlan Cattanach MacLean of Duart and Alasdair Crotach MacLeod of Harris and Dunvegan, along with such 'barons of the Western Isles' as John MacLeod of Minginish, Gilleone MacNeill of Barra, John Abrach MacLean of Coll, Ewen MacKinnon of Mishnish and Donnsleibhe MacQuarrie of Ulva. Soon afterwards, Alexander MacDonald, Captain of Clan Ranald, and Alasdair MacDonald of Glengarry entered into similar agreements. This diplomatic offensive to bring peace to the Western Isles culminated in 1521 in yet another bond of manrent given by Lachlan Cattanach MacLean of Duart, Colin Campbell of Ardkinglas and Alan Stewart of Duror among several others to Colin Campbell, third Earl of Argyll. It was made on behalf of all the inhabitants of Argyll, Lorn, Knapdale, Kintyre, Breadalbane, Balquhidder, Lennox, Menteith and Strathearn. Such an agreement is testament to the pre-eminent position that the Campbells, Earls of Argyll, had achieved in the years following the forfeiture of the Lordship of the Isles. But it was also perhaps intended to counterbalance the powerful threat posed by Alexander Mac-Donald of Dunivaig and the Glens if he was indeed recognised as Ri Innse Gall by the other septs of Clan Donald.

Meanwhile in 1510, Sir John Campbell had married Muriel, heiress of the last thane of Cawdor. She had earlier been forcibly abducted by the

Campbells after becoming the ward of the groom's father Archibald Campbell, second Earl of Argyll. Somewhat later, Sir John Campbell, now of Cawdor, acquired from John MacLean of Lochbuie various claims to the lands of Lochaber, Glencoe and Duror, which their previous proprietor had been quite unable to exercise. At first, Sir John Campbell of Cawdor was violently resisted by the Stewarts of Appin and the Camerons of Locheil, who kept hold of their lands by force of arms. However, he eventually adopted the expedient of transferring his title to the lands in question to the Earl of Argyll, his brother. The latter's prestige as the King's Lieutenant in the Isles was such that Ewen Cameron of Locheil and Allan Stewart of Duror were forced to enter into bonds of manrent with Sir John Campbell of Cawdor as their feudal superior.

Sir John Campbell of Cawdor also received a bond of manrent from Alexander MacDonald of Dunivaig and the Glens, who had evidently decided to come to terms with a family whose power and influence were evidently gaining ground in Argyll and the Western Isles, despite his own powerful position. Their agreement to become 'gossips' or godfathers to each other's children cemented the alliance between the two families. Alexander MacDonald of Dunivaig and the Glens gained in return a five-year lease of forty-five merklands in Islay, comprising nearly all his family's inheritance on the island, together with other lands in Jura and Colonsay. The lands in question had been held by John MacIain of Ardnamurchan before his death in 1518 at the hands of Donald Gallda of Lochalsh. But when he died, the wardship of his young son Alexander was granted to Colin Campbell, third Earl of Argyll, who transferred the administration of his estates on Islay to Sir John Campbell of Cawdor.

Alexander MacDonald of Dunivaig and the Glens was also favoured during these years with grants to lands in Kintyre that had previously belonged to his grandfather, Sir John Mor MacDonald of Dunivaig and the Glens, presumably at the instigation of Colin Campbell, third Earl of Argyll, and his brother Sir John Campbell of Cawdor. After regaining his Islay estates under the feudal superiority of Sir John Campbell of Cawdor, Alexander MacDonald of Dunivaig and the Glens spent much of the 1520s involved in the affairs of Ulster, where he intervened in the feud between the O'Neills and the O'Donnells, greatly strengthening his own position. Only when James V threatened to revoke the charter to his lands of Kintyre would he challenge Campbell hegemony in the Western Isles.

Rebellion against the Campbells, Earls of Argyll

During the final years of James V's minority, when the king was held in duress by Archibald Douglas, Earl of Angus, Colin Campbell as the third Earl of Argyll maintained a steadying influence on the government. Indeed, when James V broke free of the Douglases in 1528, he confirmed Colin Campbell, third Earl of Argyll, now a special confidant of the king and one of his privy councillors, in the offices as Sheriff of Argyll, Justice-General of Scotland and Master of the Royal Household. But soon after starting to rule in his own right in 1528, James V revoked all the charters that had been granted during his minority, just as his predecessors had done after coming of age. Alexander MacDonald of Dunivaig and the Glens in particular was threatened with losing his lands in Kintyre, which he had regained after the earlier rebellion of Donald Gallda in the years after 1513.

He found eager allies in the MacLeans of Duart who had their own quarrel with Colin Campbell, third Earl of Argyll, despite the bond of manrent that they and their allies had signed with Argyll in 1519. It arose from the marriage that their chieftain Lachlan Cattanach MacLean had previously made with Catherine Campbell, younger sister of the third Earl of Argyll. The marriage was not a success, as 'there was trouble behind the curtains' in the coy words of a later chronicler. Indeed, according to tradition, Lachlan Cattanach MacLean of Duart was foolishly persuaded to abandon his wife. She was left chained to an offshore rock, still known as Lady's Rock at the entrance to the Sound of Mull. As it was swept by the tides, he evidently intended that she should drown. Instead, she was rescued by some passing boatmen who conveyed her to safety with her brother Colin, third Earl of Argyll.

Unaware of his wife's rescue, Lachlan MacLean now hurried to Inveraray, intending to break the news of her unfortunate death to the Earl of Argyll as his brother-in-law, only to encounter the lady herself. Since nothing was said at the time, Lachlan MacLean of Duart apparently did not realise that the Campbells knew of his plot against his wife. Unaware of the danger, he went to Edinburgh in 1523, where he was murdered in a lodging-house by his wife's brother, Sir John Campbell of Cawdor. Such a family feud meant that the MacLeans of Duart had every reason to join Alexander MacDonald of Dunivaig and the Glens in 1529 to revenge the death of their late chief. Together, they descended upon the Campbell lands of Craignish and Rosneath which they plundered with fire and sword, killing many of the inhabitants. The Campbells or their adherents retaliated in kind by raiding the MacLean lands of Mull, Tiree and Morvern.

Such acts of savage reprisal were not expected of the Campbells since it appeared that they were taken in private revenge against the MacLeans of Duart. They were evidently not the punitive actions that might be countenanced by the Earl of Argyll in his official capacity as the King's Lieutenant in the Isles. Indeed, the suspicion arose that the Campbells, and Sir John

Campbell of Cawdor in particular, were intent on fomenting disaffection in the Western Isles so that they might be employed in putting down any rebellion to their own advantage. The royal council therefore decided to send an emissary to treat with Alexander MacDonald of Dunivaig and the Glens rather than assemble an expeditionary force, as urged by Sir John Campbell of Cawdor on behalf of his elder brother.

Submission of the Rebels

Only when the emissary failed in his mission was the Earl of Argyll ordered to proceed against the rebels. Forces were raised throughout a very wide area of western Scotland. However, the imminent prospect of vigorous action being taken against them persuaded many of the rebel chieftains to offer their submission to the king. Their names are a striking testimony to very wide support enjoyed by Alexander MacDonald of Dunivaig and the Glens as Ri Innse Gall, even if they mostly had their own quarrels with the Crown. Among their number were Hector Mor MacLean of Duart, John MacLean of Lochbuie, John Moydertach, Captain of Clan Ranald, Alexander MacIain of Ardnamurchan, Alasdair Crotach MacLeod of Harris and Dunvegan, John Cam MacLean of Coll, John MacLeod of Lewis and Donald Gruamach MacDonald of Sleat. The king offered them all safe conducts so that they might come to Edinburgh where their grievances could be aired. The Earl of Argyll was required to surrender four hostages from among his Campbell kinsmen to assure that they would return unharmed to the Western Isles.

All these preparations of a military expedition were, however, delayed by the illness and death of Colin Campbell, third Earl of Argyll, which occurred late in 1529. He was succeeded as fourth Earl of Argyll by his eldest son Archibald Campbell. He immediately took on all the hereditary offices enjoyed by his father and grandfather, except perhaps for the Lieutenancy of the Isles. Even so, it was proposed that James V should himself lead the expedition to the Western Isles, while James Stewart, Earl of Moray and the half-brother of the king as the natural son of James IV, who was now the King's Lieutenant in the North, should assemble another army in the north.

Alarmed by the scale of the forces arrayed against him, Alexander MacDonald of Dunivaig and the Glens now decided to submit in all humility to the king's authority. In June 1531, he came to Stirling under a safe-conduct where he was pardoned by James V and received back all his lands in Islay and Kintyre that he had forfeited through his rebellion. He agreed to assist the royal chamberlains in collecting the rents and other duties from the Crown lands in the southern Isles and Kintyre, to procure for them the cooperation of all the other chieftains over whom he had any control, to release all the prisoners that he held belonging to Earl of Argyll and to abstain from meddling in the lands and possessions of others.

Eclipse of Archibald Campbell, Fourth Earl of Argyll

Meanwhile, Archibald Campbell, fourth Earl of Argyll, had proceeded to the Western Isles. He was perhaps even accompanied by neutral observers from the king's household to ensure that he acted with only reasonable force against the rebels. But on his arrival, he was dismayed to find that Hector Mor MacLean of Duart and all the other rebellious chieftains were now prepared to submit to the king's authority, following the example of Alexander MacDonald of Dunivaig and the Glens. It left him with no lands to forfeit to his own advantage. Frustrated by this turn of events, he first attempted to goad the erstwhile rebels into revolt, intending that they should break the king's peace. When this tactic failed, the Earl of Argyll lodged a formal complaint with the royal council, charging Alexander MacDonald of Dunivaig and the Glens with offences against himself and his followers.

Summoned to Edinburgh to answer the charges against him, Alexander MacDonald did not hesitate to appear before the Council, much to the surprise of his accuser. He absented himself from its deliberations and, after waiting nearly a fortnight, Alexander MacDonald presented the Council with a written statement rebutting all the charges made against him. He further charged the Earl of Argyll with abusing his own office, while laying the blame for the disturbed state of the Western Isles over the last few years upon the late Earl of Argyll and his two brothers, Sir John Campbell of Cawdor and Archibald Campbell of Skipness. Such an indictment fully confirmed James V in his suspicions that the young Earl of Argyll was more concerned with pursuing his own private interests than pacifying the Western Isles in the king's name.

Already, Archibald Campbell, fourth Earl of Argyll, had revealed his own ambitions for absolute power by arguing that he should be given full authority as King's Lieutenant over Kintyre and the southern Isles, which he would exercise at his own discretion and expense. However, James V now ordered the earl's accounting of the Crown rentals from the Western Isles to be examined. It proved so unsatisfactory that Archibald Campbell, fourth Earl of Argyll, was warded in prison. Even though he was released soon afterwards, he was deprived of all his hereditary offices in the Isles which he did not regain until after the death of James V in 1542. These events mark the start of the great schism between the MacDonalds and the Campbells which reached its climax in the campaigns of Montrose in 1645 and 1646.

Clan Donald in the Ascendant

Alexander MacDonald of Dunivaig and the Glens profited greatly from the temporary disgrace of Archibald Campbell, fourth Earl of Argyll. He gained the favour of James V, who took his eldest son James to be educated at the Court in Edinburgh. Under the stern charge of William Henderson, Dean of Holyrood, he learnt to read and write, while his presence in Edinburgh guaranteed his father's own good behaviour. Alexander's proud boast that he could raise more fighting men from his own territories than the Earl of Argyll was now put to the test in 1532 when he commanded an army of 7,000 or 8,000 men in Ireland. Fighting for O'Donnell against O'Neill and his English allies, the campaign itself was intended to act as a diversion to the attacks then being made by Henry VIII of England on the Scottish borders. Its success further strengthened his family's powerful position in Antrim which would stand them in good stead for the rest of the sixteenth century.

Argyll and the Western Isles remained peaceful over the next few years, and it is recorded that James V visited the area on several occasions. Indeed, the well-known story of MacLeod's Tables may well date from one such visit. Alastair Crotach as the chief of the MacLeods of Harris and Dunvegan was dining with the king on a visit to Edinburgh when he was asked by some Lowland nobleman if he was not impressed by the magnificence of his palatial surroundings. MacLeod replied that he was willing to wager that he had on Skye an even more spacious hall with a higher roof, a richer table, and even more brilliant candlesticks. Next year, the king and his Court visited Skye, and Alastair Crotach conducted the party to the very summit of Heaval Bheag, the higher of the two flat-topped hills opposite Dunvegan, better known as MacLeod's Tables. There a great banquet was served by the light of blazing torches held aloft by MacLeod clansmen under a starry sky as the sun set in the west. The king agreed that MacLeod had won his wager. Even so, after the death of Alexander MacDonald of Dunivaig and the Glens in 1538, a further rebellion broke out in 1539 led by Donald Gorm MacDonald of Sleat. It was directed at first against the MacLeods of Harris and Dunvegan, with whom the MacDonalds of Sleat had already quarrelled over the lands of Trotternish.

Rebellion of Donald Gorm of Sleat

When Donald Gruamach of Sleat died in 1534, still holding the lands of Trotternish by force, he was succeeded by his eldest son Donald Gorm. He had earlier married the daughter and heiress of his father's ally John

MacLeod of Lewis, who was now also dead. Donald Gorm now allied himself with the legal heir to the lands of Lewis, Ruairi MacLeod, cousin of his father-in-law John MacLeod of Lewis. Even though he now held his lands of Lewis by royal charter, Ruairi MacLeod agreed to assist Donald Gorm in regaining his lands of Trotternish. They had been seized in the meantime by Alastair Crotach MacLeod of Harris and Dunvegan as their rightful tenant under the Crown. However, the conspiracy between the two rebel leaders was perhaps much wider. Donald Gorm was clearly intent on regaining the earldom of Ross, while the death of Alexander MacDonald of Dunivaig and the Glens in the previous year meant that he had a realistic claim to be recognised as Lord of the Isles at the head of Clan Donald.

Indeed, Donald Gorm was heir-male to the Lordship of the Isles, always supposing that Donald Dubh, and more especially his father Angus Og MacDonald, were illegitimate as the Crown maintained. Moreover, Donald Dubh still remained in captivity, while the position of James MacDonald as the young chief of Dunivaig and the Glens could be challenged, especially as he remained in Edinburgh undergoing an education that would assure his loyalty to the Crown. Donald Gorm could thus appeal to the age-old system of kin-based inheritance which gave him a powerful claim to the Lordship of the Isles. Doubtless he was supported by his followers, disappointed that James V had not raised Clan Donald to its former glory after the fall from grace of the Earl of Argyll. Indeed, it was the MacDonalds of Dunivaig and the Glens who were now apparently favoured by the king to the detriment of the various branches of Clan Donald in the north.

The rebellion of Donald Gorm aided by Ruairi MacLeod and his followers took place in the early summer of 1539, when he attacked Alasdair Crotach MacLeod of Harris and Dunvegan and seized the lands of Trotternish. He then directed his forces against John MacKenzie of Kintail, who was the King's Lieutenant for Wester Ross, first ravaging his lands of Kinlochewe. Donald Gorm then proceeded to Kintail, where he intended to lay siege to the Castle of Eilean Donan. It was there that his rebellion ended as suddenly as it had begun. After learning that the castle was almost deserted, Donald Gorm launched a surprise attack against the fortress. But he was struck in the foot by an arrow after he had rashly exposed himself to view under the castle walls. Not realising that the arrow was barbed, he pulled it from his flesh, cutting an artery. The medical skills of all his followers were quite unable to staunch the flow of blood, and he died soon afterwards. Although his death caused the rebellion to collapse immediately, it might otherwise have proved a formidable challenge to the king's authority in the Western Isles.

Naval Expedition of James V

James V reacted vigorously to the abortive rebellion of Donald Gorm, when he sailed in 1540 around the north of Scotland with a fleet of twelve ships, heavily armed with cannon. Cardinal Beaton, Archibald Campbell, fourth Earl of Argyll, and the Earls of Arran and Huntly were among his commanders. During the voyage, a naval surveyor mapped the coastline in great detail. The flotilla first sailed north from the Firth of Forth to Orkney where it took on supplies, and then along the north coast of Sutherland. There, the expedition seized Donald MacKay of Strathnaver before it proceeded to Lewis where Ruairi MacLeod was taken into custody. The fleet then sailed across the Minch to the west coast of Skye, where Alasdair Crotach MacLeod of Harris and Dunvegan was taken into custody.

Sailing around the north of Skye, the fleet dropped anchor off Portree. There, summoned to attend the king several chieftains of Clan Donald and its vassal kindreds were detained on board, including John Moydertach, Captain of Clan Ranald, and Alasdair MacDonald of Glengarry. Only Archibald MacDonald of Sleat, Tutor to the young son of Donald Gorm, was allowed to remain at liberty. The royal fleet with its prisoners then sailed towards Wester Ross where John MacKenzie of Kintail was held as the king's prisoner after he had come on aboard. It then passed through the Sound of Sleat, visiting the islands of Mull and Islay, before it reached Knapdale and Kintyre. Hector Mor MacLean of Duart and James MacDonald of Dunivaig and the Glens, now chief of his family after the death of his father Alexander in 1538, were likewise detained during this leg of the voyage. James V disembarked on reaching Dumbarton, but he sent the ships with all his prisoners aboard back to Edinburgh around the north of Scotland.

By taking prisoner of all these chieftains, James V was now in a very powerful position to dictate his own terms for the peaceful settlement of the Western Isles. We hardly know any of its details except that the chieftains regarded as the most disloyal were kept prisoner in Edinburgh Castle to guarantee the good behaviour of their followers. Others who seemed less of a threat were evidently released after they had surrendered hostages for their own good behaviour. The Lordship of the Isles, together with all of Kintyre, was now annexed inalienably to the Crown, while various castles were garrisoned with royal forces, including Dunaverty in the south of Kintyre and Dunivaig on the island of Islay among several others farther north. Yet all these arrangements came to nought in 1542 when James V died suddenly at the early age of thirty years, shortly after the Scottish defeat at the Battle of Solway Moss.

Chapter Three

HEADSHIP OF THE GAEL

Although James V had several illegitimate children when he died in 1542, his only legal heir was his infant daughter Mary Stuart. She became Queen of Scots when only six days old. Her minority was thus very lengthy, even by Stewart standards. She did not start to rule in her own right until 1561 when she was eighteen years of age. It was also much disturbed by religious dissension which not only culminated in the Scottish Reformation of 1560 but greatly affected Scotland's relations with England as well. Even before the death of James V, Henry VIII of England had dissolved the monasteries and made himself the head of the Church of England, rejecting the authority of the Pope as the spiritual leader of the Catholic Church in Rome.

Henry VIII had attempted to persuade James V, who was his nephew by the marriage of James IV with his sister Margaret Tudor, to follow the same policy in Scotland, but without success. Instead, the Scottish king married the French-born Mary of Guise in 1538. He thus allied himself with France in support of the Catholic Church, which now threatened a crusade against England. Even though it came to nothing, Henry VIII reacted by raiding the Scottish borders, and when James V retaliated by launching an invasion of England his divided army was utterly defeated at the Battle of Solway Moss in 1542. His death only six weeks later exposed all the latent divisions within the country. Not only were Scottish nobles now held prisoner in England where they might be persuaded to act in Henry VIII's interest, but Archibald Douglas, sixth Earl of Angus, was also exiled in England with his kinsmen after forfeiting his earldom in 1528 for holding James V captive at the very end of his minority.

The reforming zeal of the English protestants had already affected many in Scotland who formed a pro-English party, although they were not yet in a majority. The reformers first found a temporary leader in James Hamilton, second Earl of Arran, and heir-presumptive to the throne as the grandson of Mary Stewart, daughter of James II. Appointed as Governor of Scotland, he initially favoured the proposal made by Henry VIII of England that his young son Edward, Prince of Wales, should be betrothed to the infant Queen of Scotland. Henry VIII evidently intended to take the government of Scotland into his own hands as the great-uncle of the infant Queen of Scots. He was aided in this plan by the Scots nobles still held captive in England. who mostly shared his antagonism to the Catholic Church although on religious grounds. Henry VIII now demanded not only the custody of his prospective daughter-in-law, but that English garrisons should also be placed in all the fortresses of Scotland. Cardinal Beaton, Archbishop of St Andrews and the conservative leader of the pro-French party in the country. was just as strongly opposed to this marriage and all its ramifications which threatened the country's very existence as an independent and still-Catholic kingdom.

Escape of Donald Dubh

The Highland chieftains seized by James V in 1540 were mere spectators of this struggle for power among the Scottish nobility while Donald Dubh was still held in captivity as chief of Clan Donald. But this all changed when he escaped from Edinburgh Castle in 1543, where he had been incarcerated for almost forty years following the failure of his earlier rebellion. Exactly how he obtained his freedom is not known, but as Donald Gregory wrote in his classic *History of the Western Highlands and Isles* (1836): 'It is certain that he owed his liberty to the grace of God and not to the goodwill of the government.' Immediately, the forces of Clan Donald rallied to his cause. It was greatly strengthened when the government under James Hamilton. second Earl of Arran, while still opposed to the pro-French policies of Cardinal Beaton, was foolishly persuaded to release all the Highland chieftains it held captive. No doubt Arran hoped to embarrass Archibald Campbell. fourth Earl of Argyll, and George Gordon. fourth Earl of Huntly, who were among the Cardinal's staunchest allies. Already their lands were being harried by forces loyal to Donald Dubh, especially in the west. However. it was the release of John Moydertach of Clan Ranald which first greatly disturbed the country elsewhere in the Highlands. It culminated in the bloody Battle of Blar-na-Leine in 1544, in which the Frasers of Lovat were virtually annihilated.

Feud with the Frasers of Lovat

The feud of Clan Ranald with the Frasers of Lovat had its origins many years previously, when Alan MacDonald as the captain of Clan Ranald had married his second wife Isabel Fraser. daughter of Lord Lovat. He died around 1505, and was succeeded by Ranald Ban, who was his eldest son by his first marriage with Florence MacIain of Ardnamurchan. Ranald Ban only lived until 1509, when he was succeeded by his son Dugall. He proved so obnoxious to Clan Ranald, perhaps because he had entered into bonds of manrent, first with Alexander Gordon, third Earl of Huntly, and later with Sir John Campbell of Cawdor, that he may well have been murdered by his clan in 1520. However, he was certainly deposed in favour of his uncle Alexander MacDonald, younger brother of Ranald Ban by their father's first marriage.

It seems that Alexander MacDonald proved himself a popular and successful chief of Clan Ranald, even if he too allied himself to Sir John Campbell of Cawdor by another bond of manrent. He died around 1529, and was succeeded by his natural son John Moydertach as the head of Clan Ranald. Although he had supported the earlier revolt of Alexander MacDonald of Dunivaig and the Glens, he was received back into royal favour by 1531, and was granted a royal charter to lands in Moidart, Arisaig, Eigg and Uist in 1532. However, after he joined the short-lived rebellion of Donald Gorm of Sleat in 1539, he was taken prisoner by James V in 1540, as already recounted, when the king sailed around the Western Isles taking hostages of the Highland chieftains.

As long as James V held John Moydertach captive, Clan Ranald was obviously without an active chieftain. A suitable candidate was found by Hugh Fraser, third Lord of Lovat, and George Gordon, fourth Earl of Huntly. He was Ranald Gallda, eldest son of Alan MacDonald of Clan Ranald by his second marriage with Isabel Fraser of Lovat. He had been fostered from childhood by the Frasers of Lovat, so accounting for his name Gallda, meaning 'Stranger'. James V now agreed to settle lands in Moidart, Arisaig and Eigg by royal charter upon Ranald Gallda to give him a semblance of legality, and Clan Ranald was forced to accept him as its new chieftain. But as soon as John Moydertach was released from captivity in 1543, he returned to Clan Ranald as its rightful chieftain, forcing Ranald Gallda to take refuge with Lord Fraser of Lovat. The forces of Clan Ranald, assisted by the Camerons of Lochiel and the MacDonalds of Keppoch, raided as far northeast as the Fraser lands of Abertarff and Stratherrick and the lands held by the Grants of Freuchie in Urquhart and Glen Moriston. They then occupied Castle Urquhart with every sign of staying put.

Battle of Blar-na-Leine

George Gordon, fourth Earl of Huntly and Lieutenant of the North, reacted in 1544 to this invasion of Clan Ranald by mounting an expedition around four thousand strong into their heartland. He was accompanied by Hugh Fraser of Lovat and the Laird of Grant at the head of their respective clans, as well as 1,500 MacIntosh kinsmen. The forces of Clan Ranald fell back as the Earl of Huntly advanced. He eventually penetrated as far west as Inverlochy, where it seems most likely he succeeded in reducing the Camerons of Locheil and the MacDonalds of Keppoch to a surly obedience. Evidently thinking that he had scattered the forces of Clan Ranald to his own satisfaction, the Earl of Huntly now withdrew his forces from Inverlochy along the Great Glen. However, after reaching the mouth of Glen Spean, he allowed his own men to return home by way of Laggan and Badenoch. Meanwhile, Hugh Fraser of Lovat and the Laird of Grant made their own way along the Great Glen with only 400 men towards Glenmoriston and Beauly.

But apparently, Clan Ranald under John Moydertach had merely been waiting for an opportune moment to attack, since the Frasers and Grants found themselves faced by a superior force at the head of Loch Lochy. It consisted of Clan Ranald and its allies, among whom were the Camerons of Locheil, the MacDonalds of Keppoch and the MacIains of Ardnamurchan as well as their own septs of Glengarry, Knoydart and Morar. The ensuing battle was a massacre in which the Frasers and the Grants were nearly all cut to pieces. Hugh Fraser of Lovat and his young son and heir, who had only joined the battle at the last moment, together with his three brothers and Ranald Gallda all lost their lives or died later of their injuries. The battlefield itself became known as Blar-na-leine, or 'Field of the Shirts', since the day was so hot that the combatants threw off their heavy surcoats to fight in their shirts. It was essentially a battle fought by Clan Ranald to maintain John Moydertach as their chosen chieftain against the usurping pretensions of Ranald Gallda, whom the central government had imposed upon them with all the due processes of feudal law.

The descendants of John Moydertach continued to hold the Captaincy of Clan Ranald over the succeeding centuries. Indeed, although military expeditions were launched against him by the Earls of Argyll and Huntly, and afterwards by John Stewart, fourth Earl of Atholl, John Moydertach remained as Captain of Clan Ranald until his own death in 1584. He evidently still threatened the peace of his neighbours in his later years. The Grants, the MacKenzies and the MacIntoshes all entered into bonds of mutual defence against Clan Ranald, and often appealed to the Privy Council for help against the depredations of John Moydertach. Even though his lands of Moidart, Arisaig, Eigg and South Uist had been granted to others, he continued to hold them by sheer force of arms with the support of his clansmen.

Feud with the MacLeods of Harris and Dunvegan

Even before the death of John Moydertach, however, and perhaps much earlier, Clan Ranald became involved in a deadly feud with the MacLeods of Harris and Dunvegan. It apparently arose from the matrimonial affairs of his son Alan, married to a daughter of Alasdair Crotach, chief of this branch of the MacLeods before his death around 1547. However, he abandoned her for a daughter of Hector Mor MacLean of Duart, by whom he had several sons, including his two successors. Such unfaithfulness may well have aggravated the dispute between the two families over the lands of North Uist, which culminated in an escalating series of outrages and atrocities during the sixteenth century, as recorded by the seanachies of the MacLeods of Harris and Dunvegan.

According to these traditions, a MacDonald galley was first driven ashore by a gale at Loch Stockinish in Harris. Its crew of twenty-four clansmen were entertained hospitably until the MacLeods learnt that they belonged to Clan Ranald. Ordered to leave, they were all killed as they emerged one by one from the low and narrow doorway of the house. In revenge for such a gross abuse of Highland hospitality, the MacDonalds of Clan Ranald soon afterwards seized a MacLeod birlinn. Its crew of thirty-six clansmen were deliberately allowed to die from starvation, perhaps as a symbolic gesture given that their own kinsmen had themselves been refused food by the MacLeods.

Somewhat later, it is said another MacLeod galley was driven ashore by bad weather on the island of Eigg and its crew refused any provisions by the MacDonald islanders, even though they were offered payment. Driven by hunger, the MacLeods seized some cattle which they killed for food. However, while they were eating their meal, they were surrounded by a large force of MacDonalds who killed them all, apart from a MacAskill kinsman and two others. Badly mutilated, the survivors were set adrift in a small boat without any oars or a rudder. By good fortune, however, they drifted north to Skye, where Alasdair Crotach, chief of the MacLeods of Harris and Dunvegan, learnt what had happened.

Massacre on Eigg

Alasdair Crotach took his revenge by launching a ferocious attack on the island of Eigg with six galleys and several hundred men. Learning of the impending attack, the MacDonalds of Eigg and their fellow clansmen from Rhum and Canna sought safety in a great cave on the island which had a secret entrance. The MacLeods spent three days in a vain search for their enemies, only to find their hiding place when a MacDonald scout left the cave to find out what was happening. He was spotted by William MacLeod, son of Alasdair Crotach, who traced his footsteps back to the cave, taking advantage of a slight fall of snow. After much agonising among the MacLeods, or so it is said, a fire was lit at its mouth. All the MacDonalds inside the cave perished, women and children as well as men. It is said that this atrocity claimed 395 victims. Their bones were later found scattered in little heaps on the floor of the cave, as if each family had huddled closely together in death.

The MacDonalds of Clan Ranald invaded Skye three years later to take their revenge for the shocking massacre on Eigg. After landing at Ardmore Point on a Sunday, they surprised the people at worship in Trumpan Church on Waternish, which was set alight. It is said that many of the worshippers died in the fire, or in trying to escape from the flames were killed by the MacDonalds. By now, however, the MacLeods under Alasdair Crotach had rallied their own forces under the miraculous banner of the Fairy Flag, and utterly defeated the MacDonalds who were nearly all slain. Since their bodies were laid out beside a dyke or stone wall which was then pushed over them, the battle became known in Gaelic as Blar Milleadh Garaidh, or the Battle of the Spoiling of the Dyke.

There is no documentary evidence of a contemporary nature for any of these events, and it is not even known when they occurred or if indeed they took place at all. But they are so embellished with circumstantial details in the oral traditions of the Highlands that it seems likely that they did indeed occur. It was later reported to James VI that the massacre on Eigg took place in 1577, but Alasdair Crotach could not then have been involved in its execution since he died around 1547. An even earlier date of 1510 is given in the traditional accounts of the MacLeods of Harris and Dunvegan, but it is perhaps more than likely that it occurred during the reign of James V or just after his death.

The Rough Wooing

Meanwhile, late in 1543, the Scots parliament had rejected the treaty of Greenwich by which Mary Stuart, Queen of Scots, on reaching her majority would marry Edward, Prince of Wales. Instead, the 'Auld Alliance' with France was renewed as a defence against England. Already, James Hamilton, second Earl of Arran, had abandoned his pro-English stance in the face of popular opposition within Scotland. He sought instead a reconciliation with Cardinal Beaton, who had already threatened his position as Governor of Scotland by hinting that his legitimacy was not above reproach. This abrupt volte-face by the Earl of Arran greatly angered Henry VIII. The English king now tried force to get his own way, attacking Scotland first in 1544 and then in 1545 in what became known as the 'Rough Wooing'.

Meanwhile, now that Cardinal Beaton had secured the backing of James Hamilton, second Earl of Arran, as the Governor of Scotland for his own policies, he abandoned the support he had previously given Matthew Stewart, fourth Earl of Lennox. Stewart had returned from France in 1543 at the Cardinal's instigation, hoping to marry Mary of Guise, the dowager queen, so greatly strengthening his position as heir-apparent to the throne after James Hamilton. But now he lost any chance of becoming Governor of Scotland in Hamilton's place, which Cardinal Beaton had previously held out to him, nor was he offered any other office in recompense. Along with several other earls, he came out in support of the English, realising that Henry VIII was more likely to advance his own ambitions in Scotland. Almost immediately, his defection had a serious consequence. The French had dispatched a small fleet carrying military supplies, fifty pieces of artillery and ten thousand crowns, hoping to strengthen the allies of Cardinal Beaton against the English. The gold was seized by the Earl of Lennox, acting with William Cunningham, fourth Earl of Glencairn, and secured in his stronghold of Dumbarton Castle.

Naval Expedition against Scotland

After several more months of political intrigue, Matthew Stewart, fourth Earl of Lennox, went south to England in May 1544, leaving the Earl of Glencairn in charge of Dumbarton Castle. There he married Margaret Douglas whose mother was Margaret Tudor, eldest daughter of Henry VII of England and the sister of Henry VIII. As the widow of James IV by her first marriage, Margaret Tudor later married Archibald Douglas, sixth Earl of Angus, and Margaret Douglas was their daughter. By thus marrying the niece of Henry VIII, Matthew Stewart, fourth Earl of Lennox, allied himself with England while boosting his own dynastic ambitions in Scotland. Henry VIII then gave him command of a naval expedition to harry the Firth of Clyde as a diversionary tactic against the Scots. He first attacked Arran, where the Hamilton stronghold of Brodick Castle was largely destroyed, and afterwards Bute, where Rothesay Castle was seized. He then sailed towards his own castle of Dumbarton, where he landed with 300 men, thinking it was still held for him by the Earl of Glencairn.

However, unknown to him, while absent in England, his erstwhile ally had come to support Mary of Guise, the dowager queen and widow of James V. After entering the castle with only a small retinue, the Earl of Lennox became aware of disaffection. He only just escaped capture by a much larger force of 4,000 men sent to arrest him. Retreating by sea towards Bute, his ships came under attack from Archibald Campbell, fourth Earl of Argyll, whose forces were stationed in Dunoon Castle. Under the cover of a heavy bombarment from his own ships as they lay offshore, Lennox launched a counter-attack. His forces had the advantage, since they had been strengthened by a well-armed contingent from his own district of Lennox under Walter MacFarlane of Tarbet. Argyll was forced to retire after a skirmish in which his force of 700 men lost eighty of its members, mostly gentlemen. Then, after plundering Dunoon and putting it to the flames, the Earl of Lennox launched another devastating attack against the Earl of Argyll. Then sailing south, he invaded Kintyre where he laid waste the lands of James MacDonald, now chief of Dunivaig and the Glens. He was alone among Clan Donald and its vassals in supporting the Earl of Argyll, who later became his brother-in-law after he had married his sister Agnes, thus renewing an alliance between their two families.

Donald Dubh in the Western Isles

Meanwhile, early in 1543, Donald Dubh had returned to the Western Isles after escaping from Edinburgh Castle. He was welcomed with great acclaim by the still loyal clansmen of Clan Donald, who hailed him as MacDonald, Lord of the Isles. The other prisoners and hostages from the Western Isles, detained in custody by James V in 1540, were released soon afterwards. Together with Donald Dubh, they raised a force of 1,800 clansmen, which then invaded the Earl of Argyll's territories, killing many of his vassals, and carrying off a great many cattle and other plunder. Thus, when the Earl of Arran abruptly abandoned his alliance with the pro-English party in favour of Cardinal Beaton, it was almost inevitable that Donald Dubh should ally himself with Henry VIII of England against the Earl of Argyll, as indeed happened. Even so, it was not until the summer of 1545 that the Earl of Lennox finally persuaded Donald Dubh and his vassals of Clan Donald to consider abandoning their allegiance to the Scottish Crown in favour of England.

By then, Donald Dubh had resurrected the ancient Council of the Isles, which on 28 July 1545 granted a commission to two plenipotentiaries to treat with Henry VIII of England under the direction of the Earl of Lennox. Among the eighteen members of the Council were nearly all the Lords and Barons of the Isles who had once supported the great confederacy of Clan Donald under the MacDonalds, Lords of the Isles. Indeed, they included Hector Mor MacLean of Duart; John Moydertach, Captain of Clan Ranald; Ruairi MacLeod of Lewis; Alasdair Crotach MacLeod of Harris and

Dunvegan; Murdoch MacLean of Lochbuie; Archibald MacDonald, Tutor of Sleat; Alexander MacIain of Ardnamurchan; John Cam MacLean of Coll; Gilleonan MacNeill of Barra; Ewen MacKinnon of Strathordle; John MacQuarrie of Ulva; John MacLean of Ardgour; Alasdair MacDonald of Glengarry; and Angus MacDonald of Knoydart. Their names alone are a striking testimony to the enduring loyalty and allegiance that they still entertained towards Clan Donald more than fifty years after the Lordship of the Isles was itself forfeited by the Crown. Indeed, it is reminiscent of the repeated efforts made more than three centuries previously by the MacHeths to regain the earldom of Ross, and by the MacWilliams to reclaim the Scottish throne from the Canmore kings under their ancient Celtic traditions of inheritance.

Alliance with Henry VIII of England

By now, Donald Dubh had 8,000 men at his command. Four thousand men were left behind in the Western Isles to check any invasion by Argyll or Huntly. The remainder accompanied him to Knockfergus in Ireland. Aboard a fleet of 180 galleys, this contingent consisted of 3,000 footmen, and 1,000 'tall mariners, that rowed in the galleys'. The footmen were described as 'very tall men, clothed in habergeons of mail, armed with long swords and long bows, but with few guns', giving us a rare glimpse of the *daoine uaisle* or gentry of Clan Donald. Emissaries from Donald Dubh were now dispatched to the court of Henry VIII of England, where it was agreed that Donald Dubh should receive an annual pension of 2,000 crowns from the English treasury. In return, he gave an oath of allegiance that he would serve the King of England truly and faithfully with all his adherents against James Hamilton, second Earl of Arran, Regent of Scotland.

Another naval expedition was now planned against the west of Scotland, again commanded by Matthew Stewart, fourth Earl of Lennox. Donald Dubh's own forces would be joined by 2,000 Irish levies. If the expedition took action against the Earl of Argyll in his own country, Lennox was to have all of Donald Dubh's forces of 8,000 men at his command. If it invaded any other part of Scotland, and an attack on Stirling was seriously contemplated, 2,000 of Donald Dubh's men were to remain behind as a rearguard to deter any attack by the Earl of Argyll. However, before these plans could be put into effect, the Earl of Lennox was ordered to England where he was required by the Earl of Hereford in planning his own invasion of Scotland.

Inevitably, the western expedition was postponed and the delay was the ultimate cause of its failure. When the Earl of Lennox did not return immediately from England, Donald Dubh decided to withdraw to the Western

Isles with his own forces. Meanwhile, his captains were divided about how the money from the English treasury should be distributed, causing much dissension among their ranks. Eventually after returning to Ireland, Lennox found that the coalition of forces he had so laboriously assembled against the Earl of Arran had disintegrated. However, Donald Dubh was still willing to join him in another attempt on Dumbarton Castle. Accordingly, Matthew Stewart, fourth Earl of Lennox, sailed late in 1545 from Dublin with his own forces of 2,000 men aboard a formidable squadron of ships. But he abandoned the attempt to seize Dumbarton Castle for Henry VIII of England after learning that it was now held strongly by forces loyal to the Earl of Arran as the Governor of Scotland.

Death of Donald Dubh

It is not known if Donald Dubh actually joined this abortive expedition, but it certainly appears that he afterwards returned with the Earl of Lennox to Ireland. But on his way to Dublin, late in 1545, Donald Dubh died of a five-day fever at Drogheda. He was buried with great pomp and ceremony in an elaborate funeral, which was charged to Henry VIII of England at the cost of 400 pounds sterling. He left only a natural son who never pursued any claim to the Lordship of the Isles. Indeed, after the death of Donald Dubh in 1545, no serious attempt was made to restore Clan Donald to its ancient patrimony in the Lordship of the Isles for the next hundred years. Only in 1645 did Alasdair MacColla join the Earl of Montrose in his rebellion on behalf of Charles I against the eighth Earl of Argyll and the Covenanting government of Scotland, intent on restoring the MacDonell earls of Antrim to what were by then their ancestral lands in Islay and Kintyre.

Deprived of his leadership, the rebellion of Donald Dubh ended in much the same way as many another Highland insurrection. James MacDonald of Dunivaig and the Glens now put himself forward as heir-apparent to the Lordship of the Isles, despite his lack of support for Donald Dubh during the recent rebellion. However, his claim was only accepted by the cadet branches of Clan Donald and not by its vassal kindreds. He was perhaps tempted to switch his allegiance to Henry VIII of England by the prospect of receiving a handsome pension from the English treasury, as previously promised to Donald Dubh. However, no money was forthcoming, and already he had received a charter to lands in Kintyre, Islay, Jura, Sunart and Morvern. They were all erected into the barony of Barr in North Kintyre, to be held under the feudal superiority of Archibald Campbell, fourth Earl of Argyll. Now his long-awaited marriage with the earl's sister Agnes Campbell took place as well, bringing him lands in Ardnamurchan. It cemented the close relations of his family with the Earls of Argyll that would last for the next forty years.

Equally, his pretensions as the rightful heir to the Lordship of the Isles were opposed by many other kindreds who had previously supported the claims of Donald Dubh. Their belligerence was much reduced in 1546 when the Earl of Huntly with the aid of William MacIntosh, Captain of Clan Chattan, acting as the deputy Lieutenant of the North, managed to capture Ewen Cameron of Locheil and Ranald MacDonald of Keppoch. Both these Highland chieftains were among the loyal allies of John Moydertach at the head of Clan Ranald at the Battle of Blar-na-Leine in 1544 which ended with the slaughter of Lord Lovat and nearly all his Fraser clansmen. They were also implicated in the rebellion of Donald Dubh. They were briefly imprisoned at Ruthven Castle and then sent for trial in Elgin before a jury of landed gentlemen. Found guilty of treason, they were beheaded and their severed heads set above the town gates. Several of their followers were hanged. Three years later, William MacIntosh suffered a similar fate. He was charged with plotting against the life of George Gordon, fourth Earl of Huntly, now his feudal superior after being granted the earldom of Moray in 1548 by Mary of Guise. He was brought to Aberdeen, found guilty after a trial presided over by Huntly himself, and sentenced to death by beheading. Exactly how he died remains a mystery, since he was carried off to Strathbogie never to be seen again, despite the protests of the Provost of Aberdeen.

Submission of the Rebels

Such severity had a salutary effect upon the other chieftains who had previously supported the rebellion of Donald Dubh. Almost without exception they submitted to the Regent's authority. Nearly all of them were pardoned for their past offences against the realm. The MacLeans of Duart were especially favoured at this time, since Archibald Campbell, fourth Earl of Argyll, married as his third wife Catherine MacLean, daughter of Hector Mor MacLean. She was famous for her beauty, and indeed after her first husband's death in 1558 her matrimonial career rivalled that of her sister-in-law, Lady Agnes Campbell, who was now married to James MacDonald of Dunivaig and the Glens. The marriage ties of the MacLeans with the Earls of Argyll were further strengthened in 1557 when Katherine's eldest stepdaughter Janet Campbell married in 'pure virginity' Katherine's brother Hector Og MacLean, eldest son and heir-apparent of Hector Mor MacLean of Duart.

The leniency shown to the Highland chieftains who had supported Donald Dubh before his death in 1545 was doubtless made necessary by the perilous situation now facing Scotland. The country itself was threatened by the wholesale invasion of an English army under Edward Seymour, newly created Duke of Somerset and Protector of England. It ended with the utter defeat of the Scottish army at the Battle of Pinkie in 1547. Among their ranks were 4,000 men from Argyll under the command of Archibald Campbell, fourth Earl of Argyll, and his brother-in-law James MacDonald of Dunivaig and the Glens, who brought another 2,000 men from Ulster. The Scottish defeat at Pinkie meant that the Earl of Arran was now induced to pardon the Highland chieftains who still remained outlaws, offering them better terms than they could reasonably have expected. Although the Earl of Arran remained as Governor of Scotland until 1554, he became ever more susceptible to the counsels of the dowager queen, Mary of Guise, following the murder of Cardinal Beaton in 1546. She advocated a return to the Highland policies pursued by James V, arguing that central authority could only be imposed by the taking of hostages, or even by imprisoning the more turbulent chieftains themselves.

Imposition of Central Authority

Accordingly, the Earl of Arran while still Governor in 1552 summoned the Highland chiefs to meet him, first at Aberdeen and then at Inverness, to consider how the country could best be governed. Only John Moydertach of Clan Ranald refused to answer his summons. Then in 1554, the Earl of Arran resigned as Regent in favour of Mary of Guise, who was appointed in his place until her own death in 1560. She adopted a much more severe policy with regard to the Highlands and Western Isles, ordering the Earls of Argyll and Huntly to proceed by land and sea to the utter extermination of Clan Ranald, the MacDonalds of Sleat and the MacLeods of Lewis.

The Earl of Huntly failed in his commission, and he was briefly warded in prison after he had disbanded his Lowland forces who refused to follow him into the Highlands. Indeed, he was accused by his enemies of being 'the prime author of all these troubles in the North, and that for the beheading of the Laird of MacIntosh'. He was deprived for the next few years of his office of Lord Chancellor, which he had held since 1546, together with the earldom of Moray. However, it seems a seaborne expedition armed with heavy cannon and mounted by the Earl of Argyll was more successful, pounding into submission Castle Tioram, the stronghold of John Moydertach of Clan Ranald.

Mary of Guise renewed her efforts in 1555 to pacify the Highlands, now relying on the Earls of Argyll and Atholl, to prosecute her own policies. Even John Moydertach of Clan Ranald submitted to Mary of Guise, who pardoned him under favourable terms. However, he soon afterwards escaped from her custody at Perth and returned to the Highlands, along with several of his followers. A chronicler commented that she should have held the Highland fox more tightly by the ears. This failure evidently stiffened her resolve to adopt much firmer policies towards the Highland clans, since she visited Inverness in 1556, accompanied by the Earls of Argyll, Atholl and Huntly, the Earl Marischal, the Bishops of Ross and Orkney and several other members of the Privy Council.

There, Mary of Guise held courts which punished offenders with great severity and which required the clan chieftains to surrender their own followers to justice when so charged. Such measures might well have pacified the Highlands and the Western Isles had they been enforced. However, religious dissension now came to occupy her attention during the final years of her Regency to the virtual exclusion of all other matters, as the events culminating in the Scottish Reformation of 1560 reached a final crisis effectively bringing the Middle Ages finally to an end in Scotland.

Course of the Scottish Reformation

Foremost among the Protestant aristocracy in establishing the reformed religion in Scotland was Archibald Campbell, fifth Earl of Argyll. His father, the fourth Earl, despite his earlier support for Cardinal Beaton and his pro-French policies, had already embraced its tenets, of which he was a 'most zealous professor'. Indeed, along with his elder son, he was among the principal signatories to the 'Band' of the Lords of the Congregation in 1557, which united the Protestant reformers in a covenant with God against the 'superstition, idolatry and abominations of the Roman church'. Then, after his death in 1558, he was succeeded by his elder son Archibald Campbell as the fifth Earl of Argyll. Following the death of Mary Tudor in the same year, after ruling over England as a fanatical Catholic, and the accession of the Elizabeth I of England, the tide started to turn against Mary of Guise and her pro-French policies. Until then, she had done little to hinder the growing strength of Protestantism in Scotland. But now she turned against the Protestant reformers whom she charged with heresy against the Catholic Church.

The Protestants' position was greatly strengthened when John Knox returned to Scotland in May 1559. The events leading to the Scottish Reformation of 1560 now reached an abrupt climax, triggered by a riot which followed his sermon against idolatry in Perth. Faced with this challenge to her authority, Mary of Guise marched against Perth with a small but well-trained force of French troops. The Lords of the Congregation had already assembled an army in their own defence but it was poorly equipped. Hostilities came to little more than a series of marches and counter-marches, while Archibald Campbell, fifth Earl of Argyll, attempted to mediate between the two sides. However, the position changed for the worse when reinforcements arrived from France in support of Mary of Guise, causing Elizabeth I to intervene by sending an English army north to aid the Reformation forces. The French troops were besieged early in 1560 by the English army at Leith, where they were starved into surrender while Mary of Guise lay dying of dropsy in Edinburgh Castle.

Soon afterwards, following the loss of Calais in 1558, a treaty was concluded between France and England ending the hostilities between them. Its most important clause allowed the Scots Parliament to meet as a 'Concession', so that any religious differences could be resolved. Despite the moderate wording of the Treaty of Berwick, the Reformation Parliament then legislated against the Catholic Church in Scotland. It abolished the authority and jurisdiction of the Pope over Scotland, outlawed the Church of Rome and forbade the celebration of Mass. It then approved a Confession of Faith, setting forth Calvinist principles as the sole basis for the Protestant faith in Scotland. But the Parliament did not settle many questions concerning the nature of the reformed Church, and especially the role of bishops in its government, causing it great difficulty with the Crown in future years.

Role of the Fifth Earl of Argyll

Mary Stuart, Queen of Scots, returned in 1561 to rule over Scotland as a Catholic queen in a Protestant country. Among her courtiers, she greatly favoured Archibald Campbell, fifth Earl of Argyll. He was her brother-in-law by his marriage with her half-sister Jean, herself the illegitimate daughter of James V. Mary called him brother in her letters and signed herself as 'your right good sister and best friend for ever'. But he disapproved strongly of both her marriages. Indeed, after her first marriage to Henry Stewart, Lord Darnley, Archibald Campbell took to arms against her in what became known as the Chaseabout Raid. Then, upon her abdication in 1567, after Darnley's assassination and her subsequent marriage in 1567 to James Hepburn, fourth Earl of Bothwell, he acquiesced in the coronation of her infant son as James VI of Scotland. However, he rallied to her support on her escape from captivity in Lochleven Castle in 1568, only to be defeated at the Battle of Langside a few days later. When she sought refuge in England, he retired to his own country of Argyll. Despite coming to terms in 1569 with Lord James Stewart, Earl of Moray, then Regent of Scotland, the Earl of Argyll remained among the foremost leaders of the queen's party in Scotland. But after five years of civil war, he eventually reached an accommodation in November 1572 with James Douglas, Earl of Morton, acting by then as Regent of Scotland. In return, he was appointed Lord Chancellor of Scotland.

The charter under the Great Seal appointing him to this office styled him as 'Archibald, Earl of Argyll, Lord Campbell and Lorne, our Justice-General'. The latter office of Justice-General required him to administer criminal justice by presiding over justice-ayres throughout the whole of the kingdom. Along with his heritable position as Master of the King's Household, it brought him substantial rewards, since there were the profits of justice to be made. Equally, he exercised local jurisdiction over his own territories and feudal superiorities, often with powers of regality. Indeed, he was virtually independent of central authority in Argyll and the Western Isles. Quite likely, he acted as Lieutenant of the Western Isles, even if there is no actual record of his appointment, since John Carswell dedicated his Gaelic prayer-book to the Earl of Argyll in this capacity.

But closeness to the Crown, and possession of the great offices of the Crown, were not the only sources of Campbell power and wealth. Their widespread territories now dominated the western seaboard of the Scottish Highlands, south of Loch Linnhe. They stretched as far inland as Breadalbane and Loch Tay and extended south throughout Cowal, Mid-Argyll and Knapdale. They held outlying estates in Ardnamurchan, Moidart, Lochaber and North Uist as well as other lands in the Lowlands of Scotland. There was even an outpost of Campbell territory in the north-east, which the Campbells had gained by marriage of a younger son to Muriel, heiress of the last thane of Cawdor, as previously recounted.

However, as well as the Campbells of Cawdor, numerous other branches of Clan Campbell were established by the time of the fifth Earl of Argyll, often dating back more than two centuries. Among the most powerful were the Campbells of Glenorchy, afterwards the Earls of Breadalbane. All exhibited a remarkable loyalty to the Earls of Argyll, so that even the most powerful of the cadet branches were willing to serve him and his interests in their own name. Such cohesion gave added strength to the Campbells, Earls of Argyll, and indeed it formed the foundations of their territorial expansion. Such solidarity was only threatened after 1584 during the minority of Archibald Campbell, seventh Earl of Argyll, by the internecine quarrels that so often seem endemic to the other clans of the Scottish Highlands.

Marriage Alliances and Bonds of Manrent

Equally, the Earls of Argyll deliberately attempted over the years to integrate themselves with the aristocracy of Lowland Scotland by means of marriage alliances to bolster their power and influence. Their sons almost invariably married the daughters of Lowland families, unless circumstances dictated marriage with the heiress of a cadet branch which had died out in the male line in order to preserve the integrity of the Campbell estates. Otherwise, they looked for wives among the daughters of the Cunningham earls of Glencairn, the Graham earls of Menteith, the Gordon earls of Huntly, the Hamilton earls of Arran or the Stewart earls of Lennox, if they could not ally themselves with the royal line of the Stewart monarchy. Apart from Archibald Campbell, fourth Earl of Argyll, who married Catherine MacLean of Duart as his third wife in what was evidently a love-match, the Campbells never married the daughters of other Highlands clans.

The Earls of Argyll fathered more daughters than sons over the generations. Their marriages could be used to strengthen Campbell influence among the other Highland chieftains. The fourth Earl's marriage with Catherine MacLean was followed by the marriage of his eldest daughter Janet Campbell to Catherine's brother Hector Og MacLean. Then, after the death of the fourth Earl of Argyll in 1558, his widow Catherine MacLean married Calvagh O'Donnell, Earl of Tyrconnel, already the comrade-in-arms of her stepson, the fifth Earl of Argyll. It represented a widening of Campbell interests into Ulster. However, Catherine evidently abandoned her husband for his arch-enemy Shane O'Neill, Earl of Tyrone, and perhaps even betrayed him. After their deaths, she returned to Scotland, where she was safely married off for a third time to John Stewart of Appin, who was among the most trusted of the fifth Earl of Argyll's advisers. Around the same time, he arranged the marriages of Agnes Campbell, widow of James MacDonald of Dunivaig and the Glens, and of her daughter Finola, 'the dark-haired woman'. Agnes married Turlough Luineach O'Neill, successor to Shane O'Neill as Earl of Tyrone, while her daughter Finola married Hugh O'Donnell, successor to Calvagh O'Donnell as Earl of Tyrconnell.

Bonds of friendship and manrent were another powerful tool in building alliances between families that were not otherwise related to one another. Archibald Campbell, fifth Earl of Argyll, only made one bond of friendship with a fellow magnate when he entered into such an agreement in 1570 with John Stewart, fourth Earl of Atholl, intended to settle a dispute over the boundaries of their respective jurisdictions. But he entered into a great many bonds of manrent, binding numerous Highland chieftains to his own allegiance. They included such great chiefs as James MacDonald of Dunivaig and the Glens, Donald Gormson MacDonald of Sleat, John Moydertach of Clan Ranald, Hector Mor MacLean of Duart and Tormod MacLeod of Harris and Dunvegan, as well as the chieftains of many lesser clans. Their names are also encountered in the panegyrics of Gaelic poetry, composed in praise of the Earls of Argyll, which record all these clan chiefs as the allies of the Campbells. Evidently, the hegemony of Archibald Campbell, fifth Earl of Argyll, reached throughout all of Argyll and beyond to the Western Isles.

King of the Gaels

But then, as Jane Dawson has persuasively argued in her article 'The Fifth Earl of Argyll, Gaelic Lordship and Political Power in Sixteenth-Century Scotland', Archibald Campbell, fifth Earl of Argyll, was not just a Lowland aristocrat of the first rank. He was also a great Gaelic lord as well. Indeed, he was known throughout Gaeldom as MacCailein Mor, or Great Son of Colin. It was given in memory of his ancestor Sir Colin Campbell, whose grandson was rewarded by King Robert the Bruce in 1315 with the lordship of Lochawe. Praised as the 'King of the Gaels, the man who maintains the thronged court, prosperous and wealthy', Archibald Campbell, fifth Earl of Argyll, cultivated his role as a great Gaelic chieftain. According to one bard, he was only surpassed by MacDonald of Glengarry in the lavishness of his hospitality. Indeed, while living in his 'country' at Inveraray, he entertained in the opulent manner expected by Gaelic society. Among his guests was Mary Stuart, Queen of Scots, who visited Inveraray in the summer of 1563 to hunt deer in his company, accompanied by all her court. She even decided the occasion merited the wearing of Highland dress. The prospect so appalled the English ambassador in Edinburgh that he begged to be recalled to London, lest he had to traipse around the Highlands clad in a saffron shirt and a tartan plaid.

Just as importantly, Archibald Campell, fifth Earl of Argyll, patronised the Gaelic learned orders consisting of poets, bards, seannachies and physicians. The MacEwans acted as hereditary bards and seannachies to the Campbells, skilled enough to run a bardic school of the highest quality. Evidently, it attracted other Scottish and Irish poets of equal standing to Inveraray, where they expected to be entertained lavishly as befitted their status. In return, they offered poems praising their host and his generosity. By lauding him extravagantly as 'Lord of the Gael', they recognised unequivocally that the Campbells had replaced Clan Donald as the erstwhile Lords of the Isles. By now, the Campbell earls of Argyll had supplanted the MacDonald lords of the Isles at the 'Headship of the Gael', described in contemporary Gaelic poetry as the 'noblest title in all of Scotland'. Indeed, acting in just such a role, Archibald Campbell, fifth Earl of Argyll, even commissioned his private chaplain John Carswell to translate the Protestant 'Form of Prayers' into Gaelic. Campbell genealogists may have claimed descent from such prestigious figures as King Arthur and the Anglo-Norman family of Beauchamp, conflated with descent from the highest levels of ancient Gaelic society. But as Jane Dawson has stressed, the Campbells, Earls of Argyll, hardly ever neglected national politics and indeed looked beyond Scotland to an even wider stage.

Chapter Four

CLAN DONALD IN ULSTER

The death of Donald Dubh in 1545 and the collapse of his rebellion against the Scottish Crown left James MacDonald of Dunivaig and the Glens as the heir-apparent to the Lordship of the Isles. But although tempted by a pension from Henry VIII of England, which in fact never materialised, he remained loyal to the Scottish Crown under whose tutelage he had been educated after 1531. As already recounted, he was rewarded with a charter to his lands in Scotland, erected into the barony of Barr and afterwards was favoured by marriage to Agnes Campbell, sister of Archibald Campbell, fourth Earl of Argyll. But equally, his estates in the Glens of Antrim made him just as powerful a magnate in Ulster. There, he would take advantage of the rebellion of Shane O'Neill, who laid claim to his father's earldom of Tyrone in 1558, bringing the peaceful settlement of Henry VIII of England to an end in Ulster. Moreover, James MacDonald had four younger brothers to act as his loyal lieutenants when he embarked on a course of territorial aggrandisement, carving out territories for themselves farther west in the Route. Among them was Sorley Buidhe, the subject of a meticulous biography by Michael Hill entitled *Fire and Sword: Sorley Boy MacDonnell and the Rise of Clan Iain Mor, 1538–1590*. His powerful presence would dominate the history of Ulster as the ancestor of the Earls of Antrim until his death in 1589.

Already, before his death in 1538, Alexander MacDonald of Dunivaig and the Glens had established his chief stronghold at Dunanynie Castle in Antrim. It lay close to Ballycastle and its harbour, giving easy access by sea to his Scottish possessions in Islay and Kintyre. Only four miles offshore lay the heavily fortified outpost of Rathin Island. Surrounded by the treacherous waters of the North Channel with its tidal races, it offered the MacDonalds of Dunivaig and the Glens a safe haven whenever they were threatened in their mainland possessions of Scotland and Ireland. They also had a powerful fleet of swift galleys, which could be rowed by oarsmen if there was not enough wind so making them capable of outmanoeuvring sailing ships. It gave them possession of the sea lanes between their territories in Islay,

Kintyre and Antrim, lying athwart the north-western approaches to the North Channel between Scotland and Ireland.

Divided Allegiances

Politically, the MacDonalds of Dunivaig and the Glens held their lands in Islay and Kintyre from the Scottish Crown. However, their territories in the Glens of Antrim were effectively held by the sword, especially as the writ of the English government in Dublin did not then extend much beyond the Pale. The struggles in Ulster during the latter half of the sixteenth century were commonly driven by the attempts of the great Irish chieftains such as O'Neill of Tyrone and O'Donnell of Tyrconnell (now Donegal) to force the English to grant them charters to their lands, even while they still entertained hopes of independence from English rule. Engaged in such struggles, the native Irish chieftains, and indeed the MacDonalds in Antrim, could easily exploit the natural fear of England that her continental enemies such as France or Spain might gain control of an independent Ireland, so challenging her position as a great sea-power.

But equally, the protagonists in such struggles often exploited the temporary weaknesses of one another in what was a Byzantine struggle for political power and military advantage. Marked by shifting alliances and double-dealing, it seems the native Irish chieftains could never unite for long behind a single banner. The triumph of one chieftain was often the signal for his defeated rival to curry favour with the Dublin government by plotting to bring him down. This was fertile ground for the MacDonalds of Dunivaig and the Glens, for they had a ready supply of mercenary soldiers. Known as redshanks, they were recruited from among the Highland clans of Argyll and the Western Isles. Men of substance like the earlier galloglasses and often heavily armed as befitted such gentlemen, they were hired out to fight the Anglo-Irish wars that broke out in Ulster during the second half of the sixteenth century. Mostly MacLeans and MacDonalds, they could be deployed in the best interests of their own chiefs. Although they were not averse to changing sides whenever it seemed expedient, it was ultimately the Campbells, Earls of Argyll, by exercising feudal superiority over the MacLeans and the MacDonalds, who determined to what use they would be put.

Attack and Counter-Attack in Ulster

James MacDonald of Dunivaig and the Glens had been disappointed when Henry VIII of England failed to support his claim to the Lordship of the Isles in 1545. He had therefore resumed his earlier allegiance to the pro-French government of Scotland under James Hamilton, second Earl of Arran. Soon afterwards, he was rewarded with a grant of lands in Ardnamurchan from Archibald Campbell, fourth Earl of Argyll, while he was allowed to marry the earl's sister Agnes, so forging an alliance between the two families. Now living for the most part at Saddell in Kintyre, James MacDonald encouraged the actions of his youngest brother Sorley Buidhe, who spent the years after the death of Henry VIII in 1547 harrying the English forces in Ulster. Sorley Buidhe was himself loosely allied with Shane O'Neill, who had rebelled against the Dublin government after it had imprisoned his father Conn O'Neill, Earl of Tyrone under the English Crown. Together, they had attacked the English stronghold of Carrickfergus on the northern shores of Belfast Lough.

These raids in Ireland became even more menacing when England was itself threatened by a war with France after Mary Tudor, Queen of England, had married the future King Philip II of Spain. Its outbreak in June 1557 tempted Mary of Guise as the Regent of Scotland to aid France by invading England. However, she was prevented from doing so, and the Scottish border remained peaceful. Even so, the English feared a Scottish invasion might be mounted against their forces in Ireland, aided by the French army still stationed in Scotland. Already, Sir Thomas Radcliffe, Lord Fitzwalter and afterwards Earl of Sussex, acting in his capacity as Lord Lieutenant of Ireland, had mounted a military expedition in 1556 against the Glens of Antrim. It was a pre-emptive strike, intended to drive the MacDonalds from their lands. Financed by the sum of 25,000 pounds, Sussex reported it successful. Indeed, James MacDonald of Dunivaig and the Glens only just escaped with his life, fleeing under cover of darkness, while 200 of his troops were reported killed.

Yet the English account of the victory may be called into question. Although they captured the MacDonald stronghold of Glenarm Castle, another expedition was needed against the MacDonalds of Dunivaig and the Glens in 1557, when their lands in the Glens of Antrim were laid waste. However, it did not succeed in engaging James MacDonald of Dunivaig and the Glens in a pitched battle. Afterwards, the Gaelic-speaking Scots in Antrim still remained a serious threat to the English presence in Ireland. The Earl of Sussex now planned a full-scale attack on Kintyre and the Western Isles for the following year.

This expedition set sail in 1558 from Dundalk with twelve ships carrying a complement of 1,100 men. They first landed on the MacDonald island of Rathlin, killing all who resisted and laying it waste. Sussex then sailed to Kintyre, and landed at Loch Kilkerran [now Campeltown Loch]. He first burnt eight miles of the country along the east coast, together with the chief's house at Saddell. Next day, after marching across the peninsula, he harried another twelve miles on the west coast of Kintyre before attacking Dunaverty Castle on the Mull of Kintyre. He then sailed for Arran and the Cumbraes, plundering and laying them waste. However, a storm now arose and he was forced to sail to Carrickfergus rather than attacking Islay and Bute as he had intended.

Sorley Buidhe and the Route

Meanwhile, the MacDonalds of Dunivaig and the Glens had succeeded in seizing the fertile district of the Route, lying to the west of their own territories in the Glens of Antrim between the Bann and the Bush. 'Route' is a corruption of *ruada* or *riata*, so called after the district that was once the rich heartland of the ancient Irish kingdom of Riada. Fergus Mor Mac Erc and his brothers had set out from there to colonise the Scottish kingdom of Dalriada more than a thousand years earlier. The Route was held in the mid-sixteenth century by the MacQuillans. They found an erstwhile ally in Colla MacDonald, who was yet another brother of James MacDonald of Dunivaig and the Glens, when they attacked the O'Cahans west of the River Bann.

The expedition itself was so successful that it penetrated far west into Tyrconnell. Afterwards, Colla MacDonald returned to garrison his forces on the MacQuillans for the winter of 1551–2, marrying Eveleen MacQuillan, their chief's daughter. But only a few years later, his younger brother Sorley Buidhe forced the MacQuillans into submission. Then, after Colla's death in 1558, he became Captain of the Route, gaining these territories for himself. Next year, he was challenged for their possession, but succeeded in defeating the MacQuillans at the Battle of Slieve-an-Aura. After this victory, the MacDonalds of Dunivaig and the Glens were so powerful that the English now sought their help in putting down the rebellion of Shane O'Neill against the Dublin government.

Rebellion of Shane O'Neill

Shane O'Neill was the eldest son of Conn O'Neill, whom the English had recognised as the Earl of Tyrone after he had submitted to Henry VIII of England in 1542. However, the English did not recognise Shane O'Neill as the legitimate heir to his father's earldom. Instead, they favoured his father's adopted son Matthew O'Neill, Lord of Dungannon, reputedly the son of a Dundalk blacksmith. However, he was killed by his rival's followers in 1558, just a year before the death in 1559 of Conn O'Neill as the Earl of Tyrone. Already excluded from succeeding his father in 1542, Shane O'Neill had spent the years since 1551 in arms against the Dublin government. Allied at first with Sorley Buidhe, he had prevented the English from advancing far beyond the Pale towards the north of Ulster.

Even so, Shane O'Neill had his own setbacks during these years. In particular, despite superior forces of 4,000 foot and 1,000 horse, he was repulsed by Calvagh O'Donnell and his MacSweeney galloglasses in 1557 after invading Tyrconnell. When Conn O'Neill died two years later in 1559, Shane O'Neill became the chief of the O'Neills in the eyes of his followers. Meanwhile, as already recounted, the MacDonalds of Dunivaig and the Glens had borne the brunt of repeated expeditions by the Dublin government under the Earl of Sussex to expel them forcibly from their territories in the Glens of Antrim. They therefore had little reason to ally themselves with the English against Shane O'Neill. But neither did they support the rebellion of Shane O'Neill against the Dublin government. It was a policy that would later rebound against them once Shane O'Neill gained the upper hand over the English.

Role of the Fifth Earl of Argyll

Shane had succeeded his father Conn O'Neill in 1559, just a year after Elizabeth I came to the throne of England. The Scottish Reformation occurred just a year later in 1560. It was just as much a diplomatic and political revolution as a religious upheaval. It effectively brought the 'Auld Alliance' with France to an end while ushering in the prospect of a new era of friendly relations between Scotland and England. Faced with this sudden change in political circumstances, Elizabeth I of England turned to Archibald Campbell, fifth Earl of Argyll, foremost among the Protestant leaders, who had succeeded to his father's title in 1558. Early in 1560 under the Treaty of Berwick, he agreed to act as England's agent in suppressing the rebellion of Shane O'Neill in Ulster.

No doubt Argyll hoped in this way to repay his debt to Elizabeth I of England for her decisive role in defeating Mary of Guise and the pro-Catholic forces in Scotland. He could raise 3,000 men in support of the English forces in Ulster, twice as many as the whole of the English army then stationed in Ireland. In return, he was offered harquebusiers and heavy cannon for use against his own enemies in the western Highlands. should they be needed. But it seems that Elizabeth I would not authorise the necessary expenditure, so the expedition never took place. Even so, Archibald Campbell, fifth Earl of Argyll, spent several months in the western Highlands,

apparently recruiting redshanks for the proposed expedition, quite unaware
that the Earl of Sussex had made a temporary peace with Shane O'Neill.

Although Argyll's forces remained ready to serve the English interest in
Ulster for the next few years, they were never used. The Dublin government
thus lost any chance to conquer Shane O'Neill without committing their
own forces in strength. It was a golden opportunity that would not return
after 1565, when Argyll withdrew his offer to serve the English in Ireland. He
threw his weight instead behind the MacDonalds of Dunivaig and the Glens
in their own struggle against Dublin. But meanwhile, there were other ways
in which the Earl of Argyll could still support the English interest.

A few years earlier in 1555, Argyll had mounted an expedition to Donegal
in support of Calvagh O'Donnell, who was later to marry his stepmother
Catherine MacLean, his father's third wife. Together, armed with the famous
Gunna Cam, or the Crooked Gun of the Campbells, they had defeated
Calvagh's father Manus O'Donnell, Earl of Tyrconnell, and Calvagh was now
chief of the O'Donnells. Now, the Earl of Argyll dispatched 1,000 men to
Tyrconnell in 1560, hoping to strengthen Calvagh O'Donnell's position
against Shane O'Neill on his western flanks. Indeed, under Argyll's influence, Calvagh O'Donnell was now reconciled to the Dublin government,
which proposed to recognise him as the Earl of Tyrconnel.

Equally, James MacDonald and his brother Sorley Buidhe might now
be tempted to join the English and the O'Donnells in an alliance against
Shane O'Neill if they were granted a legal right to their lands in Antrim
under the English Crown. But even though this was agreed early in 1561,
the MacDonalds still remained ambivalent. Indeed, they were more inclined
to support Mary Stuart, Queen of Scots, now ruling in Edinburgh after her
return from France later that year. Faced with this setback, Elizabeth I of
England reluctantly authorised the Earl of Sussex to undertake a military
expedition against Tyrone. He was ordered not to incur any more expense
than 'necessity shall require'. But before Sussex could even marshall his
forces, Shane O'Neill seized the initiative in May 1561. He swept into
Tyrconnell, capturing Calvagh O'Donnell and his wife Catherine MacLean,
widow of Archibald Campbell, fourth Earl of Argyll. Afterwards, abandoning
Finola, daughter of James MacDonald of Dunivaig and the Glens, whom he
had earlier married, he took Catherine to bed and later married her, begetting
several sons upon her.

Shane O'Neill in the Ascendant

According to the Annals of the Four Masters, Shane's abduction of O'Donnell
and his wife Catherine allowed him to assume 'the sovereign command of all

Ulster, from Drogheda to the Erne, so that at this time he might be called with propriety the provincial King of Ulster, were it not for the opposition of the English . . .' Sussex now mounted two abortive expeditions against O'Neill. The first was defeated in Monaghan on the western flanks of Armagh. The second penetrated into Tyrone as far as Loch Foyle without even engaging the enemy who refused to give battle, melting away instead into the hinterland. Shane O'Neill now occupied such a position of strength in the autumn of 1561 that he was able to negotiate directly with Elizabeth's government in London. He even demanded a safe-conduct from the queen herself before he would leave Ulster.

On returning to Ireland in May 1562, Shane O'Neill had wrested nearly all he wanted from the London government. It had virtually conceded his claim to hegemony over the whole of Ulster. He now threatened to invade Tyrconnell in an attempt to subjugate Conn O'Donnell, whose father Calvagh was still his prisoner. Equally, James MacDonald and Sorley Buidhe were just as vulnerable on his eastern flanks. After being forced to submit to Shane O'Neill in September 1562, Sorley Buidhe took temporary refuge across the North Channel in Kintyre or the Western Isles, along with his brother.

Negotiations with Shane O'Neill

As far as the English were concerned, the situation had deteriorated alarmingly. Early in 1563, they decided to make yet another attempt to subdue Shane O'Neill by invading his territories of Tyrone once again. But still unable to gain the support of James MacDonald of Dunivaig and the Glens, they were forced to admit failure, if not defeat. Their only way forward was now to negotiate more seriously with Shane O'Neill. They were forced to recognise his claim to the earldom of Tyrone, while hoping to turn him against the MacDonalds of Antrim. In fact, the English saw the pretensions of Shane O'Neill as merely a local problem, which doubtless they could overcome given sufficient time and money. But the MacDonalds of Dunivaig and the Glens were a more serious threat to their very hold on Ulster, given the ample sources of military manpower commanded by the MacDonalds in the Western Isles. Despite holding their lands in the Glens of Antrim for the previous 150 years, the MacDonald territories in Ulster were still regarded by the English as a Scottish colony to be uprooted. Indeed, they feared that 'the MacDonalds had now become their own masters and lords'.

The treaty eventually negotiated in November 1563 with the Dublin government might well have been dictated by Shane O'Neill himself, so humiliating were its terms to the English. It simply stated:

Her Majesty receives Shane O'Neill to her gracious favour, and pardons all his offences; he shall remain captain and governor of his territory or province of Tyrone, and shall have the name and title of O'Neill, and all the jurisdiction and pre-eminences which his ancestors possessed, with the service and homage of the captains called Urraughts, and other [of] the chieftains of the O'Neill country, and he shall be created Earl of Tyrone.

In return, he promised to cooperate with the English in destroying the power of the MacDonalds in Antrim as the proof of his own good intentions. But Shane O'Neill was more concerned with advancing his own interests in Ulster rather than in serving the English. Equally, in the Machiavellian politcs of sixteenth-century Ulster, England could no doubt benefit from any internecine struggle among their Gaelic adversaries, whatever its outcome.

Campaign against the O'Donnells

Almost a year passed before Shane O'Neill moved against the MacDonalds of Antrim. But when he struck, the effect was devastating. Meanwhile, early in 1564, he had turned against the O'Donnells, ignoring his agreement with the English to release Calvagh O'Donnell from captivity and allow him to return to his lordship of Tyrconnell after the death of his father Manus O'Donnell a year earlier. Shane O'Neill swept through Fermanagh and then into Tyrconnell, occupying Lifford Castle with his forces. Still holding Calvagh O'Donnell as his prisoner, he had prevented the English from restoring the O'Donnells to power in Tyrconnell. The English were powerless, since they lacked sufficient force to challenge Shane O'Neill directly. Instead, they were forced to rely upon his loyalty in another attempt to drive out the MacDonalds from their territories in Antrim. By August 1564, Shane O'Neill had English approval for a military expedition against the Glens and the Route. But the Dublin government was unwilling to aid him materially, or otherwise become involved.

Campaign against the MacDonalds

The greatest strength of Shane O'Neill was not his courage in battle but his sense of military strategy. By early September 1564, he had gathered together enough men and supplies for a six-week campaign in Antrim. But he held his hand until April 1565 for a full-scale attack. By then, he knew the MacDonalds' strength would be greatly reduced. Sowing their crops in the spring and harvesting them in the autumn meant that their mercenary forces of redshanks only campaigned in Ireland between the festivals of

Bealtainn (1 May) and Samhain (1 November). Afterwards, they returned to the Western Isles for the winter. Shane O'Neill therefore spent the autumn of 1564 in the north, rebuilding the old castle at Culrath (now Coleraine) on the western banks of the Bann, and then dispatching a few hundred men across the river to occupy the friary on its eastern bank. It was a feint intended to distract the MacDonalds' attention from the southern approaches to the Glens of Antrim where he intended to strike early the following year. The foray was itself repulsed by Sorley Buidhe as the Captain of the Route, but his forces sustained heavy losses. It compelled him to remain ever vigilant over the coming winter against any further incursion by Shane O'Neill from the west.

Meanwhile, Sorley's elder brother James MacDonald of Dunivaig and the Glens had become involved in a long-running feud with Hector Mor MacLean of Duart over the Rhinns of Islay. It detained him in Edinburgh until early in 1565. However, Sorley Buidhe received 300 elite troops, dispatched from Kintyre by his brother in February 1565 to bolster the defence of their southern marches in Antrim. Seemingly, Sorley Buidhe was now confident that Shane O'Neill would not attack the MacDonald heartland in the Glens of Antrim. But just such an invasion took place in April 1565, after earlier forays over the previous winter had lulled Sorley Buidhe into a false sense of security. Shane O'Neill had marshalled his forces south of Loch Neagh at Easter, and then marched them north-east towards Edenduffcarrick near the present-day town of Antrim. Now thoroughly alarmed, Sorley Buidhe rushed south from Ballycastle, attempting to rally his own forces to defend the narrow pass of Knockboy, just north-east of Ballymena. It guarded not only the south-westerly approaches to the Glens of Antrim but also entry to the Route from farther south-east.

The two sides joined battle on 29 April, when Shane O'Neill with an army of 2,000 men swept aside the forces of Sorley Buidhe. Overwhelmed by sheer force of numbers, Sorley Buidhe fell back in disarray. Messengers were sent urgently to Ballycastle with instructions to light signal fires on Fair Head and Torr Head. They would alert his elder brother James MacDonald in Kintyre to the danger. Next day, Shane O'Neill advanced over the hills into the Glens of Antrim, descending Glenballyemon to reach the coast at Cushendall. There he put Red Castle to the flames and sacked the adjoining district of Glenariff to the south. As Sorley Buidhe retreated north along the coast, James MacDonald raised all his available forces in Kintyre and immediately set sail across the North Channel for Cushendun. Joining Sorley Buidhe and his small band in the early hours of the following day, they marched together over the hills past Loughareema and the headwaters of the Carey River to reach Ballycastle. Meanwhile, Shane O'Neill marched west up Glenaan from Cushendall, and then turned north across the moors to the head of Glenshesk. Descending the valley to the coast, he found the MacDonalds had abandoned Ballycastle. Instead, Sorley Buidhe and his brother James had retreated south-west along Glentaisie, where their forces camped for the night not far from their stronghold of Dunanynie.

Battle of Glentaisie

The only accounts of the ensuing Battle of Glentaisie come from the victors so it is difficult to judge what strategy Sorley Buidhe was attempting to pursue. Perhaps he hoped to draw Shane O'Neill away from the coast, expecting his other brother Alasdair Og MacDonald to land at Ballycastle with reinforcements from Kintyre. Shane O'Neill might then be trapped, forced to fight on two fronts. But Alasdair Og did not arrive in time to affect the outcome of the battle, despite the 900 men he had succeeded in raising. Indeed, when battle was joined early in the morning of 2 May, it seems likely that the MacDonalds were taken by surprise. Even so, the battle lasted much of the day until Shane O'Neill prevailed by sheer force of numbers. The remnants of the MacDonald army were forced to flee the battlefield. Out of 1,000 men, perhaps a third or more had been killed, while Shane O'Neill captured Sorley Buidhe and James MacDonald along with nineteen other gentlemen. But while Sorley Buidhe survived two years of captivity and then triumphed over Shane O'Neill, his brother James MacDonald of Dunivaig and the Glens died two months later of his wounds.

Aftermath of Glentaisie

The fortunes of Shane O'Neill were now at their zenith, while the MacDonalds of Dunivaig and the Glens had suffered their greatest reverse. By breaking the military strength of both the O'Donnells and the MacDonalds, Shane O'Neill could claim to be overlord of all Ulster. Even so, the MacDonalds had reinforcements in Scotland numbering several thousand men, ready to cross the North Channel. Indeed, when Alasdair Og arrived on the very next day and learnt what had happened, he returned to Kintyre intent on restoring his family's fortunes. Moreover, the battle itself destroyed any likelihood that the MacDonalds of Antrim and the O'Neills, Earls of Tyrone, might join together in later years to oppose the English as their common enemy.

Meanwhile, marching north with his prisoners, Shane O'Neill first captured Dunseverick Castle. He then laid siege to Dunluce Castle, which surrendered after he had threatened to starve Sorley Buidhe to death. Shane

O'Neill was now strong enough to openly defy the English, which he did by installing his own garrisons in such castles as Dundrum and Newry in the far south of Ulster. Pressed to hand over his prisoners, he adamantly refused to do so. England reacted by appointing Sir Henry Sidney as Lord Deputy of Ireland in October 1565 with instructions to pursue a more aggressive policy in Ulster. He immediately set about isolating Shane O'Neill from his natural allies.

Already, Calvagh O'Donnell had been restored to his lordship of Tyrconnell with English help. It seems that Shane O'Neill was persuaded to set him free, apparently so that he could marry Calvagh's wife Catherine MacLean, which he did in August 1565. But it seems the marriage did not prosper, since it was reported in April 1566 that he had rejected her. He apparently then hoped to marry instead James MacDonald's widow, Lady Agnes Campbell, aunt of Archibald Campbell, fifth Earl of Argyll. No doubt Shane O'Neill planned it as a diplomatic marriage, hoping to placate the MacDonalds of Dunivaig and the Glens, and especially Sorley Buidhe's only surviving brother Alasdair Og MacDonald. He may also have hoped to benefit from the powerful influence of Archibald, fifth Earl of Argyll. But although courted by both the English and Shane O'Neill, Argyll remained aloof from the struggle in Ulster and the marriage with Lady Agnes Campbell never took place. Indeed, Shane O'Neill apparently had several sons by Catherine MacLean before his own death in 1567, so their marriage perhaps flourished despite reports to the contrary.

Shane O'Neill in Rebellion

Next year, however, Argyll sent a force of redshanks to Ulster in 1566, numbering perhaps 2,000 men under the command of Alasdair Og MacDonald. Since the English were anxious that they might be used in support of Shane O'Neill's rebellion, Elizabeth I now authorised Sidney to mount an armed expedition against the overweening Earl of Tyrone. But again Shane O'Neill seized the initiative, sweeping south to besiege Dundalk towards the end of July 1566. However, he was repulsed and soon afterwards branded a rebel. A fortnight later, Sidney claimed that Alasdair Og had renounced any thought of supporting Shane O'Neill. Indeed, this did seem unlikely, given the animosity that must surely have existed between Shane O'Neill and the MacDonalds after the Battle of Glentaisie.

It was enough to persuade Sidney to take the offensive. His strategy would be two-pronged. Early in September 1566 the English landed a force of six or seven hundred men under Colonel Edward Randolph at Derry on the shores of Lough Foyle. Then, Sidney himself advanced northwards from

Armagh into the heart of Tyrone with perhaps little more than 1,000 troops. But while Shane O'Neill had the advantage of numbers, commanding upwards of 5,000 men, he still avoided a direct confrontation with the English.

Sidney was reduced to destroying all of O'Neill's castles and strongholds as he marched through Tyrone, doubtless burning the countryside and seizing all his cattle at the same time. The culmination of his campaign came when he installed Calvagh O'Donnell once again in Tyrconnell. Now he only needed to gain the support of Alasdair Og MacDonald to completely encircle Shane O'Neill in his fastness of Tyrone, who had been forced into hiding near Armagh. But Sidney's campaign suffered two blows in the autumn of 1566. Colonel Randolph was killed by accident at Derry, and then Calvagh O'Donnell died in Tyrconnell after falling from his horse. He was succeeded by his brother Hugh O'Donnell. Once allied to Shane O'Neill, it seems that Hugh O'Donnell now decided to support the English, since in November 1566 he crossed the River Finn to plunder O'Neill's lands in the north of Tyrone.

Alliance with the English

Meanwhile, after visiting Scotland during the summer, Alasdair Og Mac-Donald had returned to Antrim at the beginning of November 1566, backed by a force of 1,200 men. He then launched a foray against the district known as Clandeboy, south of the River Lagan, and held by a kinsman of O'Neill, before retreating by way of Carrickfergus to the security of the Glens of Antrim. While at Carrickfergus, he made contact with the captain of the English garrison. He reported to Sidney that Alasdair Og had assured him that he had returned to Ulster to serve the Queen of England, while even hinting that Argyll could not be trusted. Even so, it was money from Argyll given to William Piers as the constable of Carrickfergus castle that finally persuaded Alasdair Og in early December 1566 to launch an attack against the territories of Shane O'Neill across the River Bann.

Yet the English were still reluctant to encourage Alasdair Og MacDonald. Evidently, they feared an alliance with him would restore MacDonald hegemony to the Glens of Antrim against their long-term interests. Accordingly, they now proposed to plant all of eastern Ulster with their own settlers, so preventing any further influx of Gaelic-speaking Highlanders whether they came to serve Shane O'Neill or the MacDonalds of Dunivaig and the Glens. Meanwhile, although Shane O'Neill was still described as 'the only strong and rich man in Ireland' who had 'won all by the sword and so will keep it', he was encircled by his enemies, unable to obtain help from any quarter.

Downfall of Shane O'Neill

Shane O'Neill still had a sizeable force of men under arms and was able to bring as many as 5,000 men into the field. He therefore determined to break the circle closing around him at its weakest point. This he did by recklessly attacking the O'Donnells of Tyrconnell in May 1567. His gamble failed when Hugh O'Donnell counter-attacked, utterly defeating Shane O'Neill on 8 May 1567 at the Battle of Farsetmore near the head of Lough Swilly. Forced to abandon his camp with all its equipment and supplies, Shane O'Neill left around 1,300 of his men dead upon the battlefield or drowned in the tidal waters of the Swilly. Barely escaping with his life, he had suffered a devastating blow to his military power and prestige at the hands of Hugh O'Donnell, from which he would never recover.

According to Edmund Campion's *A Historie of Ireland, written in the Yeare 1571*, Shane O'Neill was 'cast in such despair, that he consulted with his secretary. . . [whether] to present himself unknown and disguised to the Deputy [Sidney], with a halter about his neck, begging his pardon.' But he still held Sorley Buidhe as his prisoner, and he had already been in touch with his brother Alasdair Og MacDonald. It seems Sorley Buidhe hoped to gain his freedom in return for an alliance between the MacDonalds and the O'Neills. Evidently, Shane O'Neill now decided to pursue just such a course, since it was reported that 'O'Neill, lacking men to defend his country, told Sorley Buidhe that, if he would procure his brother Alasdair [Og] to aid him with a thousand men, he would set him at liberty. Sorley Buidhe, desirous to be out of thralldom, wrote very earnestly to his brother for so many men as O'Neill did desire . . .' Seemingly, Shane O'Neill now agreed to visit Alasdair Og in Cushendun, so that it could be decided how their forces would be employed against the English.

Death of Shane O'Neill

Exactly how Shane O'Neill was killed at Cushendun remains a mystery, except that he lost his life in a quarrel. Riding into his enemy's camp with only fifty horsemen and accompanied by Sorley Buidhe, it seems he did not expect treachery. But by entering Alasdair Og's well-armed camp with his captive, he had surrendered his trump card. The English account of what happened comes from the Act of Attainder against Shane O'Neill, passed a few years after his death by the Dublin parliament. It suggests that he was received well enough according to the 'kindly' customs of Highland hospitality. However, apparently his arrogance got the better of his judgment at a feast, when he defended an ill-considered remark made by his secretary casting doubt upon the virtue of Lady Agnes Campbell, whom he still hoped to marry. A drunken brawl then ensued with his hosts, eager to revenge the death of their late chief, James MacDonald of Dunivaig and the Glens. They fell upon Shane O'Neill and his followers, slaughtering them all.

Even so, contemporary sources all agree that the quarrel only occurred after two or three days of serious negotiation. These include a letter written at the time by Sir William Fitzwilliam, Vice-Treasurer of Ireland, but only recently discovered. However, it is not even clear if Sorley Buidhe was implicated in plotting the murder of Shane O'Neill, although the evidence suggests he was not involved. All we know is that Shane O'Neill and all his followers were killed on 2 June during a violent argument, presumably after the negotiations had broken down. His death greatly benefited the English in Ulster, and quite possibly they had contrived at his murder. Indeed, the severed head of Shane O'Neill was pickled and then presented in a pipkin to Captain Piers, Governor of Carrickfergus. He sent it for a reward to Dublin, where it was set on a spike above the castle walls.

Aftermath of Shane O'Neill's Death

After the death of Shane O'Neill in 1567, the peace in Ulster was repeatedly threatened by the MacDonalds for almost the next thirty years until the great revolt of Hugh O'Neill, Earl of Tyrone, took place in 1595 against English rule. But first of all, the MacDonalds of Dunivaig and the Glens were able to restore their fortunes, at least in Antrim. As already recounted, James MacDonald had died two years earlier from wounds he had received at the Battle of Glentaisie in 1565. He was succeeded by his eldest son Archibald, about whom very little is known except that he died early in 1569. However, it was his uncle Alasdair Og MacDonald who had acted as effective leader of the MacDonalds of Antrim while Sorley Buidhe was still held captive by Shane O'Neill. Then, when he gained his freedom in 1567, Sorley Buidhe placed himself at their head, acting, or so he said, on behalf of Archibald's younger brother Angus MacDonald rather than Archibald himself as the chief of the MacDonalds of Dunivaig and the Glens. Alasdair Og returned to live on his estates in Kintyre until his death in 1568 campaigning in Ulster. When Archibald died in 1569, the chiefship passed to his brother Angus. His bitter quarrels with Angus's own son Sir James MacDonald would destroy them both, leading to the final extinction of their house.

Meanwhile, Sorley Buidhe seized the initiative in the summer of 1567, immediately after the death of Shane O'Neill. He first renewed his demand for a royal charter from Elizabeth I of England to his lands in Antrim. He then left for the Western Isles to recruit redshanks for service in Ulster, acting with the approval of Archibald Campbell, fifth Earl of Argyll. He had returned to Ballycastle by November, accompanied by a force of 400 men. The Scots presence in Ulster was now 1,500 strong, although they were not all under his command. Sorley Buidhe now maintained a truce with the English until May 1568 while strengthening his own position. He allied himself with Turlough Luineach O'Neill, now the chief of the O'Neills after his cousin Shane's death, while other lesser chieftains declared their support as well. Such a pan-Celtic alliance would later be sealed by the marriage of Turlough O'Neill with Lady Agnes Campbell. arranged by her nephew Archibald Campbell, fifth Earl of Argyll.

Role of Archibald Campbell, Fifth Earl of Argyll

Even before 1567, Archibald Campbell, fifth Earl of Argyll, had turned against the English in Ulster. He evidently felt aggrieved that they had failed to support James Stewart, Earl of Moray, in his abortive rebellion in 1565 against the marriage of Mary Stuart, Queen of Scots, to her cousin Henry Stewart, Lord Darnley. While the other rebels took refuge in England, Archibald Campbell simply withdrew to his own territories in Argyll. By then, his former friendship with England had turned to open hostility when he threatened to support the rebellion of Shane O'Neill before his death in June 1567. Hardly a month later, after the abdication of Mary Stuart, Queen of Scots, Archibald Campbell, fifth Earl of Argyll, parted company with James Stewart, Earl of Moray, now acting in the English interest as Regent of Scotland on behalf of the young King James VI of Scotland. Argyll's loyalty to the deposed queen overcame his adherence to the Protestant faith. He would lead her forces to defeat at the Battle of Langside in May 1568, and only later come to terms with the king's party in Scotland.

Meanwhile, Argyll could act against the English interest in Ulster. He first proposed that his aunt Lady Agnes Campbell should marry Turlough O'Neill of Tyrone. She evidently agreed, even though her husband-to-be was the heir to Shane O'Neill who had caused her second husband's death. But determined and forceful, she could see advantages in ending the feud between the two families, so protecting the interests of her children by James MacDonald of Dunivaig and the Glens. However, a wider pact was contemplated by the Earl of Argyll. It was agreed that Hugh O'Donnell of Tyrconnell would marry Lady Agnes Campbell's daughter Finola, 'the dark-haired woman'.

However, both these marriages, planned for the spring of 1568, were postponed until August 1569. The delay arose partly because English men-of-war were now patrolling the waters of the North Channel. However, the political situation had also changed once Mary Stuart, Queen of Scots, had sought refuge in England after her defeat at the Battle of Langside in May 1568. Not long afterwards, Archibald Campbell, fifth Earl of Argyll, arranged a meeting between Sorley Buidhe and Alasdair Og MacDonald of Dunivaig and the Glens, Donald Gormson MacDonald of Sleat, Hector Mor MacLean of Duart and Tormod MacLeod of Harris and Dunvegan. Seeking to resolve the apparent differences between them, Argyll only managed to bring the dispute over the Rhinns of Islay to a temporary end. He failed when he asked them to join him in supporting Mary Stuart, Queen of Scots, against the Regent Moray. Worried that he might now lose his own power and influence in Scotland, Argyll was also wary of offending England. It therefore seems likely that he put off the two proposed marriages with his kinswomen for the time being.

Turlough O'Neill on the Offensive

Once Argyll had delayed his marriage with Lady Agnes Campbell, Turlough O'Neill mounted an attack against the English, putting over a dozen towns in Ulster to the flames in early September. Two months later, Argyll presented his own ultimatum to the English. He would only agree to act on their behalf in Ulster if Elizabeth assisted Mary Stuart regain her throne in Scotland. He also offered the hand of Lady Agnes Campbell in marriage to any Irish lord of Elizabeth's choosing, but again only if the Queen of England would grant James MacDonald's widow and her son Angus a charter to their lands in the Glens of Antrim. Otherwise, he threatened to invade Ulster with an army of 5,000 men. Yet despite such threats, an uneasy calm prevailed in Ulster until the summer of 1569, when Lady Agnes Campbell, accompanied by upwards of a thousand Campbell redshanks, arrived on Rathin Island to marry Turlough O'Neill. Her daughter Finola married Hugh O'Donnell at the same ceremony. The two marriages now bound the three most powerful families in Gaelic Ulster together in a loose confederacy under the patronage of Archibald Campbell, fifth Earl of Argyll. The alliance was further strengthened by the large numbers of mercenary troops supplied by Argyll himself as dowries for his kinswomen. However, Argyll died only four years later, and the confederacy that he had succeeded in putting together with such difficulty never really survived his death. Even so, the repeated attempts made by the English to subjugate Ulster over the next thirty years came to nothing, blocked at first by the military strength of Sorley Buidhe and his MacDonald kinsmen, and then by Hugh O'Neill, Earl of Tyrone, in his rebellion against the English crown.

Meanwhile, almost immediately after their wedding feasts had ended. Turlough O'Neill and Hugh O'Donnell marched south towards Omagh at the head of an army several thousand strong. Together, they attacked the northern borders of the Pale. By the end of August 1569, more reinforcements of redshanks had joined them, mostly likely MacLeans and MacDonalds. Soon afterwards, Turlough O'Neill had reached Newry, where he posed a serious threat to the English farther south in the Pale. However, he did not have sufficient troops to take the offensive. He thus failed to take advantage of the disarray in the English ranks as they fell back to defend the Pale itself from further attack. Meanwhile, Sorley Buidhe had marched into the district of Clandeboy, south of the Glens of Antrim. He perhaps had command of the 4,000 troops which were reported from Islay in mid-August. They were ready to set sail in thirty-two galleys, bound for Lough Foyle. Little is known of this campaign except that he found an ally in Sir Brian MacFelim O'Neill of Clandeboy.

English Attempt at Plantation

The next two years saw a break in hostilities while the English reacted to the threat now facing them. No longer just prepared to seek an accommodation in Ulster, they would now adopt a more aggressive policy. The catalyst for change came from the proposal made by Sir Thomas Gerrard in March 1570 to plant a colony in Clandeboy and the Glens of Antrim as a private venture. It was intended to prevent any further influx of Highland mercenaries into Ulster from Argyll and the Western Isles. But it was Sir Thomas Smith. Secretary of State to Elizabeth I of England. who received a grant in November 1571 to the lands of Clandeboy and the Airds, held by Sir Brian MacFelim O'Neill. Sorley Buidhe reacted with anger, sweeping south to attack Carrickfergus. However, he was wounded in battle and did not recover from his injuries until the following year.

Sir Thomas Smith's natural son and namesake landed in August 1572 to establish the first English colony in the Airds. There he faced the open hostility of Sir Brian MacFelim O'Neill of Clandeboy, and indeed he was murdered only a year later. But Smith's death did not help Sir Brian MacFelim O'Neill, who now faced the enmity of the Earl of Essex. Walter Devereux, recently appointed as Governor of Ulster and Earl Marshall of Ireland. Essex had landed at Carrickfergus in August 1573, armed with a charter from Elizabeth I of England, granting him the Glens of Antrim and the Route, as well as Clandeboy, already assigned to Sir Thomas Smith. Four hundred colonists accompanied Essex, together with 1,100 troops for their defence. Although their numbers would double over the coming year, the forces at Essex's command were still inferior to the 4,000 redshanks available to Sorley Buidhe and his erstwhile allies.

Owing to Elizabeth's celebrated parsimony, Walter Devereux, Earl of Essex, did not receive sufficient resources at first from London to take the field against Sorley Buidhe for nearly two years. By then, however, Sir Brian MacFelim O'Neill was dead, slain along with many of his followers after being abducted through Essex's treachery in November 1574. But it was the peace made by the English with the ever-vacillating Turlough O'Neill in June 1575 which prompted Essex into action. Fearing that O'Neill's redshanks would now enter the service of Sorley Buidhe, he therefore marched north in early July to the Bann. He then returned to Drogheda, after engaging the enemy in little more than a few skirmishes, only to launch an expedition by sea against Rathlin Island with devastating effect.

English Raid on Rathlin Island

After an encounter with the English forces on the Bann, Sorley Buidhe had concentrated his own forces south of Ballycastle. There they could be used to counter the attack he now expected against the Glens of Antrim, or indeed against the Route. Meanwhile, he had sent all the MacDonald non-combatants to the safety of Rathlin Island. Thus, when three frigates set sail from Carrickfergus on 20 July 1575 carrying 300 foot and eighty horse, Sorley Buidhe was completely outwitted. Two days later, the English men-of-war arrived off Rathlin Island, where the fifty-strong garrison was unable to fend off the English attack. The walls of Rathlin Castle were breached after a two-day siege and 200 of its occupants put to the sword. Another 400 were hunted down and butchered as they sought refuge elsewhere on the island. Among them were the well-born wives and children of Sorley's kinsmen and no doubt many others of more humble birth.

Watching from the cliffs of Antrim, Sorley Buidhe was powerless to intervene. If he came to their rescue, Sorley Buidhe risked a devastating attack on his rear either by Turlough O'Neill, who had his own vested interests to pursue in his newly-found alliance with the English, such was the Byzantine nature of Ulster politics, or more likely by the Earl of Essex himself. Such an assault from whatever quarter it came would endanger the very existence of Sorley's hold on the Glens of Antrim. Instead, he had to content himself with attacking Carrickfergus in August 1575. But although he inflicted heavy losses by luring the English forces into a trap, he had no success in destroying the English stronghold.

Change of English Policy

The London government reacted to the bloody attack on Rathlin Island by recalling the Earl of Essex, Walter Devereux, and replacing him with Sir Henry Sidney. The English evidently feared that such aggressive actions would merely prompt Sorley Buidhe into further rebellion and perhaps tempt Turlough O'Neill into abandoning his alliance with the Dublin government. They abandoned their aggressive policy of colonisation which had failed so utterly under Essex, reverting instead to their previous policy of containing the Ulster problem. Soon after his arrival in Ireland, Sidney travelled north to meet Sorley Buidhe in the Route.

Sorley Buidhe first insisted at their meeting that Sidney withdraw the English garrison from Rathlin Island, so recently installed by Essex. Sidney justified his action to London by arguing it was too great a charge on the exchequer to keep the garrison victualled. In reality, he recognised he did not possess sufficient strength to dislodge Sorley Buidhe from his territories. Sidney therefore acknowledged Sorley's claim to the Glens of Antrim and the Route in return for a pledge of peace. An agreement between them was duly signed on 19 October 1575, but Sidney had no intention of adhering to it. Indeed, the long-term aim of English policy still remained the expulsion of the MacDonalds from the Glens of Antrim.

By appearing to recognise Sorley's claim to the Glens of Antrim, Sir Henry Sidney no doubt hoped to divide him from James MacDonald's sons, and especially Angus MacDonald of Dunivaig and the Glens. Sorley's nephew Angus laid claim to these very lands by right of inheritance as his father's eldest surviving son. His claim had the full support of his mother Lady Agnes Campbell. The English regarded her as 'a pestilent instrument, altogether Scottish' despite her marriage to Turlough O'Neill of Tyrone. But Turlough's own position was weak, since the English threatened to recognise his cousin Hugh O'Neill of Dungannon as the legitimate heir of his father Conn O'Neill, first Earl of Tyrone. An uneasy peace now descended upon Ulster until 1584, despite the occasional skirmish, which resulted in the death of Sorley Buidhe's son Donald, or so it was reported.

The years after 1575 were marked by political intrigue as the English attempted to play off Turlough O'Neill and Sorley Buidhe against one another, but with little success. Hostilities broke out intermittently, often involving several thousand Highland mercenaries from Argyll and the Western Isles, which the English usually managed to contain. Indeed, despite his best efforts and the large numbers of Highland troops at his command, Sorley Buidhe never managed to establish a military confederacy with the native Irish chiefs that lasted long enough to inflict a crushing blow against the English presence in Ulster. Indeed, the death in September 1573 of Archibald Campbell, fifth Earl of Argyll, quite likely deprived the MacDonalds of Dunivaig and the Glens of Campbell patronage. He was succeeded by his younger brother Colin as the sixth Earl of Argyll. Colin Campbell was first involved in a bitter quarrel with John Stewart, fourth Earl of Atholl, and then became enmeshed in the political intrigues that eventually destroyed James Douglas, Earl of Morton, then acting as Regent of Scotland. Preoccupied with national affairs, it seems he did not share his brother's involvement in the affairs of Ulster and the Western Isles. Indeed, he was regarded as 'weak in judgment and overmuch led by his wife', according to one estimate.

Renewed Offensive against Ulster

Then in 1584, Sir John Perrott was appointed Lord Deputy of Ireland. Despite his instructions from Elizabeth I of England to adopt a moderate policy, he determined to drive the MacDonalds from Ulster. However, he had fewer than 1,000 foot and horse under his command in all of Ireland. Even so, he undertook a military expedition into Ulster only two months after his arrival in Ireland. Reaching the north coast of Antrim after marching his forces north along both banks of the River Bann, he then laid siege to Dunluce Castle. Defended by only a small garrison, it fell soon afterwards. Sorley Buidhe and his own men fell back beyond the River Foyle to take refuge in the wilds of County Derry. Perrott returned to Dublin in September 1584 after campaigning for only ten days in the field. He had achieved almost nothing, despite his claims to the contrary, apart from the garrisoning of the castles at Culrath, Dunluce and Dunanynie. He left behind Sir John Norris who spent much of October trying to root out the huge herds of cattle, estimated at 50,000 beasts, that were Sorley Buidhe's lifeblood.

Perrot's own lieutenants seemingly doubted the success he claimed on returning to Dublin. Indeed, soon afterwards, Sir Henry Bagenal mounted an expedition from Newry against the Glens of Antrim in November 1585, consisting of 600 foot and 100 horse. But inland of Red Bay, his column was attacked by Donald Gorm, Angus's younger brother and Sorley's nephew. He was forced 'to retire shamefully'. Such a setback prompted Elizabeth I to dispatch Sir William Stanley to Ireland. Well experienced as a field commander, he joined the forces under Sir Henry Bagenal at Glenarm Castle on 30 December 1584. They first shipped their supplies north to Dunanynie Castle, just north of Ballycastle, and then marched inland under the cover of darkness, reaching Ballycastle by a circuitous route at the very beginning of January. The English commanders then divided their forces after an inconclusive skirmish with Donald Gorm who had shadowed them from

Glenarm. Bagenal returned to Dunanynie Castle, north of Ballycastle, while Stanley reconnoitred south beyond Cushendun to investigate a report that galleys had been sighted offshore.

The English forces were thus effectively cut in two when Sorley Buidhe and his nephew Angus MacDonald of Dunivaig and the Glens suddenly landed at Cushendun on 5 January 1585 with 2,000 troops. Bagenal in the north feared that Sorley Buidhe was intent on attacking Carrickfergus, so he immediately retreated south from Ballycastle by way of the Route to safety. But his sudden retreat left Stanley dangerously exposed. He managed to fall back from Cushendun over the moors to Ballycastle. There his forces were attacked at night by Sorley's men near Bunnamairgie Friary, and he himself was wounded. Despite receiving reinforcements from the west of the Bann and two companies from the north coast, Stanley was now effectively cut off from his rear. Meanwhile, Sorley Buidhe had divided his own forces leaving Donald Gorm to deal with Stanley at Ballycastle, while he himself sailed south in strength to Red Bay. There, he found that Bagenal had ventured north from Carrickfergus as far as Glenarm, perhaps intending to march even farther north to relieve Stanley. But the English commander evidently decided that discretion was the better part of valour, since he promptly fell back to the safety of Carrickfergus.

Withdrawal of the MacDonalds

Yet such success in the field nearly turned to disaster for Sorley Buidhe. Within a month, rumours were rife that the Scots intended to abandon their offensive in Ulster. Indeed, early in March 1585, Angus Macdonald of Dunivaig and the Glens took ship for Kintyre, while Sorley Buidhe and Donald Gorm retreated north as the English advanced in force upon the Glens of Antrim. Soon afterwards it was reported on 22 March that Sorley Buidhe and Donald Gorm had sailed for Scotland. Why Sorley Buidhe should suddenly abandon the field in Ulster just as he seemed poised to triumph over the English is difficult to understand. One argument advanced recently by Michael Hill suggests that Sorley Buidhe intended his original invasion as a tactical move, designed to test the English while demonstrating to the native Irish chieftains the strength of the MacDonalds. Equally, his sudden withdrawal might suggest to Elizabeth I that Perrott had made too much of the danger in Ulster. In fact, she did instruct him in the spring of 1585 to halt all military operations there.

Yet it seems more likely that Sorley Buidhe and his nephew Angus MacDonald withdrew so suddenly from Ulster to tackle a more immediate danger now facing them in the Western Isles. During the previous summer, the MacLeans of Duart had landed in force at Lough Swilly in August 1584, apparently ready to serve Shane O'Neill's sons against Turlough O'Neill of Tyrone. However, they departed just as suddenly in mid-September in the face of Perrott's invasion of Antrim. But their departure coincided closely with the death on 10 September 1584 of Colin Campbell, sixth Earl of Argyll, who had succeeded his brother Archibald Campbell to the earldom in 1573. He left a nine-year old son Archibald to inherit his title of Argyll. Until he came of age, there was a power vacuum in the Western Isles, which the MacLeans of Duart most likely exploited in resurrecting their claim to the Rhinns of Islay, held by the MacDonalds of Dunivaig and the Glens.

Angus MacDonald of Dunivaig and the Glens evidently felt so threatened that he complained to the Privy Council in Edinburgh. It issued a proclamation on 25 April 1585 against Lachlan Mor MacLean of Duart, Ruairi MacLeod of Lewis, Tormod MacLeod of Harris and Dunvegan and Donald Gormsom MacDonald of Sleat. They were all summoned to appear before the Council to answer 'touching the good rule and quieting of the Isles and Highlands'. Open hostilities may even have broken out by then. James VI was forced to write to Tormod MacLeod of Harris and Dunvegan only a few months later on 18 September 1585. He was urgently requested to come to the aid of Lachlan Mor MacLean of Duart in his feud with Angus MacDonald of Dunivaig and the Glens over the Rhinns of Islay.

Return of Sorley Buidhe to Ulster

Even so, Sorley Buidhe returned just as suddenly to Ulster in August 1585, backed by a force of 1,500 redshanks. Seizing the initiative, he recaptured Dunluce Castle in November 1585 while harrying the English forces elsewhere. By then, war had finally broken out between England and Spain over the Netherlands so there was the constant threat that Spain might invade Ireland. Even so, England was forced to commit her best officers and troops to the Netherlands, where her army had first call on what food, clothing and other military supplies were available. It left little to spare for Ireland. Equally, although urged to do so, Elizabeth I of England was not prepared to countenance the expense of hiring MacLean mercenaries to fight Sorley Buidhe, who daily grew more threatening. By February 1586, she had decided it was futile to persist in trying to subjugate Ulster by force, 'the fastest and safest ground of Ireland'. Instead, she instructed her Council to open negotiations with Sorley Buidhe. Already in 1585, she had recognised Hugh O'Neill of Dungannon as the Earl of Tyrone, hoping to strengthen the English position in Ulster. Now she was spurred to negotiate with Sorley

Buidhe on learning that Angus MacDonald of Dunivaig and the Glens was about to set sail for Ulster with 2,000 more redshanks.

But Sorley Buidhe suffered yet another twist of fate before he reached a final accord with the English when his son Alexander was killed in March 1586 after a skirmish in Tyrconnell. He was leading a force around 500 strong when he was surprised by an English detachment commanded by a Captain Merriman. Alexander challenged Merriman to single combat but a common soldier stepped forward in his place, striking Alexander with a fierce blow before he himself was killed. Captain Meririman then stepped into the fray and wounded Alexander in the leg. Alexander was later found by the English forces after he was carried from the field. They struck his head from his body. It was sent to the Lord Deputy in Dublin where the grisly object was set above the castle walls.

'Submission' of Sorley Buidhe

Perhaps the shameful death of his son Alexander prompted Sorley Buidhe to write to Dublin in April 1586, offering his submission in abject terms. However, his health was also failing, although he would live another four years. Apparently, he had incisions made to his forehead in an attempt to recover his eyesight. A month later in May 1586, Lady Agnes Campbell negotiated a grant from the English of the Glens of Antrim on behalf of her son Angus MacDonald of Dunivaig and the Glens on the understanding that Sorley Buidhe would continue to hold part of these territories with his nephew's approval. Amid rumours of renewed hostilities and the landing of redshanks from the Western Isles, Sorley Buidhe finally appeared in Dublin under a safe-conduct in June 1586. Entering the city walls, he caught sight of his son's grisly head displayed on a pike. His only response was to remark cryptically: 'my son hath many heads'.

Sorley Buidhe then submitted to Sir John Perrott as the Lord Deputy of Ireland. He acknowledged his disobedience, seeking 'favour and forgive-ness . . . in such measure as it may please her Majesty'. But such contrition was perhaps more feigned than real. The English were quite prepared to accept his absurd declaration that he was 'a man born out of this realm', so absolving him of any charge of treason against the Queen of England. Then he entered Dublin Cathedral, where it was reported to Elizabeth that he 'threw his sword down before your Majesty's picture, kissed the . . . same, [and] swore allegience to your Highness'. After such a theatrical performance, he demanded in return a charter to his lands in the Route, together with a royal pardon and a patent of denization, making him an English subject.

Indeed, the indenture he signed with Perrott on 18 June 1586 gave Sorley Buidhe nearly all he wanted, except that Rory MacQuillan was granted part of the Route, seized from his family nearly three decades previously. However, Angus MacDonald of Dunivaig and the Glens was apparently less than satisfied with the bargain made on his behalf by Lady Agnes Campbell. During the summer of 1586, he ranged far and wide in Ulster, attacking Sir John O'Dogherty in Inishowen and then expelling Rory MacQuillan from the lands he now held in the Route. By August, Angus Macdonald had sent a large force over 2,000 strong into Connacht, commanded by his brothers Donald Gorm and Alexander Carrach. But they were utterly defeated at the Battle of Ardnary on 23 September 1586. It was the greatest defeat suffered by the Highland Scots in Ulster since the time of Edward Bruce and the Battle of Dundalk in 1318. Afterwards, Angus MacDonald of Dunivaig and the Glens became ever more involved in the feud that still raged with the MacLeans of Duart over the Rhinns of Islay, while his son Randal handled his affairs in the Glens of Antrim during his lengthy absences in Scotland.

Later Divisions in Ulster

After his death in 1590, it soon became apparent how important a role Sorley Buidhe had played in keeping the MacDonalds of Dunivaig and the Glens united as a political and military force over the last four decades. A breach soon opened between Angus MacDonald of Dunivaig and the Glens and Sorley's eldest surviving son Sir James MacDonald of Dunluce. In fact, when Hugh O'Neill of Tyrone rebelled against English rule in Ireland in 1595, the relations between them were so strained they seemed quite incapable of pursuing a common policy. Indeed, within two years, Sir James MacDonald of Dunluce laid claim to Angus's territories in Kintyre and Islay, arguing to James VI of Scotland that his cousin was illegitimate.

Sir James Macdonald did not succeed in his claim. But as recounted later, Angus MacDonald of Dunivaig and the Glens now started on the downward path that would destroy his family. He first rebelled against the Scottish Crown and then quarrelled disastrously with his own son Sir James MacDonald of Islay. By 1603, he had lost all his territories in Antrim to Sir Randal MacDonald of Dunluce, who had succeeded his brother James in 1601 as the eldest-surviving son of Sorley Buidhe. Randal's loyalty to James VI, now ruling as James I of Great Britain after the death of Elizabeth I of England in 1603, was finally rewarded in 1620. He was created the first Earl of Antrim as a reward for 'reducing to civility the barbarous people' of his territories. His son Randal succeeded him as the second Earl of Antrim in 1636. He played a prominent role in the Civil Wars of the 1640s, providing men and arms to

James Graham, Marquis of Montrose, who had Randal's kinsman Alasdair MacColla as his chief lieutenant. Together, they fought a year-long but ultimately unavailing campaign on behalf of Charles I against the Scottish covenanters and their leader, Archibald Campbell, eighth Earl of Argyll.

Chapter Five

HIGHLAND FEUDS AND REBELLIONS

The descendants of Sorley Buidhe prospered as the Earls of Antrim under British rule in Ireland. However, the internecine quarrels among the MacDonalds of Dunivaig and the Glens as the senior branch of the family brought upon themselves a series of disasters leading to their eventual downfall and destruction. They were first threatened during the last two decades of the sixteenth century by a long and bloody feud with the MacLeans of Duart. The dispute itself concerned the Rhinns of Islay which were of strategic importance in guarding the sea lanes between Ulster and the island of Mull. But the seeds of discord between the two families had already been sown more than a century earlier. Apparently, John MacDonald, fourth Lord of the Isles, had then granted lands in Islay to Lachlan Og MacLean of Duart in the years after 1476. John's son Angus Og, Master of the Isles, objected so strongly to the loss of his patrimony that he took to arms against his father at the Battle of Bloody Bay. He also seems to have destroyed all evidence of the charter itself.

Only in November 1542, shortly before the death of James V, was Lachlan's grandson Hector Mor MacLean of Duart finally granted these lands in Islay. It was then said to be a renewal of the earlier grant. But he held them only briefly, since he was forced by the Earl of Argyll to renounce any claim to these lands in 1546 after the rebellion of Donald Dubh had come to an end. Instead, James MacDonald of Dunivaig and the Glens managed to regain possession of the Rhinns of Islay. A dispute then arose over the island of Gigha, which Neil MacNeill sold to James MacDonald of Dunivaig and the Glens in 1554 after redeeming it from the MacLeans of Duart. Even so, relations between the two families apparently remained friendly enough until 1562. Then, Sir James MacDonald of Dunivaig and the Glens was granted a seven-year lease to lands in Islay, including the Rhinns, where Hector Mor MacLean of Duart was now the Crown's baillie. But there was another reason for animosity between the two families. Shane O'Neill had entered into a liaison with Hector's daughter Catherine MacLean after capturing her second husband Calvagh O'Donnell in 1561. In doing so, he had rejected James MacDonald's daughter Finola whom he had married two years earlier.

Their quarrel intensified in 1562 when James MacDonald demanded that Hector Mor MacLean should recognise him as the feudal superior of the Crown lands that the MacLeans now occupied in the Rhinns of Islay. Pursuing this claim, the MacDonalds of Dunivaig and the Glens ravaged the MacLean lands in Coll, Tiree and Mull, aided by the MacDonalds of Sleat. No doubt the MacLeans retaliated by harrying the lands of the MacDonalds. The matter eventually came before the Privy Council in 1565, who decided in favour of James MacDonald of Dunivaig and the Glens. The two chieftains were each compelled to find sureties of 10,000 pounds for their good conduct. Interestingly enough, Archibald Campbell, fifth Earl of Argyll, undertook to guarantee the payment of both sureties, related as he was by marriage to both families. No doubt he acted in his own self-interest.

Renewed Feuding in the Western Isles

As we have seen, James MacDonald of Dunivaig and the Glens died in 1565 from wounds received at the Battle of Glentasie. He was succeeded by his son Angus, but probably only after the death of Angus's elder brother Archibald in 1568. His early years as chieftain were peaceful enough to judge by the lack of any government records. Indeed, he may well have been a minor at the time, since the marriage of his mother Lady Agnes Campbell to his father perhaps occurred as late as 1554 while he lived until 1614. However, hostilities were resumed between the two families after Lachlan Mor MacLean became chieftain of the MacLeans of Duart around 1578, following the deaths of his grandfather Hector Mor MacLean and then his father Hector Og MacLean only three years later.

Lachlan Mor MacLean was the nephew of the fifth Earl of Argyll, since his father Hector Og MacLean had married Argyll's sister Janet, daughter of Archibald Campbell, the fourth Earl. Raised in his uncle's Protestant household, he later married a grand-daughter of Alexander Cunningham, fifth Earl of Glencairn. His father-in-law was also a fanatical Protestant so it is likely that he embraced the tenets of the Reformed Church. Indeed, he later became the trusted ally of his cousin Archibald Campbell, afterwards the seventh Earl of Argyll, who was equally ardent in the profession of his Protestant religion.

Angus MacDonald of Dunivaig and the Glens on the other hand remained a Catholic. Nevertheless, the two families became reconciled to one another by Angus's marriage to Mary, sister of Lachlan Mor MacLean, soon after the Privy Council was once again forced to intervene in the feud between the two families. Their alliance was perhaps encouraged by Colin Campbell, now the sixth Earl of Argyll after the death of his brother Archibald in 1573. Despite this marriage, however, the feud between the two families broke out again with even greater virulence in 1585 after a quite unexpected incident. It involved Donald Gorm Mor MacDonald of Sleat.

Ten years earlier, Donald Gorm Mor had succeeded his father while still a minor as chieftain of what was the senior branch of Clan Donald. During his minority, a dispute had arisen over payment of teinds to John Campbell, Bishop of the Isles. His kinsmen Donald and Hugh MacGilleasbuig Chleirich, 'Sons of Archibald the Clerk', were outlawed as a result since they were then responsible for the family's affairs. On coming of age, Donald Gorm Mor MacDonald of Sleat decided to visit his kinsman, Angus MacDonald of Dunivaig and the Glens. Sailing from Skye past the island of Jura, he was forced by the weather to take refuge in Loch Tarbert. Unknown to him, Hugh MacGilleasbuig Chleirich, who had taken to a life of piracy, was anchored in a nearby bay. Hugh secretly landed at night with some men to carry off some cattle belonging to MacLean of Duart thinking that his kinsmen would be blamed for the theft, as indeed happened. The MacLeans attacked the MacDonalds of Sleat during the following night, killing some sixty men. Donald Gorm Mor only escaped with his life since he had decided to sleep on board his galley.

Naturally enough, Donald Gorm Mor sought retribution for the massacre of his kinsmen after returning home to Skye. He called upon the MacLeods of Lewis, the MacNeills of Gigha, the MacAllisters of Loup and the MacPhees of Colonsay among the other allies of Clan Donald to support him. The quarrel reached such a pitch that James VI was forced to write to William MacLeod of Harris and Dunvegan, urging him to assist Lachlan Mor Maclean of Duart. However, before hostilities got out of hand, Angus MacDonald of Dunivaig and the Glens decided to intervene, hoping to use his influence with his brother-in-law Lachlan Mor MacLean to mediate in his quarrel with Donald Gorm Mor of Sleat.

Kidnapping of Angus MacDonald

After visiting his kinsman Donald Gorm Mor in Skye, Angus MacDonald of Dunivaig and the Glens returned by way of Duart, intending to explain what had happened. He was received well enough at first, but the hospitality soon turned to treachery. He was seized along with his men and thrown into prison. On pain of death, Angus MacDonald of Dunivaig and the Glens had no alternative but to sign away his rights to the Rhinns of Islay. He was then released with his men but he was forced to surrender his son James, then only a child, and his brother Ranald as hostages. Returning to Islay, Angus MacDonald of Dunivaig and the Glens bided his time until Lachlan Mor MacLean arrived to claim his lands in the Rhinns, which he did in July 1586. Lachlan Mor MacLean first occupied the ruinous Castle of Loch Gorm. However, he was eventually persuaded by Angus MacDonald of Dunivaig and the Glens to visit him in his own house at Mullintrea, after repeated protestations that he and his retinue of eighty-six kinsmen and servants would come to no harm. Indeed, Angus's wife wrote to her brother urging him to accept her husband's invitation. A sumptuous feast welcomed the visitors, but after they had retired to their own lodgings for the night they were seized by the MacDonald clansmen who far outnumbered them and held captive.

While Lachlan Mor MacLean and his retinue were still held prisoner by Angus MacDonald of Dunivaig and the Glens, news came from Mull that Angus's brother Ranald, still held hostage at Duart, had been executed. Although it later turned out to be a ill-founded rumour, the revenge of the MacDonalds was swift and terrible. If we are to believe tradition, two MacLeans were executed every day until only Lachlan Mor MacLean and his uncle John Dubh were left alive. It is said that their lives were only spared because Angus MacDonald broke his leg in falling from his horse on his way to witness their execution.

General Band of 1587

These atrocities now came to the attention of James VI in Edinburgh, who was now ruling over Scotland after coming of age in the same year. Parliament now passed an Act requiring all landlords, baillies and clan chieftains to enter into a 'General Band'. This required them to find sureties proportional to their wealth and the size of their estates for the peaceable and orderly behaviour of their tenants and other adherents.

Meanwhile, after receiving a promise of a pardon for his crimes, Angus MacDonald of Dunivaig and the Glens agreed to release Lachlan Mor MacLean of Duart from captivity. Eight other hostages were to take Lachlan Mor's place. They included Lachlan's eldest son Hector, together with other hostages provided by the MacLeods of Dunvegan, the MacKinnons of Strathordle, the MacNeills of Barra and the MacLeans of Ardgour, as the allies of Lachlan Mor MacLean of Duart. Angus MacDonald of Dunivaig and the Glens and Donald Gorm Mor MacDonald of Sleat meanwhile entered into a bond of manrent with Lachlan MacIntosh, Captain of Clan Chattan. Intended to guard their northern borders, it was directed in particular against the MacLeods of Harris and Dunvegan and the MacKenzies of Kintail.

Retaliation and Counter-Retaliation

Released from captivity in 1587, Lachlan Mor MacLean quite recklessly disregarded the safety of the hostages whom he had surrendered for his own good behaviour. Indeed, no sooner had he returned to Duart than he ordered the execution of two MacDonald kinsmen who were prisoners of the MacLeans, or so it was reported to Angus MacDonald of Dunivaig and the Glens. He reacted by ordering the execution of Lachlan's uncle John Dubh, whom he still held prisoner. Lachlan Mor MacLean retaliated by ravaging the MacDonald lands of Islay and Gigha, where five or six hundred men capable of bearing arms for Clan Donald were slaughtered.

Angus MacDonald was himself besieged in his castle of Dunivaig after he had returned from the Glens of Antrim. He only gained his freedom by agreeing under duress to surrender half of his Islay possessions to Lachlan Mor MacLean of Duart. But despite his compact with Lachlan Mor MacLean, Angus then invaded the MacLean lands in Mull, Tiree, Coll and Luing with Donald Gorm Mor MacDonald of Sleat. Giving their support were the MacDonalds of Clan Ranald and the MacIains of Ardnamurchan, as well as the MacLeods of Lewis, the MacNeills of Gigha, the MacAllisters of Loup and the MacPhees of Colonsay. Ranged against them in support of Lachlan Mor MacLean of Duart were the MacLeods of Harris and Dunvegan, the MacNeills of Barra, the MacKinnons of Strathordle, and the MacQuarries of Ulva. Thus, within a century, the downfall of the Lordship of the Isles had brought about a fateful division within Gaeldom which was once united behind Clan Donald.

Intervention of James VI

As the bitter conflict between the MacDonalds and the MacLeans now threatened the peace throughout the Western Isles, James VI was again forced to intervene. He ordered that the hostages still in the hands of Angus MacDonald of Dunivaig and the Glens should be surrendered to the guardians of Archibald Campbell, seventh Earl of Argyll. Still a minor in 1587, he did not reach his majority until 1593 when he took up the Campbell tradition of acting as a loyal servant to the Crown. Equally, George Gordon, sixth Earl of Huntly, was also a minor at the death of his father in 1576. He had only returned from France after 1580, where he had been educated in the Catholic religion. He then helped the king to escape from the clutches of the Ruthven raiders in 1583 and he was later made Lord High Chamberlin in 1587. However, his religion made him an uncertain ally of the king in the eyes of the Presbyterian party. Even so, he was charged by James VI in 1587 to do everything in his power to prevent any further outbreak of violence in the northern Hebrides.

Feud with the MacIains of Ardnamurchan

James VI's intervention had little effect on Angus MacDonald of Dunivaig and the Glens. He had already forfeited all his lands after failing to release his hostages. The lands in question were then granted in life-rent to Lachlan Mor MacLean of Duart, after he had won back the favour of the Crown. Yet this settlement lasted for little more than a year since Lachlan Mor MacLean once again disturbed the king's peace. He had a particular quarrel with John MacIain of Ardnamurchan, whom he blamed for the death of his uncle John Dubh, executed the previous year by Angus MacDonald of Dunivaig and the Glens. Indeed, his execution had occurred after John MacIain had reported to Angus MacDonald, perhaps falsely, that two of his kinsmen had died at the hands of Lachlan Mor MacLean. But even earlier, John MacIain had courted MacLean's widowed mother, who was none other than Janet Campbell, daughter of the fourth Earl of Argyll. It seems that Lachlan Mor MacLean now consented to their marriage. It took place in 1588 at his residence of Torlusk in Mull.

After the wedding feast and much festivity, John MacIain retired with his bride to the bridal chamber in the main house. However, his retinue of clan gentry and servants was lodged in a nearby barn. There they were attacked at dead of night by a large party of MacLeans who slaughtered eighteen of their number without mercy. Awoken by the disturbance, John MacIain would himself have lost his life but for the desperate pleading of his wife. Even so, John MacIain was thrown into a dungeon and kept there a prisoner in chains. A complaint was made to the Privy Council in Edinburgh and Lachlan Mor MacLean of Duart forfeited all his lands and title.

Indeed, Lachlan Mor MacLean had already attacked the MacDonald islands of Rhum, Eigg, Muck and Canna. Among his forces were Spanish mercenaries from the galleon *Florida* of the Spanish armada which had taken refuge in Tobermory Bay. He then turned to ravaging MacIain's lands of Ardnamurchan, laying siege to Mingary Castle. He was only forced to retire by a superior force mustered by the neighbouring clans acting on the orders of the Privy Council. Meanwhile, the MacDonalds and their allies had harried the MacLean lands with fire and sword. aided it is said by a party of English mercenaries. Eventually, however, the hostilities ceased when the two sides agreed that the eight MacLean hostages still held by Angus

MacDonald of Dunivaig and the Glens should be exchanged for John MacIain of Ardnamurchan and the other prisoners held by Lachlan Mor MacLean of Duart who were all released.

Submission to James VI

James VI now determined to bring the king's peace to the Highlands and Western Isles. But instead of resorting to arms, the king first granted remissions under the Privy Seal in 1589 to all the MacLean and MacDonald chieftains and their principal adherents. They were all pardoned for the various crimes they had committed during their recent feuds. He then summoned Angus MacDonald of Dunivaig and the Glens, Donald Gorm Mor MacDonald of Sleat, and Lachlan Mor MacLean of Duart to Edinburgh, saying he wished to consult them about the good rule of their dominions. However, when the three chieftains arrived, they found the king absent in Denmark. They were immediately imprisoned in Edinburgh Castle, despite the safe-conducts they had received from the Privy Council.

Charged with treason, they threw themselves upon the mercy of James VI when he returned from his marriage to Anne, Princess of Denmark. He pardoned them after they had each agreed to pay a large fine for their past conduct, said to be 20,000 pounds by one account. It was a light enough punishment since they might well have paid with their lives had justice been done. But James VI was desperately short of money since the royal revenues had been squandered during his long minority. Indeed, such fines were evidently intended to recompense the king for any arrears in Crown rents from the Highlands and Western Isles. The disturbed state of the country meant they had not been collected for the past few years. Moreover, before Angus MacDonald of Dunivaig and the Glens or Donald Gorm Mor MacDonald of Sleat were set free in 1591, they had to surrender hostages to ensure they would themselves appear as required by the Privy Council on twenty days' notice. Among these hostages was James MacDonald, son of Angus MacDonald, last in the line of the MacDonalds of Dunivaig and the Glens.

Lachlan Mor MacLean of Duart was treated more leniently, and indeed he was knighted. However, he still had to surrender hostages for his good behaviour after his release from captivity. Further sureties amounting to 10,000 merks were required of all these Highland chieftains in 1592 to ensure that they would collect the rentals and other duties owed to the Crown from their lands and other possessions. Their annual rentals to the Crown were set at the same amount. John Campbell of Cawdor found surety for Angus MacDonald of Dunivaig and the Glens, and his family were later to profit greatly from the eventual downfall of this branch of Clan Donald, while

James Campbell of Ardkinglas found surety for Lachlan Mor MacLean of Duart.

It may be mentioned in passing that a merk was 13s 4d, being two-thirds of a Scots pound. The currency in Scotland became progressively debased over the years when compared with England so that the Scots pound no longer had parity with the pound sterling after 1367.

Insurrection of the Earl of Huntly

The quarrel between the MacDonalds and the MacLeans over the Rhinns of Islay was apparently just a private if very bloody feud between the two families and their followers. Even so, its effects were felt on the national stage. After the execution of Mary Stuart, Queen of Scots, which occurred in 1587, and the English defeat of the Spanish Armada in 1588, James VI was threatened early in his reign not just by the extravagant claims of the Presbyterian party, but by intrigues against his government among the pro-Catholic earls as well. They were outraged that James VI had not attacked England in revenge for Mary's execution. Although George Gordon, sixth Earl of Huntly, signed the Confession of Faith in February 1588, he was still suspected of intriguing with Philip II of Spain. Indeed, he was imprisoned briefly a year later in February 1589 after letters were intercepted expressing his regret that the Spanish Armada had failed in its attempted invasion of England.

However, soon after his release, George Gordon, sixth Earl of Huntly, joined the Earls of Bothwell, Errol and Crawford in a brief insurrection, hoping to overthrow the government of Chancellor Sir John Maitland of Thirlestane. James VI responded to the threat with vigour, quite contrary to his later reputation as lacking in physical courage. Accompanied by his Protestant lords, he marched north at the head of his army to confront the rebels at Aberdeen. Deserted by his own forces, Huntly retreated to Strathbogie, where he surrendered to those of the king. Afterwards, he was held in easy confinement for more than a year in Borthwick Castle. However, he was then released and soon restored to the favour of James VI. Indeed, the king needed all the allies he could get in his struggle against the reforming zeal of the Presbyterian Church.

Feuds among the Campbells

Three years later, Sir John Campbell of Cawdor was assassinated in 1592 during the course of a private feud among the Campbells which threatened to destroy them. However, his death was part of an even wider conspiracy, complex in its ramifications and shifting alliances. When Colin Campbell, sixth Earl of Argyll and Chancellor and Justice-General of Scotland, had died in 1584, he was succeeded by his eldest son Archibald, then only nine years old. His father's widow Agnes, Countess of Argyll, had charge of the young earl and his vast estates. But her husband had made her promise at his deathbed that she was only to act with the advice of his kinsmen. Chief among them were John Campbell of Cawdor, Dougal Campbell of Auchinbreck and Neil Campbell, Bishop of Argyll, whose signatures were required on any legal document of importance.

The young chief's kinsman Archibald Campbell of Lochnell resented being excluded from these arrangements since he regarded himself as the nearest heir-male to the house of Argyll, apart from the earl's younger brother. His resentment was encouraged secretly by Duncan Campbell of Glenorchy, who had hoped to become Tutor to the young Earl of Argyll, if not to gain the earldom for himself. As Tutor, he would have controlled all the Campbell estates during Archibald's minority and the revenues from them. When the young Earl of Argyll reached twelve years of age in 1587, he became entitled to nominate his own guardians. A further dispute then broke out within the family, ending with James Campbell of Ardkinglas and John Campbell of Cawdor being appointed as the earl's guardians.

Resentments now arose between the two guardians, since John Campbell of Cawdor failed to keep his promise to pay the 10,000 merks as surety for Angus MacDonald of Dunivaig and the Glens. His failure angered not just the king but James Campbell of Ardkinglas as well, since he was the King's Comptroller. Indeed, Ardkinglas perhaps even contemplated the assassination of John Campbell of Cawdor around this time, only to die of natural causes in 1591. It left his intended victim, Sir John Campbell of Cawdor, as the sole guardian of the young Earl of Argyll, supported by such barons as James Stewart, Earl of Moray, among many others.

Duplicity of Duncan Campbell of Glenorchy

George Gordon, sixth Earl of Huntly, now decided to exploit these divisions within the Campbell family. He evidently hoped to gain the support of Duncan Campbell of Glenorchy in his long-standing feud with James Stewart, Earl of Moray, which had recently erupted with renewed vigour. Indeed, Duncan Campbell of Glenorchy had every reason to feel aggrieved. He had been excluded as a guardian to the young Earl of Argyll ever since 1584, despite being the most powerful of all the Campbell family apart from the Earl of Argyll himself. Quite likely, he wanted the earldom for himself, or so it was said afterwards by the other conspirators. He was so disaffected that that he now agreed with George Gordon, sixth Earl of Huntly, to join a widespread conspiracy. It threatened the lives of Huntly's rival James Stewart, Earl of Moray; Archibald Campbell, seventh Earl of Argyll; Archibald's younger brother Colin Campbell of Lundie, heir-apparent to the earldom; and Archibald's guardian Sir John Campbell of Cawdor. If the plot succeeded, it was agreed that Archibald Campbell of Lochnell would become Earl of Argyll, although he may only have acted as a figurehead. He would then reward the other conspirators with grants of land.

Such a prospect was evidently sufficient for Lochnell to betray the young Earl of Argyll. It may well be that he justified his actions by appealing to the age-old system of kin-based succession in Gaeldom which gave him a powerful claim to the earldom under its archaic traditions. Chancellor Maitland was drawn into the plot so that he might defend the conspirators from its consequences. They were also joined by Duncan MacDougall of Dunollie and John Stewart of Appin who was connected by marriage with the house of Lochnell. George Gordon, sixth Earl of Huntly, also made an alliance, defensive and offensive, with Allan Cameron of Locheil. It was directed especially against the MacIntoshes of Clan Chattan and the Grants of Freuchie. It was counterbalanced by another such alliance, made between James Stewart, Earl of Moray, and James Stewart, fifth Earl of Atholl, and directed against the Earl of Huntly. It was signed among others by Simon, Lord Fraser of Lovat, John Grant of Freuchie and John Campbell of Cawdor, guardian to the young Earl of Argyll.

Feud between Huntly and Moray

George Gordon, sixth Earl of Huntly, was clearly persuaded to enter this conspiracy by his long-standing feud with James Stewart, whose death as the 'Bonnie' Earl of Moray was later lamented in the well-known ballad. Their families had been great rivals in the north, ever since the Gordon earls of Huntly had finally been deprived of the earldom of Moray by Mary Stuart, Queen of Scots. She had then conferred the fertile lowlands of Moray upon her half-brother James Stewart, namesake and father-in-law of the 'Bonnie' Earl of Moray. The ill-feeling between the two families was further exacerbated by the death of George Gordon, fourth Earl of Huntly. It happened at the Battle of Corrichie in 1562, when he was defeated by the very same James Stewart, newly created Earl of Moray.

Up to 1560, George Gordon, fourth Earl of Huntly, had been just as loyal a servant to the Crown as his predecessors. As already recounted, after the death of James V in 1542, he was appointed Lieutenant-General in the North, while he was also Lord High Chancellor of Scotland and a member of the Privy Council. Then in 1549, he was granted the gift of the lands and earldom of Moray. However, he was deprived of these lands and his other offices in 1553 after failing to put down a rising of the Camerons, as already recounted. Then, after resigning the earldom of Moray in 1555, he was restored to favour in 1557 when he was appointed Lieutenant-General of the kingdom. However, he did not receive back the earldom of Moray. Although he still remained a Catholic after the Reformation, he joined the Protestant Lords of the Congregation in demanding that French forces should leave the country in 1560, and was restored to his office of High Chancellor in 1561.

Yet Huntly did not regain his former influence in 1561 after Mary Stuart, Queen of Scots, returned to rule in her own right. Indeed, she seemed likely to grant the earldom of Moray to her half-brother James Stewart, then foremost among her supporters. Huntly's own loyalty to the Crown was further tested early in 1562 by the conduct of his younger son Sir John Gordon. He had severely wounded Lord Ogilvie in a private quarrel over an inheritance, and then after escaping twice from captivity he had returned to his estates, where he raised a sizeable force in rebellion.

Battle of Corrichie (1562)

Mary Stuart, Queen of Scots, then travelled north with a large retinue in 1562. Owing to his son's rebellious conduct, she refused to visit George Gordon, fourth Earl of Huntly, at Strathbogie. But on reaching Inverness, she was refused entry to Inverness Castle on the orders of Huntly's elder son George, Lord Gordon, afterwards the fifth Earl of Huntly and then the sheriff of Inverness. Mary raised a force from the surrounding districts, seized Inverness Castle and then returned to Aberdeen, lamenting meanwhile her own inability as a woman to lead a soldierly life. Outlawed and put to the horn, George Gordon, fourth Earl of Huntly, surely must have realised he had overreached himself. But he gathered together his own forces and marched towards Aberdeen, hoping to seize the young queen. He was especially angered by the news that the earldom of Moray had finally been granted to his rival.

However, abandoned by many of his own men, Huntly was then utterly defeated at the Battle of Corrichie by a much larger force under the command of James Stewart, now the Earl of Moray. It is said that Huntly died of apoplexy as he was led captive from the field. His two sons were captured but only Sir John Gordon was executed for high treason. Huntly's body was taken to Aberdeen to be embalmed and then brought to Edinburgh. More than six months later, a bizarre ceremony took place. The mortal remains of George Gordon, fourth Earl of Huntly, were carried into the council chamber at Edinburgh where sentence of forfeiture was pronounced against him, standing at the bar as the law required.

George, Lord Gordon, as his father's heir to the earldom of Huntly, and John Gordon, Earl of Sutherland, were both convicted of high treason and forfeited by Parliament. Only five years later, they were both restored to their earldoms in April 1567, shortly before Mary, Queen of Scots, made her fateful marriage with James Hepburn, fourth Earl of Bothwell. Then, after Mary's abdication, her half-brother James Stewart, Earl of Moray, became Regent of Scotland. He was assassinated in 1570, and afterwards his eldest daughter Elizabeth Stewart married yet another James Stewart, son of Lord Doune. Her husband thus became the 'Bonnie' Earl of Moray by right of his wife in 1581.

Death of the 'Bonnie' Earl of Moray

More than ten years later, James Stewart absented himself from court, suspected of plotting against James VI with Francis Stewart, Lord Darnley, and the fifth Earl of Bothwell, a fanatical Protestant. George Gordon, sixth Earl of Huntly, was given a commission for his capture. Trusting to a promise of receiving the King's pardon, James Stewart was staying at Donibristle House near Aberdour in Fife. He was surprised there on the night of 7 February 1592 by the Earl of Huntly and his followers, who set fire to the house. Fleeing with his clothes alight, the 'Bonnie' Earl of Moray was brutally stabbed to death in a cave on the foreshore. It is said that his presence was betrayed after a silken tassel of his cap had caught fire. Even though the Earl of Huntly was warded in Blackness Castle and deprived of all his commissions, he was released after only a week, and allowed to return north. By acting so leniently, James VI was himself suspected of plotting the death of the 'Bonnie' Earl of Moray whom he perhaps resented as 'his queen's true love'.

Murder of John Campbell of Cawdor

Three days before James Stewart, the 'Bonnie' Earl of Moray, was murdered in February 1592, Sir John Campbell of Cawdor had himself been shot dead while sitting by the fire in his house at Knipoch, south of Loch Feochain. His assassin was called Gillepatrick MacEllar. His services had been obtained by a younger brother of Archibald Campbell of Lochnell, while the weapon employed was supplied by James Campbell, the young laird of Ardkinglas. Duncan MacDougall of Dunollie sheltered the perpetrator of the crime for nearly a year. But James Campbell of Ardkinglas was suspected as well since his bitter hostility to John Campbell of Cawdor was well-known. The conspiracy against the life of Archibald Campbell, seventh Earl of Argyll, may even have been attempted. It was said that he narrowly escaped death by poisoning in 1592, although a serious illness might well have caused his symptoms.

The conspiracy against the young Earl of Argyll was eventually revealed when the two principals in the murder of John Campbell of Cawdor were captured. They were executed after torture had extracted a confession from them. John Campbell of Ardkinglas, and Duncan MacDougall of Dunollie, were arrested as well, but no action was taken against them and they were eventually set free. In fact, although John Campbell of Ardkinglas confessed all he knew of the conspiracy, there was little attempt by the authorities to bring the conspirators to justice. Indeed, Duncan Campbell of Glenorchy simply cleared his name by denying any involvement in the affair. Apparently, the government of Chancellor Maitland had an interest in concealing the truth, just as it had failed to bring the murderers of the 'Bonnie' Earl of Moray to justice.

Reconciliation among the Campbells

Not long afterwards, the Campbells closed ranks when Duncan Campbell of Glenorchy was reconciled with Archibald Campbell, seventh Earl of Argyll, through the mediation of their kinsmen and mutual friends. Even so, the Earl of Argyll was scarred for life by the affair. His Gaelic sobriquet was Gruamach, meaning 'Grim'. He felt himself surrounded by 'unkindness', unable to trust his kinsmen, whom 'he uses not as councillors but as strangers, for which cause they hold the further from him'. Indeed, it was common knowledge there was 'no love and affection' nor even 'heartliness' between them. Apart from his cousin Lachlan Mor MacLean of Duart, Argyll was only prepared to trust John Campbell of Cawdor, who had succeeded his murdered father in his estates, and Colin Campbell of Lundie, his younger brother.

Despite the marriage of John Campbell of Cawdor to the daughter of Duncan Campbell of Glenorchy in 1601, divisions still remained between the Campbells. It was not until 1619 that a formal reconciliation finally took place. Then, Sir John Campbell of Cawdor buried his differences with John Campbell of Ardkinglas and MacDougall of Dunollie. They signed a band which admitted that the murder of his father Sir John Campbell of Cawdor had caused 'prejudice, hurt, dampnage, and loss' not just to the houses of Cawdor and Ardkinglas 'but also to the whole kin and friends of the name of Campbell'. This reconciliation was timely since Archibald Campbell, seventh Earl of Argyll, had abandoned the Protestant religion by then, and fleeing abroad in 1618 had left his kinsmen to administer his estates.

Aftermath of the Murders

The murders themselves caused serious disturbances throughout the Highlands and the Western Isles. The MacIntoshes and the Grants sought revenge for the death of James Stewart, Earl of Moray, by invading the estates of George Gordon, sixth Earl of Huntly. He retaliated by persuading the Camerons of Locheil to raid the lands of Clan Chattan in Badenoch, pursuing their ancient feud against the MacIntoshes. Meanwhile, Alasdair MacDonald of Keppoch plundered the lands of the Grants in Strathspey and captured Inverness Castle. However, he was forced to surrender it to Lachlan Mor MacIntosh, who soon afterwards entered into a league with Archibald Campbell, seventh Earl of Argyll. By now, George Gordon, Earl of Huntly, became fearful of losing all the influence over Clan Chattan that he and his predecessors had exercised as Lords of Badenoch. He therefore encouraged the MacPhersons to break away from their allegiance to the MacIntoshes, and even to dispute the leadership of Clan Chattan which the MacIntoshes had held for centuries. Likewise, the murder of John Campbell of Cawdor caused the outbreak of a bloody feud with the Stewarts of Appin which lasted for many years.

These disturbances spread to the Western Isles in 1592. The murder of John Campbell of Cawdor had freed Angus MacDonald of Dunivaig and the Glens from any restraint since the surety for his good conduct was no longer in force. Lachlan Mor MacLean of Duart, Angus MacDonald of Dunivaig and the Glens and Donald Gorm Mor MacDonald of Sleat all failed to meet the conditions under which they had obtained their release from royal custody only a year earlier. They were all summoned to appear before the Privy Council in 1592. It threatened them with the forfeiture of all their lands and other possessions, with the revocation of all the pardons previously granted to them and with the execution of all the hostages they had surrendered for their own good behaviour. However, any action against them was delayed for the next two years by another outbreak of religious dissension and political intrigue within the country. It culminated in the Revolt of the Northern Earls in 1594.

Revolt of the Northern Earls

After George Gordon, sixth Earl of Huntly, was set free in 1592 from his brief period of imprisonment following the murder of James Stewart, the 'Bonnie' Earl of Moray, he continued to attract the wrath of the Presbyterian ministers in Scotland. Their suspicions of his Catholic sympathies were confirmed by the affair of the Spanish Blanks. They were blank sheets of paper signed by the Earls of Huntly, Errol and Angus, which were found in the possession of George Kerr, a Roman Catholic, as he was about to sail for Spain at the end of 1592. Torture made him reveal a plot that the Northern Earls intended to aid Spain in an invasion of western Scotland. James VI marched north to Aberdeen, whereupon the Northern Earls fled to Caithness. However, they escaped forfeiture and afterwards James VI offered them a pardon if they would submit to the Reformed Church.

Even so, the king took further action against them in 1594 at the urging of Elizabeth I of England. By then, the Northern Earls had been excommunicated by the General Assembly of the Reformed Church and their estates forfeited by Parliament. He gave the commision to Archibald Campbell, seventh Earl of Argyll, now in his eighteenth year. He was eager to avenge himself against George Gordon, sixth Earl of Huntly, for the murder of Sir John Campbell of Cawdor. He raised an ill-trained army of six or seven thousand men. It consisted of his own clansmen, together with MacLeans, MacNeils, MacGregors, MacIntoshes and Grants. Only 1,500 were musketeers and Argyll had little cavalry and no artillery. Lachlan Mor MacLean of Duart was chief among his commanders. Although forfeited only three months previously, along with Angus MacDonald of Dunivaig and the Glens and Donald Gorm Mor MacDonald of Sleat, he had afterwards paid a large sum of money in coin to James V so annulling his forfeiture.

Argyll marched north by way of Aberdeen and then proceeded into Badenoch. There he besieged Ruthven Castle which was defended by the MacPhersons for the Earl of Huntly. However, he lacked artillery to take the castle so he then marched from Strathspey through the hills towards Strathbogie, intending to meet up with Lord Forbes who had his own quarrel with the Gordon earls of Huntly. By the night of 2 October 1594 Argyll had reached Drumin at the foot of Glenlivet. There he learnt that the Earls of Huntly and Errol were nearby at Auchindoun Castle with a force of only 1,500 men. But this force consisted mostly of gentry, well-mounted and fully armed, and strengthened by a number of military veterans who had served in the Low Countries. There was also a contingent of Highlanders consisting mostly of Camerons, MacPhersons and MacDonalds from Clan Ranald. They also had five pieces of artillery.

Battle of Glenlivet

Although advised to withdraw, the Earl of Argyll trusted to his own superiority in numbers. He therefore decided to engage the enemy without even waiting for the imminent arrival of Lord Forbes. He had 1,100 cavalry at his command from the Frasers, the Dunbars, the Ogilvies and the Leslies, as well as his own kinsmen. The two armies engaged one another on the slopes of Ben Rinnes to the north of Glenlivet. Argyll had the advantage of height, so he drew up his own forces into a defensive position while the Earls of Huntly and Errol brought up their artillery pieces under cover of their own cavalry. They opened fire upon the enemy when within range, aiming especially at the yellow standard of Argyll. Although Argyll escaped with his life, Archibald Campbell of Lochnell was killed in the fusillade. It is said that Lochnell had suggested this very stratagem to the enemy, hoping to benefit from the death of his rival.

Huntly and Errol then attacked with their cavalry. Advancing slowly uphill through the heather, it was badly exposed to the withering fire of the musketeers under Lachlan Mor MacLean of Duart. Twenty gentlemen were killed, but the cavalry under the Earls of Huntly and Errol eventually routed the ill-disciplined forces of the Earl of Argyll. It was reported that the Earl of Argyll was led by his friends from the field of battle, weeping tears of mortification for his defeat, and urging them to stand and defend the honour of their name. He left some 500 men dead upon the field as his forces retreated under a rearguard action fought by Lachlan Mor MacLean of Duart.

The triumph of the Northern Earls was short-lived. News of their victory at Glenlivet was brought by the Earl of Argyll himself to James VI. He had marched north to Dundee with his own forces, accompanied by Andrew Melville, and other leading ministers of the Presbyterian party. The royal army continued north to Aberdeen, despite the lateness of the season, and then marched inland to Strathbogie. However, Huntly refused to oppose James VI in person, fleeing instead to Caithness. The royal army then burnt and razed the rebel's strongholds. Their destruction was urged on by the ministers of the Kirk, who saw it as a crusade against the ungodly. Huntly's magnificent castle at Strathbogie, and Errol's seat at Old Slains, along with the castles of Sir Walter Lindsay and Sir John Ogilvie in Angus, were all destroyed. However, James VI ignored the urgings of the Presbyterians who wanted the rebels executed for treason and allowed the Earls of Huntly and Errol to go abroad in 1595.

Huntly and Errol returned to the country only a year later without the permission of the king. After receiving them at Falkland Palace, James VI agreed that they might stay in Scotland if they came to terms with the Presbyterian religion. Accordingly, they were both received into the Reformed Church in May 1597. Then in December 1597, they were also fully restored to their titles along with the Earl of Angus. George Gordon, sixth Earl of Huntly, now a Privy Councillor, had always been a personal favourite of James VI at court. Indeed, he was created Marquis of Huntly in 1599 to mark the baptism of the king's daughter. Soon after his elevation as marquis, James VI further showed his confidence in Huntly by appointing him as Lieutenant and Justiciar in the north of Scotland, acting jointly with Ludovic Stewart, second Duke of Lennox. Huntly held these offices until 1607, when he was supplanted by Archibald Campbell, seventh Earl of Argyll.

Chapter Six

DAUNTING OF THE WESTERN ISLES

Little now disturbed the king's peace in the Highlands for the next few years. However, Clan Donald was drawn into yet another Irish revolt against English rule in Ulster. Its leader was Hugh O'Neill, Earl of Tyrone. As we have seen, Shane O'Neill of Tyrone died in 1567, when he was succeeded by his cousin Turlough O'Neill as the Earl of Tyrone. However, the English authorities did not recognise his right to the title. They eventually conferred it in 1585 on Shane's nephew Hugh O'Neill, the legitimate claimant to the earldom according to feudal law. By 1593, Hugh O'Neill had persuaded Turlough O'Neill to renounce his own position as 'chief of his name and nation'. He then entered into an alliance against English rule in Ulster with Hugh O'Donnell, Earl of Tyrconnell. Although sporadic clashes occurred in 1594 under the leadership of Hugh O'Donnell, it was not until Hugh O'Neill took the field in the spring of 1595 that the rebellion started in earnest. After three years of fighting in Ulster, he eventually inflicted a crushing defeat upon the English forces at the Battle of Yellow Ford in 1598. After his victory, much of Ireland outside the Pale around Dublin was threatened with insurrection. Another five years of fighting followed, but eventually Hugh O'Neill was forced into submission, just six days after the death of Elizabeth I of England in 1603.

Conflicting Loyalties among the Western Clans

Before he rose in rebellion against English rule, Hugh O'Neill had blundered politically when he hanged Shane O'Neill's son Hugh with his own hands since it is said he could find nobody else to act as hangman. His victim had just as legitimate a claim to the earldom of Tyrone in the eyes of his O'Neill kinsmen as his executioner. Furthermore, the victim's mother was Catherine MacLean, daughter of Hector Mor MacLean of Duart and the widow of Archibald Campbell, fourth Earl of Argyll, before she married Shane O'Neill, Earl of Tyrone. As Shane's son Hugh was the child of this later marriage, it is hardly surprising that Lachlan Mor MacLean of Duart and Archibald Campbell, seventh Earl of Argyll, failed to support Hugh O'Neill in his rebellion against English rule. Indeed, Lachlan Mor MacLean, or one of his sons, had already sent a force of 2,000 men to Ulster, where they fought alongside Shane O'Neill's sons against the pretensions of Hugh O'Neill to succeed his uncle Turlough O'Neill as chief of the O'Neills.

Such considerations did not worry Donald Gorm Mor MacDonald of Sleat or Ruairi Mor MacLeod of Harris and Dunvegan. They sailed for Ulster in the summer of 1594, each accompanied by 500 men, intending to serve Hugh O'Donnell, Earl of Tyrconnell, who was then besieging Enniskillen. After landing at Loch Foyle, they were entertained famously by O'Donnell for three days and three nights. Donald Gorm Mor MacDonald of Sleat then returned to Skye, leaving his forces behind in Ireland. However, Ruairi Mor MacLeod of Harris and Dunvegan was present at the fall of Enniskillen Castle in October 1594. He was still in Ireland in the following year, commanding 600 Islemen with Hugh O'Donnell at the siege of MacCostello's Castle in County Mayo. These same Islemen may well have defended O'Madden's Castle beyond the Shannon in 1596.

Meanwhile in 1595, another expedition left the Western Isles in support of the rebellion by Hugh O'Neill against English rule in Ulster when Donald MacDonald of Clan Ranald and John Og MacIain of Ardnamurchan sailed for Ulster with 2,000 men. However, as their fleet of galleys sheltered for the night in the Sound of Mull, perhaps landing on Calve Island just off Tobermory, it was surprised by Lachlan Mor MacLean of Duart accompanied by 1,200 men. Three hundred and fifty MacDonalds were slain in the ensuing battle and Donald MacDonald of Clan Ranald was taken captive along with several other chieftains.

The expedition mounted by Clan Ranald was apparently only part of a concerted effort by Clan Donald to help the Irish rebels, since Donald Gorm Mor MacDonald of Sleat raised yet another force in 1595, amounting to 4,000 men. They embarked for Ulster in fifty galleys, accompanied by seventy supply ships. However, the fleet was blown off course on its way to raiding the Isle of Man. English agents in Scotland had also learnt of the expedition setting sail when it obtained provisions and other supplies from ports on the Firth of Clyde. Forewarned, three English frigates attacked the fleet off Rathlin Island where thirteen galleys were sunk, and then routed the remainder off Copeland Island at the entrance to Belfast Lough where another twelve or thirteen of galleys were destroyed or captured.

Angus MacDonald of Dunivaig and the Glens had returned by then to Ulster, and Donald Gorm Mor MacDonald of Sleat joined him in the Glens of Antrim after this debacle. They evidently decided that discretion was the better part of valour. Cutting their losses, they even wrote to the Lord Deputy of Ireland, offering their services as mercenaries against Hugh O'Neill of Tyrone. Soon afterwards, however, they returned home to the Western Isles, perhaps obeying the injunction from the Privy Council of Scotland not to assist the Irish rebels. Their return from Ulster ended what turned out to be the last great expeditionary force of galleys to be launched from the Western Isles of Scotland. English sea-power was evidently now more than a match for their galleys. James VI would take advantage of the growing strength of the English navy when he became James I of Great Britain in 1603, since it gave him possession of the sea lanes around the Hebrides.

Role of Lachlan Mor MacLean

Meanwhile, Lachlan Mor MacLean of Duart sought to ally himself with Elizabeth I of England in May 1595, provided he was paid for his services. Already, Hugh O'Donnell, Earl of Tyrconnell, backed by Spanish gold, had tried unsuccessfully to elicit Lachlan's support for his own rebellion against the English Crown. However, Lachlan Mor MacLean wrote instead to the English ambassador in Edinburgh. After informing him of Hugh O'Donnell's proposal, he suggested instead that Elizabeth I of England should employ him and the Earl of Argyll to prevent the forces of Clan Donald from helping the Irish rebels. Three months later, he wrote again saying that lack of money had forced him to disband a force of 600 mercenaries, which he had used to threaten the lands of Clan Donald if they should assist the Irish rebels. Evidently, it was after this threat had been removed that MacDonald of Sleat was able to set sail with his ill-fated expedition to Ulster in the summer of 1595.

Soon afterwards, Lachlan Mor MacLean reported his victory over Donald MacDonald of Clan Ranald to the English ambassador in Edinburgh. He was later promised a reward of 1,000 crowns from Elizabeth I of England but there is little evidence he was ever paid. Then, after the rebellion of Hugh O'Neill gathered pace later in 1595, Lachlan Mor again offered his services to the English Crown. He promised to raise 4,000 men with the help of the Earl of Argyll, but again only if money was made available to pay them. Indeed, he even put forward a well-conceived strategy to defeat the Irish rebels. He would attack them in the rear with his own forces while they were confronted from the opposite direction by what English forces were already in the field. But he was not prepared to act without a 'consideration' for his services. Letters passed back and forth for the next three years, but the money needed to pay him never materialised. Eventually, any possibility of help that Lachlan Mor MacLean of Duart might have given the English in Ireland ended with his death at the Battle of Loch Gruinart in 1598.

Naval Expedition to Kintyre

Meanwhile, Angus MacDonald of Dunivaig and the Glens was still faced
with forfeiture after his return to Scotland in 1595. James VI was now in a
much stronger position after the Revolt of the Northern Earls had been
defeated in the same year but he was still very short of money. James VI now
turned his attention to increasing his revenues from the Western Isles. Early
in 1596, he sanctioned a visit to Islay by James MacDonald, eldest son of
Angus MacDonald of Dunivaig and the Glens, who had been held hostage
in Edinburgh since 1592. James VI evidently hoped that he could persuade
his father Angus to submit to royal authority.

However, James VI also realised that mere persuasion might not be
enough. He therefore laid plans for a naval expedition to the Western Isles
under his own command. Such a threat evidently persuaded Lachlan Mor
MacLean of Duart and Donald Gorm Mor MacDonald of Sleat to visit
Edinburgh where they made their submissions. Along with Ruairi Mor
MacLeod of Harris and Dunvegan and Donald MacDonald of Glengarry
they agreed to increase their rents to the Crown. Angus MacDonald of
Dunivaig and the Glens still remained obdurate until he was eventually forced
to promise James VI that he would submit to royal authority on whatever
terms that the king might choose to make.

This promise was made by James MacDonald on the authority of his
father Angus when he returned to Edinburgh in October 1596. However, it
came too late to prevent the much-delayed expedition from setting sail to
Kintyre. It was commanded by Sir William Stewart of Houston, who had
earlier been appointed as King's Lieutenant and Justiciar for the Western Isles.
James VI further ordered Ludovic Stewart, Duke of Lennox, and Archibald
Campbell, seventh Earl of Argyll, to send additional forces to Kintyre. The
king also wrote to Sir James MacDonald of Dunluce, son of Sorley Buidhe,
offering to reward him highly if he were to support the expedition against his
kinsman Angus MacDonald of Dunivaig and the Glens.

Internecine Quarrels among the MacDonalds

Such a show of force persuaded Angus MacDonald of Dunivaig and the
Glens to submit personally to the King's Lieutenant when he held a court in
Kintyre late in 1596. Then early in 1597 Angus visited Edinburgh. He agreed
under duress to vacate all his lands in Kintyre and to abandon any claim to
the Rhinns of Islay, which would be granted instead to Lachlan Mor MacLean
of Duart. He would now be allowed to occupy only his other lands on Islay.
As a test of his sincerity, he was required to find surety for the arrears in rents

he owed the Crown, to remove his clansmen and all his dependants from Kintyre and the Rhinns of Islay and to deliver up Dunivaig Castle into the king's hands. He was then allowed to return to Kintyre to fulfil these conditions. However, Sir James MacDonald, who had now been knighted as a sign of royal favour, was still to remain in Edinburgh as a hostage for his father's good behaviour.

However, after returning to Kintyre, Angus MacDonald of Dunivaig and the Glens neglected to fulfil the conditions that he had agreed with James VI for his release. Sir James MacDonald was now permitted in 1598 to visit his father for a second time. However, the strategy backfired. Sent to persuade his father Angus to comply with the king's wishes, Sir James MacDonald now seized all his father's estates. Already, Angus had given his son authority to act on his behalf in 1596. James VI held Sir James MacDonald in great affection, and Angus no doubt thought that his son could obtain better terms than himself in negotiating with the king. However, the Privy Council had not recognised the change in ownership, so Sir James MacDonald evidently now decided to put it unilaterally into effect.

He took advantage of a feud that had recently broken out among the Mac-Allisters of Loup. Their young chief Godfrey had killed his tutor or guardian on coming of age and the tutor's sons took refuge with Angus MacDonald of Dunivaig and the Glens in his residence at Askomull. Godfrey MacAllister as the young Laird of Loup now had the support of Sir James MacDonald who had recently arrived in Kintyre. Together, they surrounded the house at Askomull at the dead of night, accompanied by two or three hundred men. It was set ablaze when the tutor's sons refused to surrender themselves, even though Sir James MacDonald knew very well that his father Angus was inside with his mother. Badly burnt, they barely escaped with their lives. Afterwards, the old chief was held in irons by his son for several months.

Battle of Loch Gruinart

Sir James MacDonald now took command of his clan and he even gained the approval of James VI for his actions. However, Lachlan Mor MacLean of Duart now received the Rhinns of Islay in life-rent from the king, while he even laid claim to all of Islay on the basis of a Crown charter that he had recently been granted. His claim was strongly opposed by Sir James MacDonald. Moreover, the incident at Askomull added fuel to their quarrel. It was Lachlan Mor's sister Mary, married to Angus MacDonald of Dunivaig and the Glens, who had only just survived the fire. Sir Lachlan Mor MacLean of Duart now landed with a large body of men on Islay, intending to take legal possession of the disputed lands.

Meanwhile, Sir James MacDonald had gathered together his own forces numbering around 700 men. Their mutual friends now attempted to mediate. They were alarmed by the prospect of a bloody conflict between the two men, even though they were uncle and nephew by the marriage of Lachlan's sister Mary to James's father Angus. They for their part agreed to meet one another at Loch Gruinart to discuss their differences. Sir James MacDonald was prepared to offer half his lands in Islay to his uncle in life-rent, but only under his feudal superiority. Lachlan Mor MacLean of Duart refused to accept any such compromise, demanding instead that his nephew should surrender any claim or title to what were in fact the ancestral lands of Clan Donald on Islay.

Matters had thus reached such an impasse that the two men decided to settle their dispute by the sword. It is not clear which side had the superiority in numbers. However, the forces under Sir James MacDonald, while even appearing to retreat, managed to gain the top of a low hill. They then charged downhill in such strength that the MacLeans were routed when their vanguard collapsed upon the main body of their forces, throwing them into utter confusion. Lachlan Mor MacLean of Duart was slain, 'clad in silk with no armour and nothing about him but a rapier'. Eighty of his kinsmen and 250 clansmen were also killed, leaving only twenty survivors, or so it was said. It seems that the MacLeans had not expected a fight.

Sir James MacDonald was badly wounded in the fighting but later recovered from his injuries. Thirty of his own followers lost their lives. Hector Og MacLean, son and heir of Lachlan Mor MacLean, escaped wounded from the battlefield. He afterwards launched a devastating attack upon Islay in revenge for the death of his father. Supported by Ruari Mor MacLeod of Harris and Dunvegan, Lachlan MacKinnon of Strathordle, Ruairi MacNeill of Barra and Allan Cameron of Locheil, he encountered the MacDonald forces at Ben Bigrie near Dunivaig where they were almost annihilated. Sir James MacDonald was again wounded but he still managed to escape with a few followers to Kintyre.

MacDonald Traditions of Campbell Duplicity

Since the government did not act against Sir James MacDonald for disturbing the king's peace so violently, Lachlan Mor MacLean was presumably judged the guilty party. Indeed, within a year, the Privy Council had approved the far-sighted plan of Sir James MacDonald to establish royal authority within his own dominions. It involved the removal of all his followers from Kintyre, while handing over Dunivaig Castle to the king and paying the Crown rents, just as his father had earlier promised. Although these plans apparently came to nothing, Angus MacDonald was released from captivity to reclaim the leadership of the MacDonalds of Dunivaig and the Glens by 1600. Sir James MacDonald married a sister of Sir John Campbell of Cawdor around the same time, whose father had been murdered in 1592 as already recounted. Nothing more is known of Sir James MacDonald until 1603. However, Macdonald tradition has him acting in a very foolhardy manner during these years by accepting false advice from his Campbell brother-in-law. Indeed, Sir James Campbell of Cawdor eventually acquired nearly all of Islay at his expense in 1619.

Equally, it is said the Archibald Campbell, seventh Earl of Argyll, sup-ported Angus MacDonald of Dunivaig and the Glens to retrieve his own estates. Clearly, the death of Lachlan Mor MacLean of Duart in 1598 dealt a crushing blow to the Earl of Argyll, otherwise a cold and distant person known as Gruamach, the Grim. They had shown 'such natural love that the one will not be employed without the other'. Indeed, Lachlan Mor's death may well have first kindled the implacable hatred of Archibald Campbell. seventh Earl of Argyll, for Sir James MacDonald and his kinsmen of Dunivaig and the Glens which has subsequently smouldered between the two families down the centuries.

Angus MacDonald himself was apparently persuaded in 1603 that his son was again plotting against him. Sir James MacDonald was seized by his father, who surrendered him into the hands of Archibald Campbell, seventh Earl of Argyll. When the government learnt early in 1604 of his captivity. it ordered the Earl of Argyll to bring Sir James MacDonald before the Privy Council in Edinburgh. He was first warded in Blackness Casle, but after trying to escape he was moved to the greater security of Edinburgh Castle. He was held there until his trial for treason in 1609.

Aggrandisement by the Earl of Argyll

Thus, Angus MacDonald of Dunivaig and the Glens once again possessed his own estates after their seizure by his son, but his position seemed even less secure. Indeed, he now lost the apparent support of Archibald Campbell. seventh Earl of Argyll. It was perhaps only a ruse to deceive Angus so that Angus's son Sir James MacDonald might be captured with the help of Sir John Campbell of Cawdor. Over the next two years, Argyll used his great influence with the Privy Council to block any attempt by Angus MacDonald of Dunivaig and the Glens to gain a legal title to his lands in Kintyre and Islay. Indeed, Argyll seemed bent on procuring these lands for himself and his family.

Meanwhile, Angus MacDonald had renewed his promises of loyalty to the king following a military expedition to Kintyre in 1605. Indeed, he had paid off all the arrears in Crown rents for Kintyre and Islay. But he received no answers to the various petitions he presented to the Privy Council, nor was he allowed to attend the Court in London so that he might present his own case to James VI, now ruling over Great Britain as James I of England. Instead, protracted negotiations now took place between the Privy Council, acting with the full approval of the king, and Archibald Campbell, seventh Earl of Argyll. It was agreed early in 1607 that Argyll should be granted a charter to the lands in North and South Kintyre, and the lands on the island of Jura, previously forfeited by Angus MacDonald of Dunivaig and the Glens. The lands in question had been held by Angus's family for the last five or six centuries. Among the conditions of the grant was even a provision that no land should be leased to the MacDonalds. The grant itself is often seen as a reward to Archibald Campbell, seventh Earl of Argyll, for his persecution of the MacGregors.

Daunting of the Isles

By now, Angus MacDonald of Dunivaig and the Glens had given up any hope of keeping his ancient inheritance by peaceful means since he was reported as gathering together men and ships with a view to armed resistance. In response to this threat, the Privy Council appointed the Earl of Argyll as King's Lieutenant and Justiciar over the southern Hebrides for a period of six months. However, he lacked sufficient resources to take any effective action. It was not until 1608 that plans were laid for yet another expedition to the Western Isles. Alexander Stewart, Lord Ochiltree, and Andrew Knox, Bishop of the Isles, were then given commissions instead of Argyll to meet and confer with Angus MacDonald of Dunivaig and the Glens and Hector Og MacLean of Duart.

After much preparation, the expedition itself set sail for Islay with 900 men on board four ships and ten barques. In command was Loch Ochiltree, now appointed as the King's Lieutenant of the Isles. More ships joined the expedition off Islay, carrying additional forces from Ireland as well as a battering engine. Faced with such a formidable show of armed strength, Angus MacDonald of Dunivaig and the Glens immediately surrendered his castles of Dunivaig and Loch Gorm into the hands of Lord Ochiltree. Dunivaig was garrisoned with royal forces while the fortalice of Loch Gorm was virtually demolished.

The expedition then sailed through stormy seas to the island of Mull. On its arrival, Hector Og MacLean surrendered Duart Castle into the hands of the King's Lieutenant who garrisoned it with his own troops. Lord

Ochiltree now proceeded to hold a court at Aros Castle in Mull to which all the principal chieftains in the Western Isles were summoned. They included: Angus MacDonald of Dunivaig and the Glens; Hector MacLean of Duart and his brother Lachlan; Donald Gorm Mor MacDonald of Sleat; Donald MacDonald, Captain of Clan Ranald; and Ruairi Mor MacLeod of Harris and Dunvegan and his brother Alasdair. Also present were Lachlan MacKinnon of Strathordle, Hector MacLean of Coll and Lachlan MacLean of Lochbuie. Only Ruairi MacNeill of Barra and Ruairi MacLeod of Lewis, did not appear. Lord Ochiltree now put various proposals from the Privy Council to them. Almost unchanged, they were later enacted in 1609 as the Statutes of Iona, to be described below in the final chapter.

Surprisingly, Angus MacDonald of Dunivaig and the Glens was the only person present who was prepared to accept all the demands of Loch Ochiltree without any qualification, and he was allowed to depart. All the others were invited on board the Lieutenant's flagship to hear a sermon preached by Andrew Knox, Bishop of the Isles. Afterwards, Lord Ochiltree persuaded them to remain on board to dine with him. Only Ruairi Mor MacLeod of Harris and Dunvegan suspected any sinister design and refused the invitation. However, after the dinner, Lord Ochiltree told his astonished guests they were his prisoners by order of the king. Weighing anchor, he then set sail for Ayr. His prisoners were taken before the Privy Council in Edinburgh which ordered them to be held in Dumbarton, Stirling and Blackness Castles. Hector Og MacLean of Duart was later released so that he could accompany Andrew Knox on his visit to the Western Isles in 1609. The others were only set free after finding substantial sureties to guarantee they would attend as required any meeting of the Privy Council in Edinburgh.

Possession of Islay

Despite losing his lands in Kintyre, Angus MacDonald of Dunivaig and the Glens still held possession of his estates on Islay, although they were much reduced in extent. However, Dunivaig Castle was still garrisoned by royal forces in 1610 when James VI appointed Andrew Knox as Steward and Justice of all the Isles and Constable of Dunivaig Castle. By now, Angus was an old man, and he evidently tired of struggling fruitlessly to preserve his ancient inheritance. Possibly faced with mounting debts, he surrendered his Islay estates to his brother-in-law Sir John Campbell of Cawdor in 1612. He received the paltry sum of 6,000 merks as a 'wadset' on the land, being a mortgage which could be redeemed at any time. It was almost the final act in his long life since he died shortly afterwards in 1613.

Although Sir John Campbell of Cawdor now held the MacDonald estates of Islay, the 'wadset' was redeemed almost immediately by Sir Ranald MacDonald of Dunluce. He was a younger son of Sorley Buidhe, and a younger brother of Sir James MacDonald of Dunluce who had died in 1601. Afterwards created the first Earl of Antrim, Ranald had already been granted vast estates in Antrim by James I of Great Britain. They comprised not only the Route, which his father Sorley Buidhe had held, but also the Glens of Antrim which Angus MacDonald of Dunivaig and the Glens had also granted much earlier to his father as well. Now Sir Ranald MacDonald of Dunluce received a seven-year lease to the MacDonald lands on Islay.

Revolt on Islay

Sir Ranald MacDonald's possession of Islay was soon challenged after the death of Angus MacDonald of Dunivaig and the Glens. His tenants objected to the 'Irish laws and observances' which he imposed upon them.

At their head was Angus Og MacDonald. He was the younger son of Angus MacDonald of Dunivaig and the Glens, and the brother of Sir James MacDonald of Islay, who was still in Edinburgh Castle where he was now held captive under sentence of death. Even so, it was Angus Og's half-brother Ranald Og MacDonald, himself the natural son of Angus MacDonald of Dunivaig and the Glens, who seized the initiative. He captured Dunivaig Castle in the spring of 1614 with a few hotheads. Its capture precipitated the final downfall of the MacDonalds of Dunivaig and the Glens since Dunivaig was now the stronghold of Andrew Knox in his capacity of Steward of the Isles. Perhaps, as we shall see, the rebels were secretly encouraged by Archibald Campbell, seventh Earl of Argyll, or even Sir John Campbell of Cawdor.

Angus Og MacDonald immediately sent round a fiery cross, summoning his followers to arms so that he might recover the castle for the King. After a siege of six days, the rebels fled by sea and Angus Og MacDonald took possession of the castle. He now offered to restore the castle to Andrew Knox as its rightful owner if he was pardoned for any offence committed by himself and his followers. However, Angus Og MacDonald not only refused to deliver up Dunivaig Castle to Andrew Knox when he visited Islay soon afterwards but he had also provisioned the castle for a long siege.

The Privy Council now ordered Andrew Knox to return to Islay where he was expected to take possession of Dunivaig Castle by force. However, he delayed his departure for several months and was only able to raise seventy men for his own defence. On returning to Islay, he found Angus Og MacDonald still adamant in his refusal to surrender the castle. Quite unable to take any action against it for lack of troops, Andrew Knox now attempted to leave Islay, only to find that all his boats had been destroyed. He was only allowed to leave after entering into a treaty with Angus Og MacDonald. They agreed that Andrew Knox should try his utmost to secure Angus Og Mac-Donald a seven-year lease of Islay at an annual rental of 8,000 merks, along with possession of Dunivaig Castle, leases to all the churchlands in Islay and a pardon for all the past misdemeanours of Clan Donald.

Machinations by the Earl of Argyll

However, before leaving Islay with this commission, Andrew Knox wrote to the Privy Council in Edinburgh, revealing the true state of affairs. His letter complained bitterly of his humiliating treatment at the hands of Clan Donald. He argued it was the fault of the government, since he had not been given sufficient resources for his mission to succeed. He excused his own actions by explaining he had been forced to give up his own son and nephew as hostages before Angus Og MacDonald would even enter into negotiations for him to leave Islay. Andrew Knox further reported that Angus Og MacDonald had justified his own actions to him by claiming that Archibald Campbell, seventh Earl of Argyll, had instructed him not to surrender Dunivaig Castle to the Bishop of the Isles. Argyll had apparently also promised Angus Og MacDonald that he should receive a lease to all of Islay and possession of the castle itself. Angus Og MacDonald later declared at his trial for high treason in 1615 that he had received a message to this effect from Malcolm MacNeill, uncle to the Laird of Taynish. He had apparently heard Argyll make these very promises in his own hearing, clearly intending that they should be conveyed to Angus Og MacDonald.

Although the evidence is mostly hearsay, there can be little doubt that the Earl of Argyll was behind the rebellion of Angus Og MacDonald when he refused to give up Dunivaig Castle to Andrew Knox, Bishop of the Isles. Indeed, Argyll may well have engineered its original seizure by Ranald Og MacDonald. Just after he was captured, Ranald Og was seen to destroy a letter he had previously kept concealed about his person. The suspicion remains that it came from Argyll. However, it seems unlikely that Archibald Campbell, seventh Earl of Argyll, merely wanted the MacDonald lands of Islay for himself or his family as asserted by Clan Donald, even though these lands ultimately came into the hands of Sir John Campbell of Cawdor.

It is much more likely that Argyll's machinations were directed against Andrew Knox, Bishop of the Isles. There can be little doubt that Argyll was annoyed that Knox had ousted him from his traditional Campbell role as King's Lieutenant of the Isles which had been held by many of his prede-cessors. Indeed, Argyll may well have encouraged the rebellion of Angus Og MacDonald simply to show that Andrew Knox did not have the power and influence to act effectively in establishing and maintaining the king's authority throughout the Isles. For his part, Andrew Knox, Bishop of the Isles, criticised Argyll's role in the Western Isles when he wrote: 'I cannot think it either good or profitable to his Majesty or this realm to make the name of Campbell greater in the Isles than they are already; nor yet to root out one pestiliferous clan, and plant in another little better.'

Meanwhile, nothing came of the proposals that Andrew Knox had agreed under duress with Angus Og MacDonald. Indeed, Knox had an ally in Alexander Seton, Earl of Dunfermline, who was Chancellor of Scotland. Bypassing the Privy Council, an emissary was sent to Islay to obtain the release of the Bishop's hostages using whatever means were necessary. This he succeeded in doing, and he convinced Angus Og MacDonald not to surrender Dunivaig Castle to Sir John Campbell of Cawdor without the authority of the Lord Chancellor and the Privy Council. He thus left Angus Og MacDonald determined to remain in possession of Dunivaig Castle until his terms were agreed.

Intervention of Sir James Campbell of Cawdor

By now, however, the Privy Council had accepted the offer of Sir James Campbell of Cawdor to pay 9,000 merks in feu-duty as an annual rental in perpetuity for the lands that he had temporarily lost in Islay. Cawdor then took on a commission to reduce Angus Og MacDonald to obedience, largely at his own expense. Only the artillery and ammunition needed to besiege Dunivaig Castle were to be provided at public expense, although 200 men and six cannon were later sent from Ireland for this purpose. Sir John Campbell of Cawdor sailed for Islay towards the end of 1614, and after a siege of several weeks eventually forced the surrender of Dunivaig Castle.

Fourteen rebels were immediately tried and executed. Angus Og Mac-Donald and several of his followers were brought to Edinburgh where they were examined by the Privy Council. Any evidence exonerating Angus Og MacDonald was suppressed by the Earl of Dunfermline, the Lord Chancellor, and Archibald Campbell, seventh Earl of Argyll, who was Justice-General of Scotland. He was eventually condemned to death for high treason, and executed at the Mercat Cross in Edinburgh on 8 July 1615. However, his fate had perhaps been sealed two months earlier when Sir James MacDonald finally succeeded in escaping from Edinburgh Castle.

Escape of Sir James MacDonald

Held captive ever since 1603, Sir James MacDonald remained quite powerless to influence the impending catastrophe as it overtook his line of Dunivaig and the Glens. Indeed, he had actually been tried in 1609 for 'high and manifest treason'. He was then condemned to death for his part in setting fire to the house at Askomull and imprisoning his father Angus MacDonald of Dunivaig and the Glens. However, the sentence was never carried out. He remained a prisoner until May 1615, when he escaped from Edinburgh Castle with the help of Alasdair MacDonald of Keppoch and John MacDonald, the young Master of Clan Ranald.

Crossing the Forth by boat to Burntisland, the fugitives fled north by way of Perth towards Loch Rannoch. There they were sighted by their pursuers, chief among whom were the Earl of Tullibardine and George Gordon, sixth Earl and first Marquis of Huntly. However, they evaded capture and, taking to the woods, the fugitives were met by a party of Keppoch's men who brought them safely to Lochaber. Then after passing through Morar and Knoydart, they finally reached Sleat on the island of Skye, where they conferred with Donald Gorm Mor MacDonald. Taking ship, they then sailed south to the island of Eigg, where they were joined by Colla Ciotach MacDonald, the 'Left-Handed', and his followers. He was the 'Old Colkitto' of the history books, who had taken a prominent part in the recent rebellion of Angus Og MacDonald on Islay. However, when Dunivaig Castle was surrendered to Sir John Campbell of Cawdor, he had managed to escape. He was now engaged in a life of piracy on the high seas with Malcolm MacLeod of Lewis.

Final Rebellion by Sir James MacDonald

After a very enthusiastic welcome by his clansmen on Eigg, Sir James Mac-Donald now sailed south for Islay with a sizeable force of several hundred men which daily increased in numbers. He first landed on Colonsay, and then reached Islay, scarcely a month after escaping from Edinburgh Castle. He captured Dunivaig Castle with little difficulty and then set about expelling all the followers of Sir John Campbell of Cawdor from the island. After securing Islay, Sir James MacDonald then crossed to Kintyre where he seized the whole peninsula with a force now nearly 1,000 strong, augmented as it was by his former tenants.

Throughout this campaign, Sir James MacDonald acted moderately, enforcing a strict discipline upon his own forces. Clearly, he hoped to convince the government that he was prepared to cooperate if he was restored to his ancestral lands. He adopted the same tone in writing to various noblemen whom he hoped would influence the Privy Council on his behalf. He further justified his escape from Edinburgh Castle in a petition to the Privy Council, saying that Sir John Campbell of Cawdor had secured a

warrant from James VI for his instant execution under the sentence of death
already passed on him at his trial in 1609. He implored the king

> not to yield to my [enemies], to root me and my whole race out, being
> 5 or 6 hundred years [in] possession . . . If his Majesty be not willing
> that I should be his Highness's tenant in Islay, for God's cause let his
> Majesty hold it in his own hand; for that is certain I will die before I see
> a Campbell in possession . . . I trust in God that all the Campbells in
> Scotland shall not recover [Islay] so long as they live . . . My race has
> been ten hundred years kindly Scotsmen, under the Kings of Scotland.

He begged that 'I may have this piece of old possessions, which is Islay, to
sustain myself and all my kin, that now follows me.' But he was even willing
to accept 'any poor part of that which our forebears had'.

When Sir James MacDonald first escaped, the Privy Council reacted by
offering a reward of £2,000 for his capture, dead or alive. The sum was later
increased to £5,000. Before learning of his presence on Islay, all of the
Western Isles and the adjacent mainland of Scotland were placed under a
state of alert. Archibald Campbell, seventh Earl of Argyll, was appointed as
King's Lieutenant, but he was absent in London where he had taken refuge
from his creditors in Scotland. The Privy Council repeatedly urged him to
return to Scotland, but he delayed his return to Edinburgh until the middle
of August. Another fortnight passed before he had mustered his forces at
Duntroon on Loch Crinan to begin operations against the rebels.

Argyll's Campaign against the Rebels

As well as the support of the English navy, Archibald Campbell, seventh Earl
of Argyll, had a well-armed force of 400 mercenaries, along with another
1,200 of his own men. Meanwhile, his own spies reported that Sir James
MacDonald was camped with his own forces on the west coast of Kintyre,
opposite the island of Cara at the southern end of Gigha, where his galleys
were anchored. Argyll now divided his forces. Sending 800 of his men by
ship towards Gigha along the west coast of Knapdale, he sailed south with
the remainder of his forces along along Loch Fyne to Tarbert, where he
was joined by more reinforcements under John Campbell of Ardkinglas.
Argyll now advanced by land on the rebels' camp with his own forces, while
the other detachment attacked the island of Cara from the sea.

The King's Lieutenant had such a superiority in men and armament that
the rebels were thrown into utter disarray. Alasdair MacDonald of Keppoch
fled south to the Mull of Kintyre, where he narrowly escaped by sea from his
pursuers. Sir James MacDonald managed to reach Rathlin Island, while

Colla Ciotach made for Islay, where he occupied Dunivaig Castle. Argyll now crossed to the island of Jura. There he learnt that Sir James MacDonald had returned to Islay where he was encamped with 500 men near the isle of Orsay at the southern end of the Rhinns of Islay. Reinforced by two more warships, the Earl of Argyll now crossed to Islay, landing without any opposition at the harbour of Loch Leodomais, now Port Ellen.

Exile and Death of Sir James MacDonald

Sir James MacDonald first attempted to reach a temporary truce with the Earl of Argyll. But it broke down through the intransigence of Colla Ciotach who would not surrender the Castles of Dunivaig and Loch Gorm. Sir James MacDonald was therefore forced to abandon all hope of effective resistance. Argyll's strategy was to attack him by night, hoping to take his forces by surprise. But his followers lit beacons on the Mull of Oa, warning Sir James MacDonald of the danger. Now determined to escape by sea, his principal tenants begged him to stay and fight it out. According to tradition, they all declared that they would die at his feet, defending him from his enemies. They had already risked their lives for him and they could expect no mercy if they were captured. But their entreaties fell on deaf ears. Sir James MacDonald embarked with forty of his closest kinsmen for the remote island of Inishtrahull off the coast of Donegal, never to return to the Western Isles. So ended the last great struggle of Clan Donald to defend their ancestral lands of Islay and Kintyre against Campbell aggrandisement. Apart from the MacDonalds, Earls of Antrim, only the northern septs of Clan Donald still held their lands in Skye and the Outer Hebrides and elsewhere on the Scottish mainland north of Glencoe, Lochaber and the Great Glen.

Abandoned by Sir James MacDonald in so cavalier and shameful a fashion, his devoted clansmen had their worst fears fully realised. Colla Ciotach turned king's evidence when he surrendered the Castles of Dunivaig and Loch Gorm in return for a guarantee of his own safety. He sought pardons for several of his own followers, but betrayed nineteen of his fellow-rebels from among the principal inhabitants of Islay. Ten of them were instantly brought to trial and executed by Argyll, along with another nine men, executed soon afterwards. Archibald Campbell, seventh Earl of Argyll, left Islay in the possession of Sir John Campbell of Cawdor and returned to Kintyre, where more summary executions took place.

By now, Sir James MacDonald had reached Galway where he sought refuge with some Jesuits. They arranged for his escape to exile in Spain. Alasdair MacDonald of Keppoch had accompanied him on his flight to Ireland. However, he first returned to Lochaber, where he remained an outlaw until 1618. He then escaped to exile in Spain where he joined Sir James MacDonald. Curiously enough, they were soon afterwards joined by none other than their arch-enemy, Archibald Campbell, seventh Earl of Argyll. It is said that they spent many hours together, plotting against James VI of Scotland.

Much of the recent animosity between Clan Donald and the Campbell earls of Argyll and their closest allies, the MacLeans of Duart, was caused by religious differences. However, after Archibald Campbell, seventh Earl of Argyll, married his second wife in 1610, she converted her husband to the Catholic religion. Argyll himself spent much of his time after 1610 in England, since his wife was English, only returning to Scotland on royal commissions. He evidently remained in great favour with James VI until 1618, when he was permitted to go abroad for the sake of his health. It was then discovered that he had gone to the Spanish Netherlands, entering into the service of Philip III of Spain.

James VI now commanded Argyll to appear before the Privy Council within sixty days, but he failed to do so. He was proclaimed a traitor early in 1619 and forfeited his earldom. His change in faith had evidently remained a secret, since it was now reported to the Privy Council that Argyll 'has not only made apostasy and defection from the true religion and goes openly to mass, but with that he is secretly reconciled with his Majesty's proclaimed traitor and rebel, Sir James MacDonald.' However, the king's resentment evidently did not last for very long and he was restored to his title in 1621. Although free to return to Scotland, he remained abroad until 1627 when he settled in London. Afterwards, he only visited Scotland once in 1635, when he persuaded the Privy Council in Edinburgh to overturn the sale of Kintyre to Randal MacDonald, eldest son of the first Earl of Antrim. Returning to London without even visiting Inveraray, he died in 1638.

The fall from grace of the Earl of Argyll in 1619 restored the MacDonalds to favour with James VI. Sir James MacDonald and Alasdair MacDonald of Keppoch were both recalled to London in 1620, and they received pensions from the Crown. Alasdair MacDonald of Keppoch was eventually allowed to return to his estates in Lochaber, which he occupied peacefully until his own death in 1635. Only subsequently did a feud break out over the possession of these lands with the MacIntoshes of Clan Chattan, which was not resolved until 1688. However, Sir James MacDonald stayed south of the Border, since the Privy Council was reluctant to allow his return to his native land despite the king's intercession on his behalf. When he died in London in 1626, he left no heirs and the house of Dunivaig and the Glens became extinct.

Chapter Seven

AGGRANDISEMENT OF
THE MACKENZIES

The forfeiture of the earldom of Ross in 1476 by John MacDonald, fourth Lord of the Isles, was greatly to the advantage of Alexander MacKenzie of Kintail, known as Ionraic or 'Upright', and his descendants. While still a youth, he was among the Highland chieftains summoned to attend the Parliament called by James I at Inverness in 1427. Detained by the king, he was sent south to be educated at the High School in Perth where the Court often resided. He remained a loyal servant of the Crown throughout his long life, and afterwards his descendants maintained this tradition. Indeed, their loyalty was such that the only MacKenzie ever said to have received a remission or pardon for offences against the Crown was Colin MacKenzie of Kintail. His offence was committed at the Battle of Langside in 1568, where he fought on behalf of Mary Stuart, Queen of Scots, against James Stewart, Earl of Moray, then acting as Regent for the infant James VI of Scotland.

Alexander Ionraic MacKenzie of Kintail was rewarded for such loyalty in 1477, when he was granted a charter from the Crown confirming him in his lands of Kintail and granting him the lands of Strathconon, Strathgarve and Strathbraan. John MacDonald, fourth Lord of the Isles, while still the Earl of Ross, had granted him these lands in Easter Ross in 1463, but they had afterwards been forfeited to the Crown in 1476. The MacKenzies probably abandoned their Castle of Eilean Donan in Wester Ross around this time to make Kinellan Castle near Strathpeffer their main residence. Then in the seventeenth century, the MacKenzies under Colin MacKenzie, first Earl of Seaforth, built Brahan Castle. It was destroyed in 1815, as prophesied by the Brahan Seer. Their other stronghold in Easter Ross was Castle Leod, which was built around the same time by Sir Roderick MacKenzie of Coigach, ancestor of the present Earls of Cromartie. By then, the MacKenzies were masters of much of the ancient province of Ross, stretching from the fertile churchlands of the Black Isle to the island of Lewis in the Outer Hebrides.

Early History of the MacKenzies

After gaining possession of the fertile valleys of Easter Ross around the head of the Beauly Firth in 1477, Alexander Ionraic MacKenzie of Kintail and his son Kenneth resisted the attempts of the MacDonalds to regain the earldom of Ross by force. Kenneth MacKenzie died early in 1492, only a few years after his father and not long after his victory in 1491 over Alexander MacDonald of Lochalsh at the Battle of Blar-na-Pairce. He was succeeded by his son Kenneth Og MacKenzie. Then, soon after the Lordship of the Isles was forfeited by Clan Donald in 1493, Kenneth Og MacKenzie and his brother-in-law Farquhar MacIntosh of Clan Chattan were arrested and imprisoned in Edinburgh Castle by James IV. The king perhaps feared their influence upon the Highland clans still loyal to the MacDonalds, since it is said, although on doubtful authority, that their mothers were both daughters of John, last Lord of the Isles. They managed to escape from captivity in 1497, but Kenneth Og MacKenzie was killed at Torwood near Stirling, resisting arrest by the Laird of Buchanan. His severed head was brought in triumph to James IV. Farquhar MacIntosh was captured at the same time and imprisoned until after the death of James IV at the Battle of Flodden in 1513.

Since Kenneth Og MacKenzie had died without any heirs, a struggle for power then broke out among the MacKenzies. He was succeeded by his half-brother John MacKenzie of Killin, born of his father's second marriage with Agnes Fraser. However, as he was still a child, his uncle Hector Roy MacKenzie of Gairloch became Tutor to the clan. Exactly how Hector gained a title to his lands in Gairloch, which were originally held by a sept of the MacLeods of Lewis, remains a mystery. However, according to tradition, Hector's sister had earlier married Allan MacLeod of Gairloch, who was then murdered by his brother Ruairi MacLeod, fearful that the MacLeod lands of Gairloch would pass to the MacKenzies by this marriage. For good measure, he also killed his two young nephews, born of this marriage.

Learning of this outrage against his two grandsons, Alexander Ionraic MacKenzie apparently sent their uncle Hector Roy MacKenzie to Edinburgh with their bloodstained shirts to demand retribution from James IV. He returned with Letters of Fire and Sword against Ruairi MacLeod who had killed his sister's husband, and a charter to his lands of Gairloch. James IV perhaps wished to appease Hector Roy MacKenzie. He had fought for James III at the Battle of Sauchieburn in 1488, when the future James IV was party to the rebellion that ended with his father's death. Whatever the truth of this tradition, Hector Roy MacKenzie certainly did receive a charter to the lands of Gairloch. The Sheriff of Inverness was ordered to give him possession of these lands in 1494, while he later received further charters to these lands in

1508 and 1513. However, these events marked the start of a bitter feud with the MacLeods of Gairloch, which lasted for the next hundred years before the MacKenzies were able to take full possession of their lands in Gairloch.

Hector Roy MacKenzie now tried to keep hold of the chiefship of the MacKenzies by questioning the legitimacy of his young nephew, John MacKenzie of Killin. However, he was opposed by Hugh Fraser of Lovat, who was John MacKenzies's maternal uncle, together with Sir William Munro of Foulis, Justiciar of the Sheriffdom of Inverness, and James Stewart, Duke of Ross, younger brother of James IV. Sir William Munro decided on a show of force. It ended in disaster when 900 of his own followers were surprised at Bealach 'n Cor just west of Loch Ussie by a much smaller force under Hector Roy MacKenzie. The Munros were routed with heavy losses, and the place where they fell is still known as Tobar nan Ceann, or Well of the Heads. Even so, Hector Roy MacKenzie eventually became reconciled with his nephew, who inherited all the MacKenzie lands in Easter Ross lying around the head of the Cromarty Firth, as well as the lands farther west in Kintail.

Territorial Expansion

John MacKenzie of Killin throughout his long life gained further estates in Easter Ross and elsewhere, as did his grandson Colin Cam MacKenzie after 1574, while the MacKenzie lands of Kintail were erected into the free barony of Eilean Donan in 1508. John MacKenzie fought at the Battle of Flodden in 1513, and after the Scottish defeat, he was made King's Lieutenant for Wester Ross, charged with defending his country against the rebellion of Donald Gallda MacDonald of Lochalsh. More than twenty years later, he was further rewarded for his part in bringing the rebellion of Donald Gorm MacDonald of Sleat to an end in 1539. By 1544, he was sufficiently powerful to ignore the orders of George Gordon, fourth Earl of Huntly, then acting as Lieutenant-General of the North, but he took part in the Battle of Pinkie in 1547 where he was captured by the English. Released after his tenants raised a ransom on his behalf, he later became a Privy Councillor to Mary of Guise when she was Queen Regent before the accession in 1561 of her daughter Mary Stuart, Queen of Scots. He died at a great age in the same year and was succeeded by his only son Kenneth.

Kenneth MacKenzie of Kintail did not long survive his father, dying in 1568. His skills on the battlefield, displayed long before his father's death, were evidently matched by his prowess in the bedchamber, since he had four sons and six daughters by his marriage with Elizabeth Stewart, daughter of the Earl of Atholl. They nearly all made advantageous marriages with other leading families in the Highlands. He was succeeded in 1568 by his eldest surviving son Colin Cam, meaning 'One-Eyed', who was then still a minor. By the time of his death in 1594, the MacKenzies had profited greatly from the Scottish Reformation of 1560, obtaining lands in the Black Isle previously held by the Church. This territorial expansion brought them into conflict with their neighbours, especially the Munros and the Rosses to the north and the Frasers to the south. However, these years were dominated by a bitter feud with the MacDonalds of Glengarry. It eventually left the MacKenzies in possession of nearly all the western seaboard of the northern Highlands, stretching from Kintail in the south to Eddrachillis in the north. They also acquired the island of Lewis in dubious circumstances, following the destruction of the MacLeods of Lewis early in the seventeenth century. Soon afterwards, Colin Cam's eldest grandson became the first Earl of Seaforth.

MacDonalds of Glengarry

The MacDonalds of Glengarry trace their ancestry from Donald, grandson of John MacDonald, first Lord of the Isles. His father was Ranald, the eponymous ancestor of Clan Ranald, who was himself the eldest son of John's first marriage with Amie MacRuairi. However, the early history of the MacDonalds of Glengarry is very obscure. Donald was made Steward of Lochaber before his death in 1420. His son Alexander held lands in Glengarry and Morar according to a later charter of 1538. Alexander's son John succeeded him in 1460, and John's son Alasdair had succeeded him by 1501, if not earlier. It is said that he took part in the expedition of his future father-in-law Alexander MacDonald of Lochalsh against Easter Ross in 1491, and later joined the rebellion of Lochalsh's son Donald Gallda in the years afer 1513, raiding the lands of John Grant of Freuchie in Easter Ross.

After Donald Gallda's death, Alasdair MacDonald made his peace with the Crown, entering into bonds of manrent with Colin Campbell, third Earl of Argyll. Even so, he was drawn into the rebellion of Alexander MacDonald of Dunivaig and the Glens in the years after 1528. Although he submitted to James V in 1531, his lands of Invergarry were then granted to Ewen Cameron of Locheil. It was not until March 1539 that Alasdair MacDonald of Glengarry finally received a royal charter to his lands of Glengarry and Morar. Indeed, his father had evidently held his lands of Morar without any title ever since the Lordship of the Isles was forfeited in 1493. Even earlier, Alasdair's grandfather had perhaps held Knoydart in a similar fashion, since the feudal dues of non-entry had not been paid since 1467. Alasdair's father had apparently held his lands of Glengarry by force of arms as well, since they were leased on various occasions by the Crown to the Camerons of Locheil, and the Gordon earls of Huntly.

This grant of March 1539 also gave Alasdair MacDonald of Glengarry a half-share in the lands of Lochalsh, Lochcarron and Lochbroom. They had come to him through his marriage with Margaret, daughter and co-heiress of Sir Alexander MacDonald of Lochalsh, after Donald Gallda and her other brothers had died childless. However, she had a sister Janet, who in marrying Thomas Dingwall of Kildun had conveyed the other half-share in the lands of Lochalsh, Lochcarron and Lochbroom to her husband. But no sooner had Alasdair MacDonald of Glengarry received a royal charter to all his possessions in 1539 than he rebelled against the Crown by joining Donald Gorm of Sleat in his insurrection of the same year. He was forfeited and James V bestowed his lands of Laggan, Kilfinnan and Invergarry upon John MacKenzie of Kintail. It was the cause of a long and bitter feud that broke out forty years later between the MacKenzies of Kintail and the MacDonalds of Glengarry, and lasted until the early years of the seventeenth century.

As already recounted, Alasdair MacDonald of Glengarry was among the Highland chieftains forcibly detained by James V when he sailed around the north of Scotland in 1540. However, he was set free by James Hamilton, Earl of Arran, then acting as Regent after the death of James V in 1542. Soon afterwards, Alasdair MacDonald allied himself with John Moydertach in his successful attempt to seize the chiefship of Clan Ranald from Ranald Gallda. It ended with their victory over the Frasers of Lovat at the Battle of Blar-na-Leine in 1544. Alasdair afterwards joined the short-lived rebellion of Donald Dubh in 1545 and acted as a member of his Council of the Isles. By then, the Grants, MacIntoshes, MacKenzies and some other clans in Easter Ross had formed a league against the MacDonalds of Clan Ranald and Glengarry and the Camerons of Locheil, aimed at driving these clans out of Ross-shire.

Indeed, James Grant of Freuchie was given a Crown grant to all the lands of Glengarry in 1546, after Alasdair MacDonald and his family had failed to compensate James Grant of Freuchie and John Mor Grant of Glenmoriston for the losses they had suffered after the Battle of Blar-na-Leine. Even so, James Grant of Freuchie was quite unable to take possession of these lands against the bitter opposition of Alasdair MacDonald of Glengarry and John Moydertach of Glen Ranald. Then, after Scottish defeat at the Battle of Pinkie in 1547, the rebel chieftains were both pardoned for their past behaviour. Even so, their lands were not restored to them, and they still remained defiant of central government, despite the attempts of the Earls of Argyll, Huntly and Atholl to bring them to heel.

Marriage Alliances and Bonds of Manrent

Alasdair MacDonald of Glengarry had died by 1566, presumably at a great age, and he was succeeded by his son Angus. By then, James Grant of Freuchie was dead as well, and his claim to the lands of Glengarry passed to his son John Grant of Freuchie. His daughter Barbara then married Colin Cam MacKenzie of Kintail in 1570, who received as her dowry a half-share in the lands of Lochbroom, which had originally belonged to Alasdair MacDonald of Glengarry. The marriage alliance between the two families was further buttressed by a bond of manrent, whereby Colin Cam MacKenzie of Kintail agreed to defend John Grant of Freuchie against Clan Ranald and the MacDonalds of Glengarry.

Even so, nearly all his ancestral lands came back into the possession of Angus MacDonald of Glengarry after 1571 when he married as his third wife Janet, sister of Colin Cam MacKenzie of Kintail, so cementing an alliance between the two families. It was further agreed in the same year that Angus's son Donald should marry Helen, daughter of John Grant of Freuchie, who in return resigned his claim to all of Glengarry's lands dating back to their forfeiture in 1546. Angus MacDonald of Glengarry also gave a pledge to defend John Grant of Freuchie against any aggressor, except Clan Ranald and the king. The culmination of all these alliances came in 1574 when Angus MacDonald of Glengarry was granted a Crown charter to his lands of Glengarry, along with twelve merklands of Morar, twelve merklands of Lochalsh and four merklands of Lochcarron. Only his half-share in the lands of Lochbroom remained in the hands of his brother-in-law Colin Cam MacKenzie. But Angus died later that year and was succeeded by his son Donald, whose long life was full of vicissitudes before he died in 1645 at the great age of 102.

Hostility of the Earl of Argyll

Donald MacDonald of Glengarry was first faced by the antagonism of Colin Campbell, sixth Earl of Argyll, soon after he had succeeded to his title in 1574. Already, Argyll had quarrelled with John Stewart, fourth Earl of Atholl, concerning their powers of jurisdiction over the Camerons of Locheil, which Colin Campbell claimed for himself by virtue of his hereditary office of Justice-General of Scotland. Soon afterwards, he retired to Argyll where he was accused of oppressive and illegal conduct, invading the island of Luing, and imprisoning persons of rank without warrant. Around the same time, he was also charged by the Privy Council with levying his vassals with the intention of attacking Donald MacDonald of Glengarry.

Glengarry had apparently offended Argyll in some way, perhaps by entering into an alliance with the Grants of Freuchie or the MacKenzies of Kintail, since his family had earlier held a bond of manrent with the Campbell earls of Argyll. The Privy Council acted promptly under Regent Morton, instructing the Tutor of Lovat, MacKenzie of Kintail, Grant of Freuchie, the Chief of MacIntosh, Munro of Foulis, Ross of Balnagown, MacDonald of Keppoch and the Chief of Chisholm, who were all to defend Donald MacDonald of Glengarry if he were attacked by the Earl of Argyll. Not long afterwards, however, Colin Campbell, sixth Earl of Argyll, was made Lord Chancellor in 1579, after which he played a more law-abiding role in the affairs of the realm.

Feud with the MacKenzies of Kintail

Donald MacDonald of Glengarry now became a prey to the acquisitive ambitions of Colin Cam MacKenzie of Kintail over the lands of Lochalsh and Lochcarron. After the death of Sir Donald Gallda MacDonald of Lochalsh in 1519, it may be remembered, these lands were divided between his two sisters and a half-share came by marriage into the hands of the MacDonalds of Glengarry. The other half-share was likewise acquired by Thomas Dingwall of Kildun, but it was sold by his son in 1554 to Kenneth MacKenzie of Kintail. After his father's death in 1568, Colin Cam MacKenzie of Kintail inherited his half-share of these lands, but he evidently decided in 1581 to seize the remaining lands of Lochalsh and Lochcarron, now held by Donald MacDonald of Glengarry.

Colin Cam MacKenzie found a pretext by alleging that the MacDonalds of Glengarry were mistreating their tenants in a cruel and tyrannical manner. Faced with this threat to his territories, Donald MacDonald of Glengarry took up residence at Lochcarron, while placing a strong garrison in his Castle of Strome. Despite these precautions, however, the quarrel over land quickly deteriorated into a savage and bloody feud between the two families. Only a year later in 1582, Donald MacDonald of Glengarry appeared before the Privy Council in Edinburgh, alleging that his lands had been invaded by Colin Cam's brother Ruairi MacKenzie of Redcastle with 200 followers. After much plunder and slaughter they had captured himself and his uncle Ruairi, along with three of his sons and many of their friends and servants. Apart from himself, they had all been put to death in a cruel and barbaric manner and their bodies left prey to dogs and other ravenous beasts without a Christian burial.

Faced with this dreadful indictment, Colin Cam MacKenzie of Kintail was first ordered to return Strome Castle to Donald MacDonald of Glengarry, so it had evidently been captured by the MacKenzies. However, after pleading ignorance of any summons against him, the castle was eventually surrendered into the keeping of Colin Campbell, sixth Earl of Argyll. Indeed, little effective action was taken against Colin Cam MacKenzie of Kintail, and his brother Ruairi MacKenzie of Redcastle. However, their guilt was recognised in 1586 when they were granted a remission by the Privy Council for all the crimes that they had committed against the MacDonalds of Glengarry. Indeed, Colin MacKenzie of Kintail was briefly warded in Blackness Castle. By then, James VI had confirmed Donald MacDonald of Glengarry in possession of all his lands in Lochalsh and Lochcarron. However, it seems that these lands still remained in dispute, since Sir William Stewart of Houston acting in his capacity of King's Lieutenant had a commission to occupy Strome Castle in 1596.

Renewed Feuding with the MacKenzies

Colin Cam MacKenzie of Kintail died in 1594 and was succeeded by his son Kenneth who two years later became a member of the Privy Council. However, it was not until 1602 that the feud over the lands of Lochalsh and Lochcarron broke out again with renewed violence. It seems that the MacDonalds of Glengarry were now the aggressors, since Kenneth MacKenzie of Kintail was given Letters of Fire and Sword against the MacDonalds of Glengarry. Led by Donald's son Angus, they had attacked the MacKenzie lands of Torridon and 'cruelly slaughtered all the aged men with many women and children'. Although it is not clear exactly how Kenneth MacKenzie of Kintail obtained his commission against the MacDonalds, and they later accused him of sharp practice, he now invaded Glengarry's lands of Morar which he devastated without any mercy, putting many of its inhabitants to the sword. The MacDonalds retaliated by plundering Lochalsh and the district of Applecross which had previously been held inviolate as a sanctuary.

The feud now threatened to involve the other septs of Clan Donald so Kenneth MacKenzie of Kintail visited Mull, hoping to gain the support of Hector MacLean of Duart, his nephew by marriage. Meanwhile, Angus MacDonald of Glengarry invaded Lochcarron by sea, laying waste to the land and carrying off much plunder. However, returning south through the Sound of Kylerhea, his overladen galley was attacked by night by the MacKenzies who had marshalled their forces in two boats. Taken by surprise by a volley of shots, the MacDonalds crowded to the opposite side of their galley which overturned in the water. Many were drowned while others were slaughtered on reaching the shore. Angus MacDonald was himself among the dead. This victory allowed Kenneth MacKenzie of Kintail on his return from Mull to beseige the ill-defended Castle of Strome, which was captured from its MacDonald garrison and partly destroyed.

The final act in this bitter feud occurred in 1603, when Alan MacDonald of Lundie made a sudden descent upon the MacKenzie lands in the Black Isle. According to the MacKenzie traditions, it supposedly culminated in the burning of the church at Kilchrist, when the whole congregation perished as the Glengarry piper marched around the building, playing the pibroch known for ever afterwards as Kilchrist. However, the MacDonald historians are adamant that this massacre never took place, arguing that the church at Kilchrist was no longer used for worship in 1603, and indeed was then just a ruin.

Whatever the truth of the matter, and the Raid of Kilchrist is now just another legendary page in Highland history, it seems that Donald MacDonald of Glengarry now tired of his efforts to keep hold of his lands in Wester Ross. By 1607, they had all been granted by James VI to Kenneth MacKenzie of Kintail and erected into the barony of Lochalsh. Two years later Kenneth MacKenzie was himself made a peer of the realm as the first Lord MacKenzie of Kintail and granted the barony of Glenelg. The island of Lewis was already among the lands included in the barony of Lochalsh, and the MacKenzies of Kintail were now to profit from the downfall of the MacLeods of Lewis and the eventual destruction of their family after their lands had been granted by James VI to the Fife Adventurers.

Early History of the MacLeods of Lewis

The MacLeods have long claimed descent from the Norse kings of the Isle of Man, who held sway over the Hebrides before their power was challenged in the mid-twelfth century by Somerled, King of Argyll and the Western Isles. However, William Matheson now contends in his study of 'The Ancestry of the MacLeods of Lewis' that they are really descended from a Norseman from Caithness, who fled to the Hebrides around 1139. He perhaps married Helga, daughter of the Norse steward of Skye, from whom he received the lands of Dunvegan. His name was Olvir Rosta, the 'Unruly', whom the sagas describe as 'the tallest of men, and strong in limb, exceedingly overbearing, and a great fighter'. His great-grandson was Leod, from whom the MacLeods take their name. Mere conjecture suggests that Leod married a sister or daughter of Magnus Olavson, last of the Norse kings of Man. However, Leod's son was almost certainly Tormod, and he had a son Gille-Caluim, rendered into English as Malcolm, who founded the family now known as the MacLeods of Harris and Dunvegan. However, according to an Irish genealogy, Tormod had another son Murchadh, and it was Murchadh's son Torquil who was the ancestor of the MacLeods of Lewis. Tradition has it that Murchadh married a daughter of the Nicholsons of Lewis and then seized her father's lands in Lewis for his own son Torquil.

After the Wars of Scottish Independence, the MacLeods of Lewis became the vassals of the MacDonalds, Lords of the Isles, when they were granted the island of Lewis by David II in 1343. Torquil MacLeod of Lewis was also granted a charter in 1343 to the lands of Assynt with its castle by David II. It is a MacLeod tradition that he first gained these lands by marriage with an heiress of the MacNicols of Assynt, together with the MacLeod lands of Coigach. Another grant made by David II in 1343 favoured the MacLeods of Harris and Dunvegan, who received Glenelg. However, it was not until Alexander MacDonald, third Lord of the Isles, became the Earl of Ross in 1437 that the MacLeods of Harris and Dunvegan finally came under the feudal superiority of the MacDonalds, Lords of the Isles.

Gairloch was another acquisition of the MacLeods of Lewis, but how they came to possess it during the course of the fifteenth century is quite unknown. Possibly, it once belonged to the MacDonalds, Lords of the Isles and Earls of Ross, who then granted it to a cadet family of the MacLeods of Lewis. As already recounted, Gairloch later came to be held by the Mac-Kenzies of Kintail. Raasay also belonged to the same branch of the MacLeods of Lewis, even if it was originally churchland. However it came into his hands, Raasay was bestowed in 1510 by Malcolm MacLeod of Lewis upon his second son Malcolm Garbh. He was the progenitor of the family known as the MacLeods of Raasay. His descendants survived the downfall and extinction of the MacLeods of Lewis in the direct line as the sole representatives of this ancient family.

All these possessions of the MacLeods of Lewis and their cadet families were put at risk when Torquil MacLeod of Lewis supported the rebellion of Donald Dubh when he first attempted to seize the Lordship of the Isles in 1503. After their estates had been forfeited, Assynt and Coigach were given in life-rent to Iye Roy MacKay of Strathnaver. However, he died in 1517, and these lands were restored to the MacLeods of Lewis. By then, Torquil MacLeod of Lewis was also dead. However, his own son John MacLeod was excluded from the succession, perhaps on account of his youth or inexperience. Instead, his estates on Lewis were granted by royal charter in 1511 to Torquil's brother Malcolm. He remained in full possession of all his estates despite his subsequent support for the rebellion of Sir Donald Gallda MacDonald of Lochalsh which followed the death of James IV at the Battle of Flodden in 1513, as already recounted.

Malcolm MacLeod of Lewis had died by 1524. His estates were then seized by Torquil's son John MacLeod of Lewis, who regained them with the help of Donald Gruamach MacDonald of Sleat, as already recounted. John MacLeod of Lewis died around 1532, leaving no sons to succeed him. However, his daughter Margaret married his ally's son Donald Gorm MacDonald of Sleat, thus reinforcing the existing alliance between these two families. Ruairi MacLeod, eldest son of Malcolm MacLeod, now became the chief of Lewis under the kin-based system of inheritance. It was his matrimonial troubles which caused the eventual destruction of his family, together with machinations of the MacKenzies of Kintail and the enmity of the MacLeods of Raasay.

Marriages of Ruairi MacLeod

Tradition has it that Ruairi MacLeod of Lewis first married Janet MacKenzie, said to be a daughter of John MacKenzie of Killin. She was apparently a lady of mature charms and the widow of Angus Roy MacKay of Strathnaver. However, there is some doubt about her identity, since Angus Roy MacKay apparently married Agnes, who was the sister of John MacKenzie of Killin, rather than his daughter. After marrying Ruairi MacLeod of Lewis, she gave birth to a son Torquil. He was known as Torquil Connanach, since he was fostered among his mother's family in Strathconon. Perhaps mistreated by Ruairi MacLeod, she then eloped with her husband's nephew John MacLeod of Raasay, otherwise known as Iain of the Axe. She later married him after Ruairi MacLeod of Lewis had divorced her and disinherited her son Torquil Connanach, whom he claimed was not his own. Indeed, it is not even certain that Ruairi MacLeod was Torquil's father, since long afterwards Uisdean Morison, Brieve of Lewis, confessed on his deathbed that he had committed adultery with Torquil's mother, claiming Torquil to be his own son.

Ruairi MacLeod of Lewis was foremost among the rebels who took part in the ill-fated insurrection of 1539 which ended with the death of Donald Gorm MacDonald of Sleat at Eilean Donan. A year later, he was detained by James V during his voyage around the north of Scotland in 1540, along with many other Highland chiefs. He seems then to have regained the king's favour since he was allowed to make an advantageous marriage in 1541 when his lands were erected into the free barony of Lewis. His second wife was Barbara Stewart, daughter of Lord Avandale, the Lord Chancellor, and she bore him another son, also called Torquil. He was known as Torquil Oighre, meaning the Heir, to distinguish him from his half-brother Torquil Connanach.

Even though he was now restored to favour, Ruairi MacLeod of Lewis was party to Donald Dubh's rebellion after his escape from captivity in 1543, and indeed acted as a member of his Council of the Isles. However, after Donald Dubh's death in 1545 and the collapse of his rebellion, Ruairi MacLeod of Lewis was pardoned for his treasonable actions against the Crown. However, he continued to act quite independently of central government. Indeed, Letters of Fire and Sword were issued in 1554 for the utter extermination of Ruairi MacLeod of Lewis, John Moydertach of Clan Ranald and Donald Gormson MacDonald of Sleat after they had all refused to attend a Parliament at Inverness.

Forceful Claims to Patrimony

When Mary Stuart, Queen of Scots, ascended the throne in 1561, the disinherited Torquil Connanach and his legitimate half-brother Torquil Oighre were already young men, while their father Ruairi MacLeod of Lewis had another thirty-four years to live. However, the claim of Torquil Connanach to be acknowledged as his father's heir came to a head in 1566. It followed the death of his half-brother Torquil Oighre, drowned while crossing the Minch with sixty of his followers. Torquil Connanach now captured his supposed father Ruairi MacLeod and kept him prisoner in dreadful conditions for the next four years. He only gained his freedom by agreeing to recognise Torquil Connanach as his rightful heir. Torquil Connanach now brought Ruairi MacLeod of Lewis before the Privy Council in 1572, when he was forced to resign all his estates of Lewis, Assynt, Coigach and Waternish to the Crown. They were then granted to Torquil Connanach as his lawful heir while he himself only received them back in life-rent. There is little doubt that Torquil Connanach acted with the full support of Colin Cam MacKenzie of Kintail, now chief of the MacKenzies after the death of his grandfather in 1561 and his father in 1568, among whom Torquil had spent his childhood.

Massacre of the MacLeods of Raasay

The charter of 1572 recognised Malcolm MacLeod of Raasay as the heir of Torquil Connanach should Torquil die without lawful issue. According to tradition, Malcolm MacLeod was the sole survivor of a notorious massacre that probably occurred in 1568 or 1569. John MacLeod of Raasay had already offended his clansmen by his earlier marriage with Janet (or Agnes) MacKenzie, mother of Torquil Connanach, after she had abandoned his uncle Ruairi MacLeod of Lewis, so allying himself with the MacKenzies of Kintail. He further incurred their displeasure by allowing a daughter of this marriage to marry a grandson of Hector Roy MacKenzie of Gairloch. Then, after his first wife had died, John MacLeod of Raasay married a sister of Ruairi Nimhneach MacLeod of Gairloch, meaning 'Venomous'.

Ruairi Nimhneach MacLeod of Gairloch now plotted the destruction of the MacLeods of Raasay so that their lands might come to his own nephew, born of his sister's second marriage to John MacLeod of Raasay. Accordingly, he invited John MacLeod of Raasay, along with the sons of his first marriage, to the island of Isay at the mouth of Loch Dunvegan on the pretext of consulting them about some weighty matter. After a feast ended the day's business, Ruairi MacLeod of Gairloch left the banqueting chamber and then summoned each of his guests in turn. Ushered into his presence, they were all murdered by a pair of hired assassins, lying in wait for them on either side of the doorway. Only Malcolm MacLeod, youngest son (or perhaps grandson) of John MacLeod of Raasay, escaped with his life since he was then living with his foster-father Malcolm MacNeil who conveyed him into the care of Sir John Campbell of Cawdor. When he came of age in 1571, he managed to oust Ruairi Nimhneach MacLeod from occupying his own lands and thereafter ruled as chief of the MacLeods of Raasay until his death in 1610.

Internecine Strife among the MacLeods of Lewis

Meanwhile, Ruairi MacLeod of Lewis, after he had regained his liberty in 1572, revoked the agreement he had just made with the Privy Council recognising Torquil Connanach as his lawful heir. Not surprisingly, this further aggravated the bitter feud between the two men and they were both summoned to appear again in Edinburgh in 1576. Torquil Connanach was again recognised by the Privy Council as the rightful heir to Ruairi MacLeod of Lewis and granted a charter to the lands of Coigach. Interestingly enough, Ruairi MacLeod of Lewis had the support of Colin Campbell, sixth Earl of Argyll, who surrendered a surety of 5,000 pounds for his good behaviour, perhaps hoping to counter the interests of the MacKenzies. This reconciliation lasted until 1583 when their ancient quarrel was resumed with even greater bitterness.

By then, Ruairi MacLeod of Lewis had married a daughter of Hector Og MacLean of Duart as his third wife, and he now had two sons of this marriage, called Torquil Dubh and Tormod Uigach. He also had a number of natural sons, among them Donald and Murdoch MacLeod who became divided among themselves after Ruairi MacLeod of Lewis had recognised Torquil Dubh as his rightful heir. Hostilities broke out between the two half-brothers when Tormod Uigach was murdered by Donald, who was then seized by his natural brother Murdoch. Donald managed to escape and then turned the tables on Murdoch, whom he captured and imprisoned in Stornoway Castle.

Torquil Connanach now came to the rescue of his half-brother Murdoch, whom he released after capturing Stornoway Castle. Once again, Ruairi MacLeod of Lewis was detained by Torquil Connanach and held prisoner in Stornoway Castle by Torquil's son John. Meanwhile, Torquil Connanach carried off all the family charters, which he later lodged with Colin Cam MacKenzie of Kintail. However, Torquil's son John was killed by his uncle Ruairi Og MacLeod, yet another of Ruairi MacLeod's natural sons, who freed his aged father from captivity. In revenge, Torquil Connanach had his half-brother Donald executed at Dingwall. After this storm of internecine strife had abated, Ruairi MacLeod of Lewis was left in possession of Lewis for the rest of his 'troublesome days', while Torquil Connanach continued to occupy Coigach.

Before Ruairi MacLeod of Lewis died in 1595, aged ninety-four, he had probably placed his affairs in the hands of Torquil Dubh MacLeod as his elder son from his third and final marriage. Yet Torquil Connanach still had a legal title to all the estates now held by his half-brother, while he now enjoyed the powerful backing of Kenneth MacKenzie, afterwards Lord MacKenzie of Kintail, who had succeeded his father Colin Cam MacKenzie in 1594. Indeed, Torquil Connanach received yet another charter to the lands of Lewis, after Torquil Dubh had devastated his lands of Coigach in 1596 with a force of seven or eight hundred men as well as plundering the MacKenzie lands of Lochbroom. Summoned to appear before the Privy Council, Torquil Dubh MacLeod was declared a rebel when he failed to answer the summons.

Despite his popularity with his own clansmen in Lewis, Torquil Dubh MacLeod was betrayed soon afterwards by the Brieve of Lewis, chief of the Morisons of Ness. Despite his judicial duties, it seems he was not averse to acts of piracy since he captured a Dutch ship with its cargo of wine in 1597 and brought it into Ness in the north of Lewis. Torquil Dubh MacLeod suspected nothing amiss when he was invited on board to sample the wine, but he was seized immediately he went below decks, along with several of his companions. They were all transported to Coigach, where Torquil Connanach, acting on the instructions of Kenneth MacKenzie of Kintail, made them all 'shorter of their heads without doom or law', executing them in what was an act of summary justice.

Chapter Eight

PLANTATION OF THE ISLES

The death of Torquil Dubh MacLeod in 1597 did not greatly benefit Torquil Connanach MacLeod nor even Kenneth MacKenzie of Kintail immediately, because James VI now put his plans for the improvement of the Highlands and Western Isles into effect. The country itself remained racked by clan feuds and struggles over rival jurisdictions so that it was arguably in a worse state than ever. James VI was easily convinced that such disorder was depriving him of much-needed revenue, 'whereof his Majesty is very scarce', as Donald Gorm Mor MacDonald of Sleat was astute enough to remark. The long and troublesome years of his minority had left James VI starved of Crown revenues while he had very extravagant tastes. He soon came to suspect that he was receiving an inadequate return from his Crown lands in the Western Isles, which he thought enjoyed an 'incredible fertility of corn', and more reasonably 'a store of fishings'.

The economic resources of the Western Isles had already been greatly exaggerated by Dean Munro in 1549. Now it seems that James VI commissioned another glowing report which was just as misleading. Written in the years before 1595, it greatly magnified the economic potential of the Western Isles as a source of Crown revenue. It convinced James VI that the country only remained so poor because of the deplorable character of his Gaelic-speaking subjects. Such endemic disorder not only made it very difficult to collect the Crown revenues, especially from the Western Isles, but James VI now entertained high hopes of greatly increasing these revenues as well. Indeed, the clan chiefs regularly failed to pay their rents, especially if their lands had been forfeited. They were also accused of attacking fishing boats in their waters, pursuing what was a jealously guarded monopoly only enjoyed by the merchants of the royal burghs.

1597 Act of Revocation

James VI now decided to embark on a deliberate policy of granting out territories in the Highlands and Western Isles to new and more trustworthy proprietors. They would not only be required to pay a much higher rent for their land, but they could also be expected to enforce law and order much more effectively than the previous landlords. Moreover, they were to be Lowland Scots, better able to maintain orderly government. The new land-lords would thus enrich themselves and the country by their industry and enterprise. This policy was put into effect by an Act of Parliament in 1597, which required all landholders to exhibit their title deeds to the Lords of the Exchequer by May 1598. They were also to find sureties for the regular payment of their rents to the Crown and for the peaceful and orderly behav-iour of themselves and all their adherents. Since any failure to meet these conditions was to result in forfeiture of all their lands, there is little doubt that the Act itself was deliberately designed to bring about this very end.

James VI and his advisers knew very well that several chieftains had lost their title deeds, so that the Act itself was little more than legalised robbery on the part of the Crown. Needless to say, many of the Highland chieftains were quite unable to produce the necessary documents which had been lost or destroyed over the years, if indeed they had ever existed. Others were unwilling to cooperate with such an imposition of royal authority. Even if they were able to satisfy the Lords of the Exchequer by exhibiting their title deeds in Edinburgh, they were then required to find sureties for the regular payment of their rents to the Crown and for their own good conduct, while they were to take responsibility for the peaceable and orderly behaviour of all their tenants and other followers. Often, they were quite unable to raise the money needed to guarantee these sureties, which were deliberately set at too high a level for most chieftains to pay.

No doubt, James VI intended in this summary manner to expropriate as much land as possible from the native inhabitants of the Highlands and the Western Isles and rent it out to other proprietors. He evidently regarded their 'barbarous inhumanity' as excuse enough for depriving them of their hereditary possessions. Indeed, according to the preamble to the Act, the inhabitants of the Highlands and Islands had not only failed to pay their annual rents and to perform the services due to the Crown for their lands. They had also made the Highlands and the Western Isles, naturally so valuable from the fertility of the soil and the richness of the fisheries, altogether unprofitable to themselves and their fellow-countrymen. The extravagant claim was even made that the natural resources of Lewis were among the greatest in the kingdom.

Unfortunately, the record of the Parliament held in May 1598 has been lost so that we do not know exactly what happened. However, the MacLeods of Lewis were certainly forfeited of all their lands, despite the fact that Kenneth MacKenzie of Kintail now held their charters given to him by

Torquil Connanach for safe-keeping. Ruairi Mor MacLeod of Harris and Dunvegan declined to appear before the Privy Council. He feared imprisonment if he came to Edinburgh, even under a safe conduct, since he had supported the MacLeods of Lewis after the death of Torquil Dubh. The consequence was that he too suffered forfeiture of all his lands in Harris, Skye and Glenelg. Likewise forfeited were the disputed lands of Trotternish in Skye, even though Donald Gorm Mor MacDonald of Sleat had recently been granted a lease of these lands.

Scheme for the Plantation of Lewis

James VI now wasted no time in trying to plant the island of Lewis with Lowlanders. A contract was drawn up in June 1598 with a company of twelve gentlemen under the leadership of Ludovic Stewart, Duke of Lennox. He was the king's cousin and among his greatest favourites at Court. Since they mostly came from Fife, they later became known as the Fife Adventurers. They undertook to 'plant policy and civilisation in the hitherto most barbarous Isle of Lewis . . ., and to develop [its] extraordinarily rich resources for the public good and the King's profit'. Moreover, they were to overcome 'the evil disposition and barbarity' of the inhabitants, since it was perfectly known to the king that the island of Lewis is

> by special Providence and blessing of God enriched with an incredible fertility of corn and store of fishings . . . far supplanting the plenty of any part of the inland [mainland]. And yet, nevertheless, the same are possessed by inhabitants who are void of any knowledge of God or his religion, and naturally abhorring all kind of civility, who have given themselves over to all kinds of barbarity and inhumanity . . ., occupying in the meantime and violently possessing his Highness's proper lands without payment . . .

The plantation of Lewis was likely to be hazardous and expensive, so the annual rental of 140 chalders of barley for the lands of Lewis, Rona and the Shiant Isles was assigned to Ludovic Stewart, Duke of Lennox, for the first seven years. Two years later, it was agreed that the yearly duty should be reduced to 1,000 pounds, along with 1,000 codling, 1,000 lingfish, and 1,000 skate. The Earl of Lennox was also appointed as the King's Lieutenant in Lewis. However, his freedom of action was restricted, since he had to consult the king or his councillors before taking any initiative. The intention was 'to plant Lowlandmen in the Isles and transport the inhabitants to the mainland, where they might learn civility'. It was a policy applied with more lasting effect in Ulster only a few years later.

Given the family feuds among the MacLeods of Lewis, which still raged despite the death of Torquil Dubh, the scheme might well have succeeded if avarice had not tempted James VI to cast his net wider than Lewis. However, he granted the Fife Adventurers not just Lewis, but also the lands recently forfeited in Skye by Ruairi Mor MacLeod of Harris and Dunvegan and the district of Trotternish recently leased to Donald Gorm Mor MacDonald of Sleat. James VI thus created by his own actions a powerful party among the chieftains of the Western Isles dedicated to frustrating and discouraging the settlers by any means in their power. Moreover, Donald Gorm Mor MacDonald of Sleat had himself a dubious claim to Lewis, given his grandfather's marriage with Margaret, daughter of Torquil MacLeod of Lewis.

Although Torquil Dubh MacLeod had left several sons when he was executed in 1597, Donald Gorm Mor of Sleat now put himself forward as the rightful heir of Ruairi MacLeod of Lewis, especially as there was every reason to suspect that Torquil Connanach was not Ruairi's son. Pursuing his claim to Lewis, he invaded the island with a strong body of followers who did much damage before they were repulsed by the MacLeods. However, it was the secret hostility of Kenneth MacKenzie of Kintail, whose long years of scheming to gain possession of Lewis looked like coming to nothing if the Fife Adventurers were successful, that posed the greatest threat to the plans of James VI.

First Expedition of the Fife Adventurers

The Fife Adventurers set sail for the island of Lewis towards the end of 1598, accompanied by five or six hundred troops and a number of artisans and craftsmen, whom they had hired for the purpose. The island itself was held by Murdoch and Neil MacLeod who were now the only natural sons of Ruairi MacLeod still alive. When the Fife Adventurers landed early in December, they first laid siege to Stornoway Castle, which they captured with some difficulty after overcoming the local inhabitants. However, they now found themselves in difficulties. Not only were supplies scarce and their own equipment inadequate, but they also lacked proper shelter against the winter weather. They started construction of what was later described as 'a pretty town', but their ranks were soon decimated by an outbreak of dysentery. They were also harried by guerilla attacks, launched against them by Neil MacLeod who remained in hiding on the island.

James Learmouth of Balcomie was now chosen from among the Fife Adventurers to sail around the north of Scotland to the Lowlands, where they hoped to procure more provisions and perhaps report back to James VI. However, his ship was captured by Murdoch MacLeod off Coigach where he had taken refuge with Torquil Connanach. James Learmouth was held captive on the Summer Isles at the mouth of Loch Broom and only released with two of his companions after he had signed a bond agreeing to pay his captors a large ransom. Soon afterwards, he died from ill-treatment. Meanwhile, Neil MacLeod with 200 'barbarous, bloody and wicked High-landmen' had suddenly attacked the Fife Adventurers on the island of Lewis. They killed twenty-two of their number, burnt property to the value of 20,000 merks and carried off horses, cows, oxen, sheep and other beasts worth 10,000 pounds.

Capture and Execution of Murdoch MacLeod

Faced with all these difficulties, the Fife Adventurers now resorted to diplo-macy, hoping to exploit the divisions between Neil MacLeod and his brother Murdoch. Indeed, Murdoch still favoured the Morisons of Ness whom Neil blamed for the death of Torquil Dubh. The colonists therefore offered Neil MacLeod a grant of land in Lewis, promising him a free pardon from the king for all his past offences if he were to deliver Murdoch MacLeod into their hands. This he did, capturing him along with twelve of his followers who were immediately executed. Their severed heads were sent as grisly relics in a sack to Edinburgh where they were impaled above the city gates. Murdoch MacLeod was himself brought to Fife, where he was tried by a court in St Andrews, and sentenced to be hung, drawn and quartered. Neil MacLeod accompanied the leaders of the Fife Adventurers back to Edinburgh where he obtained a pardon from the king.

Before his execution, however, Murdoch MacLeod had evidently accused Kenneth MacKenzie of Kintail of obstructing the Fife Adventurers, since he was apprehended and held in ward at Edinburgh Castle. He only escaped trial through the influence of his friends at Court, and especially that of the Lord Chancellor, James Graham, third Earl of Montrose. However, Kenneth MacKenzie did enter into a compact with the Fife Adventurers whereby each party agreed to maintain friendly relations with one another. Its terms clearly show at the very least that Kenneth MacKenzie of Kintail had encouraged the attacks made by Murdoch MacLeod on the Fife Adventurers.

By now, bolstered by their agreement with Neil MacLeod, the Fife Adven-turers had apparently managed to gain a secure foothold at last on the island of Lewis. Indeed, ambitious plans were now laid for the future of the colony. The building of churches and schools, the construction of harbours, the establishment of inns for travellers, the erection of burghs of barony and the holding of weekly markets and annual fairs were all envisaged. Yet the true state of the Western Isles was revealed by the sudden outbreak of yet another bitter if short-lived feud in 1601, quite unrelated to the presence of the Fife Adventures on the island of Lewis.

Feud between Dunvegan and Sleat

Donald Gorm Mor MacDonald of Sleat rejected his wife, who was a sister of Ruairi Mor MacLeod of Harris and Dunvegan. Legend has it that she was sent back to her family, mounted on a one-eyed horse, led by a one-eyed groom and followed by a one-eyed dog. It was a common enough embellishment of such tales in the Highlands, almost too good to waste. Enraged by this slight, Ruairi Mor MacLeod promptly called out his men. They devastated Trotternish which was still held by the MacDonalds of Sleat despite the forfeiture of 1598. Donald Gorm Mor MacDonald retaliated by attacking the MacLeod lands in Harris. Ruairi Mor MacLeod then raided North Uist, sending his cousin Donald Glas MacLeod and forty followers to carry off the goods placed for safety by the local people within the Church of the Holy Trinity at Carinish. However, the MacLeods were surprised while eating breakfast in the church by a small party of twelve MacDonalds led by a celebrated warrior of Clan Ranald called Donald MacIain 'ic Sheumais. Donald Glas MacLeod and all but two of his men were ambushed and killed as they pursued the MacDonalds, tricked into thinking that they only faced a handful of their enemies.

The Battle of Carinish had a curious sequel. Travelling to Skye to report his victory to Donald Gorm Mor MacDonald of Sleat, Donald MacIain 'ic Sheumais was forced to take shelter from a storm at Rodil on Harris. There he was entertained hospitably enough by Ruairi Mor MacLeod of Harris and Dunvegan, even after he had learnt of the identity of his guests. However, the MacDonalds did not strain the limits of Highland hospitality too far. They left secretly after nightfall, and it was wise that they did so since their quarters were set alight by the MacLeod clansmen, unknown to their chief. The feud now became ever more deadly as both sides repeatedly raided one another to their 'utter ruin and desolation'. The local people were reduced to such extremities that they were forced to eat horses, dogs, cats and other 'filthy beasts'.

Battle of Coire na Creiche

Donald Gorm Mor MacDonald of Sleat was now determined to end the feud with a decisive victory over the MacLeods of Harris and Dunvegan. He took advantage of the absence of Ruairi Mor MacLeod who had gone to seek the assistance of Archibald Campbell, seventh Earl of Argyll. Mustering his forces, he now decided upon an all-out invasion of the MacLeod lands in the north of Skye, directed in particular against Minginish and Bracadale. The cattle seized in this raid were seemingly driven back to a rendezvous at Coire na Creiche, or Corrie of the Foray. It overlooks the head of Glen Brittle from the north-western slopes of the Cuillin Hills. There, the fighting strength of the MacLeods led by Alexander MacLeod, brother of the absent chief, caught up with the MacDonalds, intent on seizing back their cattle. The Battle of 'Benquhillan' was joined late in the day and lasted well into the night. It ended with the utter defeat of the MacLeods after 'a cruel and terrible skirmish' fought 'with terrible obstinacy'. Alexander MacLeod was taken prisoner along with thirty of his principal kinsmen. It is memorable as the last clan battle fought on the island of Skye.

The Privy Council now intervened in the summer of 1601 and brought the feud to an end. Donald Gorm Mor MacDonald of Sleat was ordered to surrender himself to George Gordon, sixth Earl of Huntly and now the Marquis of Huntly. Ruairi Mor MacLeod of Harris and Dunvegan was to place himself in the hands of Archibald Campbell, seventh Earl of Argyll. Soon afterwards, the two men were reconciled with one another through the good offices of their mutual friends such as Angus MacDonald of Dunivaig and the Glens and Lachlan MacLean of Coll among others. After Donald Gorm Mor MacDonald of Sleat had agreed to release his prisoners, their bloody feud was formally ended by three weeks of feasting and other festivities at Dunvegan Castle. Although their quarrel briefly flared up again in 1603, the old adversaries pursued their differences through the law courts with such vigour that their pugnacity for legal dispute became just as renowned as their earlier battles with the sword.

Defeat of the Fife Adventurers

The abrupt ending of the bloody feud between the MacDonalds of Sleat and the MacLeods of Harris and Dunvegan seemed an augury of more peaceful times in the northern Hebrides. But the plantation of Lewis now received a sudden and unexpected reverse. Soon after Neil MacLeod had returned in 1601 from Edinburgh with his pardon, he broke off all friendly relations with the Fife Adventurers. It seems he was insulted by James Spens of Wormiston who was among their leaders. Spens now set out with a troop of soldiers on a dark December night, hoping to capture Neil MacLeod. However, the alarm was raised, and the Lowlanders lost sixty men. killed by the Lewismen as they were chased for two or three miles back to their camp. Learning of this setback to the Fife Adventurers, Kenneth MacKenzie of Kintail now played his trump card in the person of Tormod MacLeod. He was the younger brother of Torquil Dubh MacLeod, who had been so summarily executed by Torquil Connanach in 1597.

Around the time of his brother's execution, Tormod MacLeod had himself been kidnapped by Kenneth MacKenzie of Kintail, while he was still only a schoolboy in Perth. He had been held captive ever since, despite the repeated orders of the Privy Council for his release. He was now set at liberty by Kenneth MacKenzie of Kintail, who promised him help if he were to join Neil MacLeod in attacking the Fife Adventurers. Returning to Lewis, he was warmly welcomed as the rightful heir of old Ruairi MacLeod of Lewis. Together, they quickly joined forces to attack the Fife Adventurers in their camp. The defenders resisted the attack stoutly, only to suffer heavy losses when the camp was stormed by the MacLeods. The Fife Adventurers were forced to surrender unconditionally. Tormod MacLeod only agreed to their release after receiving a promise that they would 'purchase' a remission from the king for himself and his followers for all their offences against the Crown. Moreover, the Fife Adventurers also agreed to resign all their rights in the island of Lewis, never to return. James Spens of Wormiston and his son-in-law were left behind as hostages to this agreement while the rest of the Fife Adventurers returned to the Lowlands of Scotland.

Renewed Plans for the Plantation of Lewis

Tormod MacLeod was not to remain long in undisputed possession of Lewis. By 1602, enfuriated by this affront to his dignity, James VI tried without success to persuade Parliament to finance another expedition to Lewis. He argued that the people of England would see a king who could not rule a handful of 'barbaric' inhabitants of Lewis as unfit to govern them. However, rebuffed by Parliament, any plans for a second attempt to settle Lewis were abandoned for the time being in 1603 when James VI of Scotland became James I of Great Britain, France and Ireland after the death of Queen Elizabeth of England. Plans for a fresh expedition to Lewis were therefore delayed for another two years.

The morale of the Fife Adventurers was fatally weakened by the failure of their first attempt to colonise Lewis. Indeed, only Sir James Spens of Wormiston, who had now been knighted, was still willing to take part in another expedition. He was joined by a newcomer Sir Thomas Ker of Hirth. They were appointed as the King's Justices and Commissioners in Lewis for a year and given Commissions of Fire and Sword to take whatever action they thought necessary to pacify the island. Later, two more members joined the expedition after they had acquired the rights of the original shareholders.

Meanwhile, all the chieftains of the northern Hebrides were ordered to deliver up their castles to the officers appointed to receive them, removing themselves and their servants within twenty-four hours. If they refused, their castles were to be besieged with 'warlike engines' and their defenders treated as rebels and traitors. Furthermore, all owners of galleys, birlinns and other vessels throughout the northern Hebrides and the adjacent mainland were ordered to surrender them at Loch Broom. Only then did the Fife Adventurers set sail for Lewis in August 1605, accompanied by Kenneth MacKenzie of Kintail, Donald Gorm Mor MacDonald of Sleat and Uisdean Dubh MacKay of Strathnaver.

Return of the Fife Adventurers

After landing in force on Lewis, the colonists took formal possession of the island. They then offered terms to Tormod MacLeod. They promised him that if he submitted they would send him to London so that he might obtain a pardon from James VI. Now realising the strength of the forces opposed against him, Tormod MacLeod agreed to their terms, much against the advice of Neil MacLeod. However, James VI was certainly not going to abandon his plans for Lewis, despite it being said that he was impressed by Tormod MacLeod's modest and gallant bearing. Any hope that he might influence the king in his favour was destroyed by the intrigues of the colonists' friends at Court. They prevailed upon James VI to keep Tormod MacLeod warded in Edinburgh Castle, where he languished without trial for the next ten years. Eventually he was allowed to leave the country for Holland where he entered the service of Maurice, Prince of Orange. He never saw Lewis again and it seems that he died without any heirs to succeed him.

Meanwhile, the leaders of the Fife Adventurers returned south, leaving the island garrisoned for the winter. Neil MacLeod and his followers were still at large, and they repeatedly harassed the colonists with guerilla attacks. By the summer of 1606, money was running short and the soldiers of the island's garrison had started to desert, along with some of the craftsmen and other artisans. Already, the colonists had apparently learnt of a rising planned against them, even if it came to nothing. Then, later in 1606, Kenneth MacKenzie of Kintail received a Commission of Fire and Sword against Ruairi MacNeill of Barra and Sir Donald MacDonald, Captain of Clan Ranald. They had come to the aid of Neil MacLeod, attacking the Fife Adventurers on Lewis, where their followers had 'committed barbarous and detestable murders and slaughters'.

'Extirpation of the Country People'

By the spring of 1607, James VI had evidently lost confidence in the Fife Adventurers. He now planned a much more ruthless means of pacifying the

Western Isles and the island of Lewis in particular. His determination to take drastic action was greatly reinforced in April 1607 when Neil MacLeod launched another devastating attack with 300 well-armed men upon the colony at Stornoway after he had tricked the Fife Adventurers into thinking that he was reconciled to their presence. Indeed, he had even offered his own services in promoting the prosperity of the colony to gain their trust.

Even before the sudden outbreak of this insurrection, James VI had urged the Privy Council in Edinburgh to enter into negotiations with George Gordon, first Marquis of Huntly. He was evidently prepared to accept a grant of Uist, Eigg, Canna, Rhum, Barra, Raasay, St Kilda and all the other islands, apart from Skye and Lewis, which were still held by the Fife Adventurers once he had reduced all their inhabitants to obedience. He would be given full powers as the King's Lieutenant north of the Dee. However, he was required to meet all the expenses of the operation, which was to be concluded within a year.

However, immediately after Neil MacLeod had once again rebelled against the Fife Adventurers, the Privy Council put further proposals to the Marquis of Huntly. It was suggested to him that 'he should end the service, not by agreement with the country people, but by extirpating them'. There can be very little doubt that this brutal condition was instigated by James VI himself, or with his full knowledge, since it is hardly credible that such a proposal should be made without his authority. The Marquis of Huntly for his part was quite willing to undertake the 'extirpation of the barbarous people of the Isles, within a year', provided that a suitable rent could be agreed for the lands in question. But given the difficulty and expense of the enterprise, he was only prepared to offer 400 pounds, and no more, while the Privy Council had in mind the sum of 10,000 pounds.

The Privy Council, in demanding such a large rent, perhaps hoped to take advantage of the hostility of the Presbyterian Church to the Marquis of Huntly. Indeed, the prospect of his gaining even more power in the north of Scotland, where he had been King's Lieutenant and Justiciar since 1601, may well have alarmed the Reformed Church and its fanatical leaders, given his pro-Catholic sympathies. However, George Gordon was first ordered by James VI to 'extirpate and rout out the Captain of Clan Ranald, with his whole clan and their followers within the isles of Knoydart and Moidart, and also Ruairi MacNeill of Barra with his clan, and the whole of Clan Donald in the north', and plant a civilised people in their place. But before he could take any such action, he was charged with failing to attend Church to hear the sermon, suspected of instructing his family against the tenets of the Presbyterian religion. James VI was forced to dismiss him from his office of King's Lieutenant and Justiciar in the north of Scotland in favour of

Archibald Campbell, seventh Earl of Argyll. Even so, it was Kenneth Mac-Kenzie of Kintail who ultimately benefited most from his downfall.

By now, the Fife Adventurers were close to abandoning the island of Lewis yet again when a final blow was struck against them, this time by Ruairi Mor MacLeod of Harris and Dunvegan. He had forfeited his lands in Skye in 1598, which were later granted to the Fife Adventurers in 1606, after he was declared a rebel for refusing to surrender Dunvegan Castle. Now seriously alarmed, he sought the support of Archibald Campbell, seventh Earl of Argyll, hoping for a reconciliation with James VI. But no sooner had he succeeded in regaining the king's favour than the ties of kinship again proved too strong and he went to the assistance of Neil MacLeod. Landing at Stornoway in 1607 with a body of his clansmen, he captured Stornoway Castle in a surprise attack and refused to give it up. Instead, he handed the castle over to Neil MacLeod, and the last remnants of the Fife Adventurers left in despair for the south.

Aggrandisement by MacKenzie of Kintail

Even before the second attempt to colonise Lewis had failed, Kenneth MacKenzie of Kintail had adroitly persuaded the Lord Chancellor, who was now Alexander Seton, Earl of Dunfermline, to grant him a charter to the island. Early in 1607, Kenneth MacKenzie of Kintail, after resigning all his lands to the Crown, received them back again in another grant, which now included the MacLeod lands of Lewis, Assynt and Waternish as well. Indeed, he had already purchased a legal title to these lands from Torquil Connanach MacLeod, who in turn had received a grant to all these lands from the Crown in 1596, after the death of Ruairi MacLeod of Lewis in 1595. Torquil Connanach included his own lands of Coigach in the sale to Kenneth MacKenzie of Kintail, who now granted these lands to his brother Roderick MacKenzie, ancestor of the Earls of Cromartie.

Faced with this *fait accompli* over their lands in Lewis, the surviving members of the Fife Adventures complained bitterly to James VI. They were now reduced by death or resignation to only three in number, and their ranks were to be further reduced in 1609 when James. Lord Balmerino, was accused of high treason. This left only Sir James Spens of Wormiston from among the original partners, and Sir James Hay of Netherliff who now acquired an interest in the enterprise. James VI now ordered Kenneth MacKenzie of Kintail to return the island of Lewis immediately to the Fife Adventurers. They received yet another grant to the island, along with all the lands once held by Ruairi Mor MacLeod of Harris and Dunvegan and by Donald Gorm Mor MacDonald of Sleat as well as the Crown lands of Trotternish.

Final Expedition of the Fife Adventurers

However, another two years passed before the Fife Adventurers attempted another expedition north to Lewis in 1609. The island was still held by the arch-rebel Neil MacLeod, and their efforts were also thwarted by Kenneth MacKenzie of Kintail who secretly encouraged Neil MacLeod to resist the Fife Adventurers. To allay any suspicion, he now sent his brother Roderick MacKenzie of Coigach with 400 men to support the Fife Adventurers when they renewed their attempt to colonise Lewis in 1609. However, Kenneth MacKenzie of Kintail was also responsible for supplying provisions to the Fife Adventurers on Lewis. Accordingly, he shipped a cargo of provisions to the colonists, while secretly advising Neil MacLeod of its despatch so that the vessel might be seized.

The Fife Adventurers were relying utterly on these supplies, and when they never arrived they were forced to abandon their enterprise before it had hardly begun. Disbanding their forces, Spens and Hay as the leaders of the expedition sailed back to Fife, leaving only a small garrison in Stornoway Castle. The Castle was captured soon afterwards by Neil MacLeod, who sent its garrison safely home to the Lowlands. By now, Spens and Hay were so discouraged by their repeated failures to colonise Lewis that they finally agreed to sell their interest in the island to Kenneth MacKenzie of Kintail in 1610. He thus acquired by right what he had so long tried to seize by force.

Acquisition of Lewis by MacKenzie of Kintail

Kenneth MacKenzie of Kintail lost no time in pressing his claims to Lewis. Issued with a Commission of Fire and Sword from the government, he landed with a large force of his own clansmen on the island and quickly reduced nearly all the islanders to obedience. Indeed, they may well have submitted more readily to Kenneth MacKenzie of Kintail than the Fife Adventurers. He at least was one of their own, since they were otherwise faced with conquest by Lowland Scots with their foreign language and alien culture. Only Neil MacLeod and some thirty followers held out for the next three years.

They first sought refuge on the remote and rocky Stack of Birsay at the mouth of Loch Roag on the west coast of Lewis. It had previously been provisioned for just such an emergency. But after this 'infamous byke [wasp nest] of lawless and insolent lymmaris [outlaws]' was destroyed, Neil MacLeod sought refuge in Harris. He surrendered at last to Ruairi Mor MacLeod of Harris and Dunvegan who agreed to take him to London. However, if Neil MacLeod had hoped to obtain a pardon from James VI, perhaps on the grounds that he had previously captured a notorious pirate and handed him over to the authorities, he was sorely disappointed. On reaching Glasgow, Ruairi Mor MacLeod was ordered by the Privy Council to deliver up his prisoner to the authorities in Edinburgh. Charged with high treason, Neil MacLeod was found guilty and executed in April 1613. Only Ruairi Mor MacLeod continued to London, where he was knighted for his services to the Crown and returned to Scotland as Sir Roderick MacLeod of Harris and Dunvegan.

Still alive were only the three young grandsons of Ruairi MacLeod, eleventh and last chief of Lewis, by his third marriage. What became of them is a mystery. They all disappeared from the historical record, leaving only the MacLeods of Raasay to represent their ancient line. Nearly all the natural sons of Ruairi MacLeod of Lewis were dead as well. After the execution of Neil MacLeod in 1613, his eldest son Donald was banished from Scotland in the same year, only returning two years later with his younger brother to raid Lewis. Afterwards he settled in Holland, where he died. He had three cousins, who were the sons of Ruairi Og MacLeod, another natural son of old Ruairi MacLeod of Lewis, but William and Ruairi were captured and executed by Sir Roderick MacKenzie of Coigach, now Tutor of Kintail. This left Malcolm Mor MacLeod, who managed to escape from captivity. He joined the rebellion of Sir James MacDonald in 1615 and afterwards took to a life of piracy. By then, the MacKenzies of Kintail were the undisputed masters of Lewis and nearly all of Wester Ross.

MacKenzies, Earls of Seaforth

Kenneth MacKenzie of Kintail had already been created Lord MacKenzie of Kintail in 1609, two years before his death in 1611. His son Colin MacKenzie became the first Earl of Seaforth in 1623, taking his title from his territories in Lewis. During his minority, the affairs of the family were handled by his uncle Roderick MacKenzie of Coigach. He became notorious as the 'Tutor of Kintail' in repressing disorder among the lawless Highlanders. Indeed, as the Gaelic proverb had it: 'There are two things worse than the Tutor of Kintail: frost in spring, and mist in the dog-days.' He was later knighted by the Crown for bringing peace to the island of Lewis and reducing Mull, Morvern and Tiree to order. He then bought the lands of Tarbat north of the Cromarty Firth, which were erected into a barony in 1623. It was his grandson George who became the first of Earl of Cromartie in 1703.

Chapter Nine

CONFLICTS OF
THE NORTHERN CLANS

The forfeiture in 1476 of the earldom of Ross by John MacDonald, fourth Lord of the Isles, and his subsequent loss of the Lordship itself in 1493 hardly affected the northern earldoms of Caithness and Sutherland. Instead, the history of the far north of Scotland during the sixteenth century was dominated by almost constant hostility between these two earldoms. Meanwhile, the MacKays of Strathnaver supported one side and then the other, as they each sought to gain mastery over its rival, often acting in the name of the Crown. The earldom of Caithness was held throughout this time by the Sinclairs. They had gained what was then the Norse earldom of Orkney in 1379, before they were created earls of Caithness in 1455, shortly before Scotland acquired Orkney and Shetland from the Norwegian crown. Their descendants, who held the title until 1765, became so powerful in the north during the sixteenth century that they were able to challenge the supremacy of the Gordons, Earls of Sutherland. However, it was a challenge that they could not ultimately sustain.

As already recounted, the Gordons were most likely granted the earldom of Huntly in the same year as the Sinclairs were created Earls of Caithness. Over the next two generations, the Gordons established for themselves a strong position as the King's Lieutenants in the North, often acting as Justiciar north of the Forth. They were later appointed as hereditary sheriffs of Inverness and Aberdeen with jurisdiction throughout the north of Scotland. George Gordon, second Earl of Huntly, eventually became Lord Chancellor of Scotland shortly before his death in 1501, while his second son Adam married Elizabeth, daughter of John, eighth Earl of Sutherland. It was through this marriage that Alexander Gordon, third Earl of Huntly, engineered the downfall of the Earls of Sutherland in their ancient line. It has been described as 'one of the most notable pieces of skulduggery in the annals of the north'.

Downfall of the ancient Earls of Sutherland

John, eighth Earl of Sutherland in the ancient line, had succeeded his father in 1460. According to tradition, his first wife was a daughter of Alexander MacDonald, third Lord of the Isles and Earl of Ross. It was perhaps this family connection which lead to John's downfall in 1494, only a year after the forfeiture of the Lordship of the Isles. Declared incapable of managing his own affairs, a brieve of idiotry was issued against him by James IV. It is said that the king acted at the insistence of Adam Gordon, second son of George Gordon, second Earl of Huntly, whose father was then Justiciar of the North. Yet John had exercised control over his earldom of Sutherland for more than thirty years and he was later judged to be responsible for his actions. Nevertheless, his brother-in-law Sir James Dunbar of Cummock was made his legal guardian or curator.

Acting in this capacity, Sir James Dunbar afterwards pursued Alexander Sutherland of Dirlot for some debts. He responded by raiding Dunrobin Castle in 1498, when he murdered James's brother Alexander Dunbar who had married Janet Sutherland, the Earl's sister. Iye Roy MacKay of Strathnaver now came to the aid of Sir James Dunbar. He captured the murderer, Alexander Sutherland of Dirlot, who was his own brother-in-law by the marriage of his sister or perhaps his nephew by this marriage. The captured man was brought to James IV at Inverness and executed along with ten of his accomplices.

Iye Roy MacKay benefited greatly as a result, since he was rewarded in 1499 with a royal charter to various lands in Strathnaver, Sutherland and Caithness. They included the lands of Farr, Armadale and Strathy, forfeited by Alexander Sutherland of Dirlot. MacKay received a further charter from the Crown in 1504, confirming his possession of the lands that his distant ancestor Angus Dubh MacKay had received in 1415 from Donald MacDonald, second Lord of the Isles. By then, he was active in suppressing the rebellion of Donald Dubh, grandson of the last Lord of the Isles, which broke out on his escape from captivity in 1503. Doubtless, the grant was a reward for his efforts on behalf of the Crown.

Meanwhile, the marriage had taken place of Elizabeth Sutherland, daughter of the eighth Earl of Sutherland, to Adam Gordon, second son of George Gordon, second Earl of Huntly, shortly before the latter's death in 1501. When the eighth Earl of Sutherland died around 1508, he was succeeded by his eldest son John. It seems he also suffered from mental weakness, or so it was alleged by the Gordons, Earls of Huntly. He was made a ward of the Crown on succeeding his father and later judged as incapable of managing his own affairs in 1514, just like his father. Even so, he was still capable of declaring that his sister Elizabeth and her husband Adam Gordon were his closest heirs, while he entered into a voluntary agreement at the same time preventing him from making improper settlements or conveyances of his estate. The suspicion remains that he was unduly influenced by his strong-minded sister and her Gordon husband. It seems they took advantage of the disturbed state of the country after the Battle of Flodden in 1513 to advance their own interests.

Disputed Inheritance

John, ninth and last Earl of Sutherland in the ancient line, died within a month of these proceedings in 1514. The manner of his death and its place is not recorded, and neither is it known where he was buried. His death opened the succession to his sister Elizabeth, except that it was disputed by her half-brother Alexander Sutherland. But he was unable to produce any documents naming him as the heir to the earldom and he had earlier renounced any such claim while still a minor in 1509, acting on the advice of his guardians. Alexander Sutherland complained bitterly that he was even prevented from appearing before the court to pursue his claim to the earldom by the hostility of the sheriff who was none other than Alexander Gordon, third Earl of Huntly. He was evidently determined that his brother's wife should succeed to the earldom of Sutherland, so favouring his own family. Elizabeth Sutherland was thus served heir to the title as Countess of Sutherland in 1515 after her brother's death the previous year, and Adam Gordon was then recognised as the Earl of Sutherland in right of his wife.

Thus deprived of his rightful inheritance by such sharp practice, Alexander Sutherland reacted by forcibly occupying Dunrobin Castle in 1515 and seizing some Crown revenues. Adam Gordon now appealed to John Sinclair, third Earl of Caithness, for help in regaining his possessions. It seems that they were successful since it is recorded that Alexander Sutherland was afterwards held captive in Edinburgh Castle early in 1517. However, he must have escaped, as he seized Dunrobin Castle for a second time in 1518. He evidently held it for well over a year, since the Earl of Caithness was put to the horn in 1519 for not fulfilling his promise to take and hold Dunrobin Castle for Adam Gordon. Alexander Sutherland was finally defeated in his efforts to regain the earldom of Sutherland in 1519 or 1520, when he was killed in a skirmish near Kintradwell by forces sent north to capture him. His severed head was left to bleach in the sun from the top of Dunrobin Castle as a grisly warning.

Adam Gordon, now styling himself Earl of Sutherland, afterwards strength-ened his own position in the far north of Scotland by granting out land to his supporters and by entering into bonds of friendship with John Sinclair, third Earl of Caithness, and Iye Roy MacKay of Strathnaver among several others. Even so, it seems that Adam Gordon and his wife Elizabeth, Countess of Sutherland, did not even reside within the earldom and took little part in its affairs. Instead, they left its administration in the hands of their eldest son Alexander Gordon, Master of Sutherland, until they eventually resigned the earldom in his favour in 1527. Afterwards, they hardly ever appear in the records of the time. Then in 1530, after the death of Alexander Gordon, Master of Sutherland, the earldom passed to Alexander's son John who was then only five years of age, even though his grandparents were still both alive.

Only a few months after Alexander's death in 1530, William Sutherland of Duffus was murdered in Thurso. What motive lay behind his violent death remains obscure, and it is not even known who committed the crime. However, Sir Robert Gordon alleged that he was murdered by the Gunns, acting at the instigation of the Bishop of Caithness. As a distant descendant of Nicholas Sutherland, second son of Kenneth, fourth Earl of Sutherland, it is possible that William Sutherland of Duffus was plotting to restore the ancient earldom of Sutherland to his family when he fell foul of Andrew Stewart, Bishop of Caithness.

Alexander Gordon, Master of Sutherland, had married Janet Stewart, eldest daughter of John Stewart, second Earl of Atholl, while the Bishop of Caithness was Atholl's younger brother. As Janet Stewart's uncle, he perhaps had every reason to advance the interests of her family in such a murderous fashion. In any event, several of the bishop's clergy were afterwards summoned to attend a justice-ayres at Inverness for their part in the slaughter of William Sutherland of Duffus, while the bishop evidently thought it best to seek refuge with his kinsmen in Atholl.

Feuds of the MacKays

Meanwhile, John MacKay had succeeded his father Iye Roy MacKay of Strathnaver in 1517. Almost immediately he abandoned his father's 'good and true service' to the Crown which had brought the family such rewards. He renewed the long-standing feud with the Morays over the lands of Strathfleet, which reached a climax at the Battle of Torran Dubh near Rogart. Then, after John MacKay of Strathnaver had died in 1529, he was succeeded by his brother Donald. He allied himself with John, Master of Forbes, and Sir John Campbell of Cawdor in pursuing a feud which ended with the death of Alexander Seton of Meldrum. Although they claimed common ancestry with the Forbeses, why the MacKays ever became involved in such a distant feud is not clear, since there were 'broils enough at home'. But it threatened the fortunes of the MacKays, since James V would not recognise Donald MacKay of Strathnaver as the heir of his brother John. Instead, the king granted his lands in Strathnaver to William Sutherland of Duffus, who was murdered the following year as already recounted. Donald MacKay was pardoned in 1536 for his part in the feud with the Setons, and then granted a charter to his lands in 1539 when they were erected into the barony of Farr. In return, he had to pay 700 merks to the only son and heir of the late William Sutherland of Duffus in compensation for his losses.

The following year, as already recounted, James V undertook his great expedition by sea around the north of Scotland, and Donald MacKay of Strathnaver accompanied the king back to Dumbarton. After remaining at court for some time, he returned north, where he raised a levy for the Scottish army that was defeated at the Battle of Solway Moss in 1542. His eldest son Iye Dubh MacKay was captured during the battle, remaining for nearly ten years in England where he entered the service of Henry VIII. Although he seemingly did not fight for the English at the Battle of Pinkie in 1547, he was certainly present when Haddington was captured in 1548. He also came during these years under the reforming influence of the Protestant Church of England which had been established in 1532. Indeed, after the death of James V in 1542, he joined the English party as it attempted to promote the marriage of the infant Mary Stuart, Queen of Scots, to Henry VIII's son Edward, Prince of Wales.

Diplomacy of the Bishop of Caithness

Meanwhile, Andrew Stewart, Bishop of Caithness, was succeeded after his death in 1542 by Robert Stewart, younger brother of Matthew Stewart, fourth Earl of Lennox. He was destined to become the seventh Earl of Lennox in 1578. But long before this happened, the Scots Parliament had repudiated the Treaty of Greenwich in 1543 in favour of the 'Auld Alliance' with France. As already recounted, his elder brother soon afterwards left Scotland to enter the service of Henry VIII of England, accompanied by the newly elected Bishop of Caithness. He left his Castles of Scrabster and Skibo under the protection of George Sinclair, fourth Earl of Caithness, and Donald MacKay of Strathnaver, along with his churchlands. Not surprisingly, he was forfeited for treachery along with his brother Matthew Stewart, fourth Earl of Lennox.

George Gordon, fourth Earl of Huntly, evidently took advantage of the Bishop's downfall by nominating his own younger brother Alexander Gordon to the now vacant diocese of Caithness. However, their attempt to seize the rich churchlands of Caithness was apparently foiled by George Sinclair, fourth Earl of Caithness. He prevented them from advancing north of Helmsdale Water with a force of 2,500 men, drawn up in battle array. However, Robert Stewart was soon afterwards restored as the Bishop of Caithness by Cardinal David Beaton, Archibishop of St Andrews. He then bought out his ecclesiastical rival in 1548 by granting him a yearly pension of 500 merks out of his own revenues. Shortly afterwards, the Bishop of Caithness arranged for his sister Eleanor to marry John Gordon, tenth Earl of Sutherland. This alliance was further bolstered by a bond of friendship between the Bishop and the Earl of Sutherland. The latter agreed to support the clergy in collecting their teinds and other rents, while the bishop agreed to pay him a pension of 100 pounds a year for this service.

Meanwhile, Robert Stewart, Bishop of Caithness, pursued much the same policy with regard to the other magnates in the north. He granted out lands to George Sinclair, fourth Earl of Caithness, later erected into the barony of Mey, while Donald MacKay of Strathnaver received a grant of fifteen davochs of churchland in Durness. The Bishop of Caithness even induced John Gordon, tenth Earl of Sutherland, George Sinclair, fourth Earl of Caithness, and Donald MacKay of Strathnaver to enter into a bond of mutual friendship with one another, apparently on quite equal terms by which they agreed to staunch their ancient quarrels. The bond was sealed by a meeting with the bishop at Girnigoe Castle in 1549 where they each swore to be faithful to one other for all the days of their lives.

Such skilful diplomacy on the part of the Bishop of Caithness meant he was now accepted into favour by the French party in Scotland. Indeed, he went to France with the dowager queen mother Mary of Guise in 1550, accompanying the Earls of Huntly and Sutherland on this diplomatic mission to ally Scotland against England. It was perhaps their absence abroad that prompted Donald MacKay of Strathnaver to launch yet another raid against the Rosses of Balnagown which occurred around this time. However, Donald MacKay died soon afterwards and his son Iye Dubh MacKay returned north to claim his inheritance. This was no easy matter since he had spent the years since the Scottish defeat at Solway Moss in 1542 in the service of England.

Rebellion of Iye Dubh MacKay

No sooner had Iye Dubh MacKay returned to Strathnaver than George Gordon, fourth Earl of Huntly and now Lord Chancellor of Scotland, had him disinherited at a meeting of Parliament in 1551. The grounds were entirely spurious. It was alleged that his father Donald MacKay was illegitimate, given that the marriage of his grandfather Iye Roy MacKay was not canonical. However, Iye Roy MacKay had received a precept of legitimation for both his sons from James IV in 1511 which thus made his grandson Iye

Dubh MacKay the rightful heir to his father's estates. Nevertheless, he was deprived of a legal title to his lands by such means, and they were granted instead to Robert Reid, Bishop of Orkney.

The following year, the dowager queen mother Mary of Guise, and James Hamilton, second Earl of Arran, who was still acting as Regent of Scotland, called a Parliament at Inverness. Iye Dubh MacKay and George Sinclair, fourth Earl of Caithness, were both summoned to attend, but neither appeared. Evidently, they did not trust the good faith of George Gordon, fourth Earl of Huntly and Sheriff of Inverness. Indeed, only two years earlier, he had summarily executed Lachlan MacIntosh of Clan Chattan on a trumped-up charge of plotting against his life. But it was only in 1554 that John Gordon, tenth Earl of Sutherland, was authorised to raise levies in the north to order to bring Iye Dubh MacKay to justice after he had apparently attacked the lands of Navidale. The earl's half-brother, Hugh Kennedy of Girvanmains, received a commission at the same time to sail from Leith in the *Lion*, armed with cannon and manned by fifty marines and twenty men-at-arms.

The forces at the command of John, tenth Earl of Sutherland, concentrated their attack upon the MacKay fortress of Borve Castle, situated on the north coast of the Aird of Farr overlooking the Pentland Firth. When the *Lion* arrived from Leith, her cannon were hauled up the cliffs and mounted as a battery on the eastern headland of Borroged, known afterwards as Ru-nan-Gunnach or Gun-Point. From this vantage point, a barrage of fire was unleashed with devastating effect against Borve Castle and the MacKay stronghold fell. Even so, it was only late in 1554 that Iye Dubh MacKay surrendered to prevent any further destruction of his country. He was held prisoner in Dumbarton Castle for much of 1555.

Rewards to the Earl of Sutherland

John Gordon, tenth Earl of Sutherland, was rewarded greatly for his actions against Iye Dubh MacKay of Strathnaver. Mary of Guise, now acting as Regent of Scotland, granted him a pension of 1,000 merks a year and made him baillie of the lands of Farr which had been forfeited to the Crown. Already he had received the earldom of Ross as its tenant, and a lease of the earldom of Moray, granted in 1549 to George Gordon, fourth Earl of Huntly, before he fell from favour in 1553. John Gordon, tenth Earl of Sutherland, also profited greatly from his marriage to Eleanor, sister of Robert Stewart, Bishop of Caithness, who made him the baillie of his diocese in 1553.

However, this was merely a prelude to further grants in 1557, 1559 and 1560 whereby the Bishop of Caithness conveyed many churchlands in

Caithness and Sutherland to his sister and brother-in-law in return for the payment of feu-duties. They came to a total of £683 4s 8¹/₂d, thus exceeding the rental received in 1546 from the whole earldom of Sutherland. The Earl of Sutherland also became the hereditary constable of the bishop's palace at Dornoch, as well as his castle at Scrabster. Such transfers of land greatly impoverished the Church after the Reformation, while the Bishop of Caithness continued to enjoy a very substantial income. Indeed, it is said that the bishop 'turned with the times and became Protestant, but still bore the title of Bishop of Caithness, and enjoyed the revenue until his death'.

Changes of Fortune in the Far North

Meanwhile, George Sinclair, fourth Earl of Caithness, had suffered a series of reverses after 1552 when he failed to appear before Parliament at Inverness. Even if he was treated more leniently than Iye Dubh MacKay, Robert Stewart, Bishop of Caithness, accused him of various crimes which were chiefly committed by his own retainers against the bishop's clergy. He was detained after he was summoned in 1553 to appear at Inverness before George Gordon, fourth Earl of Huntly, and Robert Stewart, Bishop of Caithness. Brought to Edinburgh, it is said that he only purchased his liberty with a large sum of money. Afterwards, he received a pardon in 1556, but further charges were brought against him only five days later.

Intent on strengthening his position against the growing power of the Earl of Sutherland, George Sinclair, fourth Earl of Caithness, now entered into a marriage alliance with Alexander Sutherland of Duffus in 1559. It was agreed between them that Elizabeth Sinclair, eldest daughter of the Earl of Caithness, or her sisters starting with the next eldest, should marry Alexander Sutherland, eldest son of the laird of Duffus, then only five years old, or his brothers starting with the next eldest, until a marriage was completed between the two families. The marriage did indeed take place in 1568 when the bridegroom Alexander Sutherland was fourteen years of age. After his death, his brother William inherited their father's estates of Duffus in 1579 when he married Margaret Sinclair as another daughter of the fourth Earl of Caithness who was next in line under the terms of this marriage contract.

Meanwhile, the momentous events of the Scottish Reformation intervened, and Mary Stuart, Queen of Scots, came to the throne only a year later in 1561. George Sinclair, fourth Earl of Caithness, was evidently restored to favour, appearing as a member of the Privy Council by the end of 1561. Not long afterwards, George Gordon, fourth Earl of Huntly, rebelled against the Crown, only to meet his death at the Battle of Corrichie in 1562. His downfall also brought down John Gordon, tenth Earl of Sutherland, who was implicated in Huntly's rebellion against the Crown. The Earl of Sutherland was forfeited of all his lands and titles in 1563 after he had fled the country to take refuge in Flanders. His disgrace greatly benefited Iye Dubh MacKay who was pardoned in 1562, but he did not receive back a legal title to his lands, as he could well have expected. However, several other families did gain charters to their lands from the Crown which they had previously held under the feudal superiority of the Gordons, Earls of Sutherland.

Even if the first few years of Mary Stuart's reign may be judged a success, her difficulties started in July 1565 when she married her first cousin Henry Stewart, Lord Darnley, eldest son of Matthew Stewart, fourth Earl of Lennox. The marriage itself caused such dissension among the nobility, led by her own half-brother, James Stewart, Earl of Moray, that she was forced to seek allies among the Catholic lords. Already the Gordons, Earls of Huntly, had been restored to favour in 1564 when George Gordon, now the eldest surviving son of the late Earl of Huntly, was appointed as Lord Chancellor. He was restored a few years later in 1567 as the fifth Earl of Huntly. John Gordon, tenth Earl of Sutherland, was also encouraged to return to Scotland in 1565, only to be captured by the English off Berwick. Released the next year, he soon afterwards received a new charter to his lands in the earldom of Sutherland. However, it was not until 1567 that his forfeiture was finally rescinded.

Not long afterwards, Mary Stuart, Queen of Scots, confirmed George Sinclair, fourth Earl of Caithness, as the hereditary Justiciar for the whole diocese of Caithness, which then consisted of the districts of Caithness, Sutherland, Strathnaver and Assynt, laying the foundation for much future trouble. The queen now took the disastrous step of marrying James Hepburn, fourth Earl of Bothwell, less than a month after he had abducted her in April 1567 and only three months after Lord Darnley had himself been murdered at Kirk O'Field in February 1567. By then, the queen had restored George Gordon to his title as the fifth Earl of Huntly, and evidently hoping to gain his much-needed support for her marriage, granted him the lands of Farr, which Iye Dubh MacKay had lost when he was disinherited in 1551.

Plot against the Earl of Sutherland

John Gordon, tenth Earl of Sutherland, was among the very few nobles to witness the queen's marriage to the Earl of Bothwell on 15 May 1567, which earned her so much opprobrium from even her most loyal followers. Just a month later, she surrendered to a confederacy of noblemen who had mustered an army against her at Carberry Hill near Musselburgh, and soon afterwards she abdicated in favour of her infant son James VI. By then,

John Gordon, tenth Earl of Sutherland, had returned north to Sutherland, where he and his countess died from poison in June 1567. It was administered to them in their food or drink while staying at Helmsdale by Isabel Sinclair, wife of the earl's uncle Gilbert Gordon of Garty. She was the daughter of Alexander Sinclair of Dunbeath, who was himself the uncle of George Sinclair, fourth Earl of Caithness. Their son would have succeeded to the earldom of Sutherland if Alexander Gordon, only son of John Gordon, tenth Earl of Sutherland, had shared his father's fate as the plotters evidently intended, but he managed to escape to Skibo Castle.

It is not known if George Sinclair, fourth Earl of Caithness, was himself involved in the plot. However, he benefited in any event by purchasing the ward and marriage of the young Alexander Gordon, now eleventh Earl of Sutherland after his father's death. George Sinclair promptly married off his ward Alexander Gordon while still a youth of fifteen to his own daughter Barbara Sinclair, then thirty-two years of age. The young heir to the earldom of Sutherland evidently objected to such treatment, since he escaped in 1569 to take refuge in Strathbogie with George Gordon, fifth Earl of Huntly. After coming of age in 1573, he divorced his first wife, and married Huntly's sister Lady Jean Gordon, whom the Earl of Bothwell had divorced to marry Mary Stuart, Queen of Scots. Meanwhile, George Sinclair, fourth Earl of Caithness, was ensconced in Dunrobin Castle, where it is said he destroyed all the Sutherland writs and charters that he could find.

Disorders in the North

It seems likely that disorder had become endemic in the far north ever since John Gordon, tenth Earl of Sutherland, was forfeited in 1563, along with the Gordons, Earls of Huntly. Iye Dubh MacKay had already laid waste to the barony of Skibo in 1566 with the help of Neil MacLeod of Assynt, setting fire to the town of Dornoch and returning later to attack Strathfleet. Then, his ancestral lands of Farr were granted in 1567 to Alexander Gordon, fifth Earl of Huntly. Only a few years later, Iye Dubh MacKay joined forces with John Sinclair, eldest son of George Sinclair, fourth Earl of Caithness, harrying Sutherland far and wide. Together with the Sutherlands of Duffus, they expelled such adherents of the young Earl of Sutherland as the Morays and Gordons. Again, Dornoch was burnt and the cathedral put to the flames. No doubt, the actions of John Sinclair, Master of Caithness, were intended to avenge his sister's desertion by the young Earl of Sutherland.

John Sinclair then became embroiled in a feud with Lawrence, Lord Oliphant, after he had attacked the latter's castle of Old Wick in July 1569. However, it seems unlikely that John Sinclair as the Master of Caithness had the backing of his father in pursuing such a lawless course. Indeed, it seems George Sinclair, fourth Earl of Caithness, afterwards held his eldest son as a prisoner in the dungeon of Girnigoe Castle, where he was 'kept in miserable captivy for the space of seven years, and died at last in prison of famine and vermin'. His death was said to be caused by thirst resulting from a diet of salt beef, washed down only by brandy.

Restoration of Iye Dubh MacKay

The fortunes of Iye Dubh MacKay improved somewhat after the abdication of Mary Stuart, Queen of Scots, and the appointment of James Stewart, Earl of Moray, as Regent of Scotland. He came north to Inverness in 1569, when George Gordon, fifth Earl of Huntly, promised that he would convey the lands of Strathnaver into the hands of Iye Dubh MacKay for a payment of 4,000 merks, to be held from the Crown. However, he reneged on this promise after the Regent was assassinated in January 1570. He offered instead to restore Iye Dubh MacKay to his lands for the sum of 3,000 merks, but only on condition that they were held under his own superiority. Acting on the advice of Lord Forbes, Iye Dubh MacKay reluctantly agreed to this proposal. He was thus restored to his ancestral lands, even if he did not come to hold them from the Crown in the manner of his ancestors.

It was almost the last event in his long life since Iye Dubh MacKay died two years later in 1572. He was succeeded by Uisdean Dubh MacKay as the eldest son of his father's second marriage. His succession was not accepted by all his clansmen since Iye Dubh MacKay had sons from an earlier union with Helen MacLeod of Assynt who was his first cousin. They had a better claim to be recognised as Chief of MacKay under the kin-based system of inheritance, but their father's marriage to their mother was not recognised by the Church, since it was within the forbidden degrees of consanguinity. The young heir was barely eleven years of age and his wardship was granted to George Sinclair, fourth Earl of Caithness, who took him into his household at Girnigoe Castle and indeed married him off to his daughter Elizabeth Sinclair.

Divisions within Clan MacKay

The clan was first governed in his absence by the young chief's cousin, John Mor MacLeod of Assynt. However, he was murdered soon afterwards at Girnigoe, which he had been inveigled into visiting, it seems, at the instigation of George Sinclair, fourth Earl of Caithness. The young chief's elder half-brother John Beag MacKay then became Tutor of Strathnaver, but he was killed in 1579 during a skirmish at Durness, after he was attacked in his house at Balnakiel. His assailants were the MacLeods of Assynt and a sept known as the Abrach MacKays, descended from Ian Abrach MacKay, younger son of Angus Dubh MacKay, who had died in 1433. Whether this attack was incited by George Sinclair, fourth Earl of Caithness, or by Alexander Gordon, eleventh Earl of Sutherland, who had reached his majority in 1573, remains a mystery, but they have both been blamed.

The Gunns were involved as well, since William Gunn was killed at the same time as John Beag MacKay while staying with him at Balnakiel. The sequel was a long and bloody feud between the Gunns and the Abrach MacKays over the next few decades. Even more serious were the divisions that it opened up within the clan itself, now with Uisdean Dubh MacKay at its head, bitterly opposed by the Abrach MacKays. They sided for their part with Alexander Gordon, eleventh Earl of Sutherland, while the Gunns supported the Sinclairs, Earls of Caithness.

Sutherland and Huntly

Alexander Gordon, eleventh Earl of Sutherland, came of age in 1573. He then divorced his first wife, Barbara Sinclair, who had been forced upon him against his will by her father and his guardian, George Sinclair, fourth Earl of Caithness. As grounds for divorce, he cited her adultery with Iye Dubh MacKay of Strathnaver, although it was never proved. Alexander Gordon then married Lady Jean Gordon, sister of George Gordon, fifth Earl of Huntly, so reinforcing the close relations between the two families. Not long afterwards, George Gordon, fifth Earl of Huntly, died suddenly in 1576 from a fit while playing football. He was succeeded by his eldest son George Gordon, who became the sixth Earl of Huntly while still a minor of fourteen years and afterwards the first Marquis of Huntly.

It was Alexander Gordon, eleventh Earl of Sutherland, as his uncle by marriage, who was appointed the legal guardian to the young Earl of Huntly. George Gordon, sixth Earl of Huntly, was educated abroad in France, only returning to Scotland by 1583 when he came of age. Almost his first act on attaining his majority was to grant the superiority of the MacKay lands in Strathnaver to his guardian, receiving in return the lordship of Aboyne. Alexander Gordon, eleventh Earl of Sutherland thus gained a legal title over Uisdean Dubh MacKay and his descendants. who afterwards held their lands of Strathnaver under the feudal superiority of the Gordons, Earls of Sutherland. The next few years would see a struggle for supremacy in the north, as Alexander Gordon, eleventh Earl of Sutherland, attempted to detach Uisdean Dubh MacKay from his allegiance to the Sinclairs, Earls of Caithness.

Chapter Ten

SUPREMACY IN THE NORTH

George Sinclair, fourth Earl of Caithness, died in 1582 after holding the earl-dom for fifty-three years. He was succeeded by his grandson George Sinclair, who became the fifth Earl of Caithness at the age of sixteen years. When he died in 1643 at the age of seventy-eight, nearly all the power and influence of the earldom of Caithness had been lost by his actions. By dint of some manoeuvring, Alexander Gordon, eleventh Earl of Sutherland, arranged in 1585 for the young Earl of Caithness to marry Jean Gordon, only daughter of George Gordon, fifth Earl of Huntly. This marriage threatened to destroy the complicated web of marriages and other alliances by which his grand-father had attempted to bind the Sutherlands of Duffus, the MacKays of Strathnaver and the Gunns to his house of Caithness. Indeed, after Alexander Sutherland of Duffus had married Elizabeth Sinclair in 1568, as already recounted, his younger brother William married her younger sister Margaret in 1579, so renewing the terms of the original contract between their two families. Then, after her first husband had died, Elizabeth Sinclair was given in marriage by her father to Uisdean Dubh MacKay of Strathnaver, who had come of age in 1583.

Battle of Altgawn and its Aftermath

Even before George Sinclair, fourth Earl of Caithness, had died in 1582, his wide powers as Justiciar over the whole diocese of Caithness had been greatly reduced by the Privy Council at the urging of Alexander Gordon, eleventh Earl of Sutherland. He now championed the right of his kinsman George Gordon, sixth Earl of Huntly, to inherit the hereditary office as Sheriff of Inverness, Ross and Caithness which had been held by his family for several generations, and the Privy Council agreed. Alexander Gordon, eleventh Earl of Sutherland, now determined to destroy the alliances of the young Earl of Caithness, backed as he was by the Abrach MacKays and the MacLeods of Assynt.

Alexander Gordon first plotted the destruction of the Gunns. They were the staunch supporters of Uisdean Dubh MacKay of Strathnaver as well as the erstwhile allies of the Sinclairs, Earls of Caithness. It is said that he only agreed to George Sinclair, fifth Earl of Caithness, marrying Jean Gordon, sister of the young Earl of Huntly, if the bridegroom were to help him in their destruction. After threats from George Gordon, sixth Earl of Huntly, acting in his capacity as the King's Lieutenant-General, the Earl of Caithness was forced in 1586 to join a two-pronged attack against the Gunns. His own forces from Caithness were to invade the uplands of Braemore from the east, while the forces under the Earl of Sutherland were to approach from the south and west, so trapping the Gunns. However, as the Gunns had earlier been among the staunchest allies of his family, it seems that the Earl of Caithness salved his conscience by warning them of the impending attack.

When the two expeditions set off, it so happened that the Gordons of Sutherland first encountered William MacKay, later of Bighouse, and the younger brother of Uisdean Dubh MacKay. He was returning with cattle from a raiding party against James MacLeod of Assynt, himself an adherent of the Earl of Sutherland. Fighting a rearguard action, William MacKay fell back towards Ben Griam where the Gunns had taken refuge, threatened as they were by the Sinclairs advancing from the east. Meeting up early next morning at Altgawn, the MacKays and the Gunns resolved to attack the Sinclairs first, hoping to surprise their enemies with their new-found strength. Indeed, they routed the Sinclairs as they advanced uphill, killing their leader, Henry Sinclair, cousin of the young Earl of Caithness, and seven score of his men. When they learnt of this reverse, the forces of the Earl of Sutherland melted away of their own accord.

Meanwhile, Uisdean Dubh MacKay of Strathnaver had gone to visit Girnigoe Castle, hoping to influence his brother-in-law George Sinclair, fifth Earl of Caithness, on behalf of the Gunns. When news arrived that the Sinclair forces had been defeated by the Gunns and his own clansmen at Altgawn, he was forced to flee for his very life back to Strathnaver at the dead of night. Thus, without striking a single blow, Alexander Gordon, eleventh Earl of Sutherland, achieved his aim of separating the Earl of Caithness from the Gunns and the MacKays, who had previously been among his staunchest supporters.

However, despite their great victory at Altgawn, the Gunns were still harried by the forces of Alexander Gordon, eleventh Earl of Sutherland, and George Sinclair, fifth Earl of Caithness. It seems Uisdean Dubh MacKay now advised the Gunns to seek refuge in the Western Isles, saying that he was no longer able to protect them from their enemies. A party of Gunns apparently made their way across country towards Wester Ross, where they encountered the Abrach MacKays and the MacLeods of Assynt near the head of Loch Broom at Leckmelm, losing thirty-two of their men. However, not long afterwards, the Abrach MacKays were heavily defeated at the Battle of Syre in Strathnaver, fighting against the forces of Ian Ruadh MacKay, or so Sir Robert Gordon recorded. It seems the MacKays were still weakened by their internecine quarrels arising from the skirmish at Durness in 1579.

Confrontation at Helmsdale

A dispute now arose which destroyed the fragile and one-sided alliance between George Sinclair, fifth Earl of Caithness, and Alexander Gordon, eleventh Earl of Sutherland. Bent on territorial aggrandisement, Alexander Gordon, eleventh Earl of Sutherland, now sought to recover the lands in the Strath of Kildonan which his great-grandfather had granted in 1516 to John Sinclair, then Earl of Caithness. He also attempted to exercise jurisdiction over the churchlands in the earldom of Caithness which his father had received at the Reformation from Robert Stewart, Bishop of Caithness. Already offended by these demands, the Earl of Caithness was further incensed when his horses had their tails docks by a Gordon who held lands in the Strath of Kildonan. Swearing revenge for this insult to his honour, he secretly gathered together a body of men in February 1587 who crossed the Ord of Caithness and attacked the culprit, killing him. Alexander Gordon, eleventh Earl of Sutherland, retaliated against this incursion by raising his own forces. They included some MacIntoshes, the MacKenzies of Redcastle, the Munros of Cortalich and a party from the MacLeods of Assynt.

Marching north to Helmsdale in early March, Alexander Gordon, eleventh Earl of Sutherland, was confronted by just as strong a force under the Earl of Caithness, consisting of men from Caithness, Strathnaver and Orkney. Uisdean Dubh MacKay was present as the leader of the Strathnaver contingent, despite his earlier support for the Gunns. The two forces first faced one another for several days with only a minor skirmish. Alexander Gordon, eleventh Earl of Sutherland, then sent MacIntosh in secret across the river to parley with Uisdean Dubh MacKay, offering to reward him if he were to desert the Earl of Caithness. After meeting with a flat refusal from Uisdean Dubh MacKay, another emissary was sent from the Earl of Sutherland. He entered into a treaty with the Earl of Caithness from which Uisdean Dubh MacKay was deliberately excluded. After learning that the Earl of Caithness was prepared to abandon him without a scruple just as he had earlier betrayed the Gunns, Uisdean Dubh MacKay promptly withdrew his forces in disgust, marching his men back to Strathnaver.

Pact between MacKay and Sutherland

Now wary of the Earl of Caithness, Uisdean Dubh MacKay had little choice but to seek an accommodation with Alexander Gordon, eleventh Earl of Sutherland, who held the superiority of his lands in Strathnaver. The earl for his part was just as eager to reach an agreement with Uisdean Dubh MacKay. A meeting between the two men was held at Inverness in the autumn of 1588. It evidently persuaded Uisdean Dubh MacKay to acknowledge the superiority of Alexander Gordon, eleventh Earl of Sutherland, who in return granted him a charter to his lands of Strathnaver in 1589. Indeed, so anxious was the Earl of Sutherland to secure the allegiance of Uisdean Dubh MacKay that he was even prepared to forgo the non-entry dues for the lands of Strathnaver, amounting to 50,000 pounds, which were owed to him by Uisdean Dubh MacKay. They sealed the compact between their two families when Uisdean Dubh MacKay married the earl's eldest daughter Jane Gordon. Then aged only fifteen, she was described as 'a lady of excellent beauty and comeliness, witty, imbued with sundry good qualities both of mind and body'. Since he had already divorced his first wife Elizabeth, sister of George Sinclair, fifth Earl of Caithness, he must have decided that the future lay with the Gordons, Earls of Sutherland.

Invasion of Caithness

Thus strengthened by his alliance with Uisdean Dubh MacKay of Strathnaver, Alexander Gordon, eleventh Earl of Sutherland, was now able to launch a devastating attack upon George Sinclair, fifth Earl of Caithness, and his erstwhile ally of only a few years ago. It took place in February 1589 once he had obtained Letters of Fire and Sword from Chancellor Maitland against the Earl of Caithness. His commission gave him the legal right to invade the earldom of Caithness, seeking justice for the death of the Gordon tenant who had docked the horse's tails. He first dispatched 200 men to lay waste the coastal districts from Dunbeath to Latheron, held by the Sinclairs of Dunbeath and the Sutherlands of Forse. A few days later, the Earl of Sutherland himself crossed the Ord of Caithness with a much larger force, among whom were the MacKays of Strathnaver and the Gunns. He then advanced farther north to beseige the Sinclair stronghold of Girnigoe Castle which, however, was too strong to capture without any cannon.

George Sinclair, fifth Earl of Caithness, now agreed to submit their dispute to the arbitration of George Gordon, sixth Earl of Huntly. The Earl of Sutherland therefore withdrew his forces after laying waste to the surrounding countryside and plundering the town of Wick. Indeed, its sacking became known as La na Creiche Moire, or Day of the Great Spoil, such was the booty. The Gordons even broke into the burial vault of the Sinclairs, Earls of Caithness, and destroyed the leaden casket containing the heart of the late earl. It is said that the Gordons lost 300 men during this expedition, so savage was the fighting.

Settlement in the North

This great raid was followed by attacks and counter-attacks between the various adherents of Sutherland and Caithness over the next few months. Eventually, however, the two earls came together at Elgin, where they agreed that all their quarrels should be settled in the future by George Gordon, sixth Earl of Huntly. However, their agreement did not prevent George Sinclair, fifth Earl of Caithness, from invading Sutherland in the autumn of 1590. He penetrated as far south as Dunrobin and then fell back north along the coast, carrying away a great number of cattle. The raiding party was attacked at Kintradwell by the hastily raised forces of the Earl of Sutherland, but they did not manage to retrieve the cattle. Meanwhile, Uisdean Dubh MacKay had mounted a diversionary attack over Druim Hollistan in the north. He laid the country waste as far as Thurso and returned to Strathnaver laden with much plunder. As such disorder spread throughout the country to the alarm of the great landholders, the Earl of Sutherland eventually persuaded George Sinclair, fifth Earl of Caithness, to visit the Earl of Huntly at Strath-bogie in the spring of 1591. There they finally settled the dispute between themselves.

It may well be that such an accommodation was forced upon them by the Act of Parliament of 1587, commonly called the 'General Band', whereby they had to find caution for their own good conduct, which now came into effect. The Earl of Sutherland had to find caution in 20,000 merks, Uisdean Dubh MacKay in 10,000 pounds (or 15,000 merks), and the Earl of Caithness in 20,000 pounds (or 30,000 merks). After so much bloodshed over their possession, the Earl of Caithness simply resigned the disputed lands in the Strath of Kildonan to the Earl of Sutherland, receiving various churchlands in Caithness in return. James VI in confirming this latter grant added as his own gift the patronage of the churches of Wick, Thurso, Latheron and Halkirk, 'understanding the burning zeal of the said George [Earl of Caithness] for the promotion of the glory of God'.

Death of the Earl of Sutherland

Any prospect of maintaining the king's peace in the far north of Scotland was now upset when Alexander Gordon, eleventh Earl of Sutherland, died in December 1594 at the early age of forty-two years. He was succeeded by his young son John, then eighteen years of age. Soon after his father's death, John Gordon, now twelfth Earl of Sutherland, visited the Earl of Caithness at Girnigoe Castle, hoping to renew his father's bond of friendship with his rival. However, while he was there, the Sutherlands of Berriedale slipped across the Ord of Caithness to attack the Strath of Kildonan, threatening the life of a Gunn kinsman. It is not known if the Earl of Caithness was behind the attack, but the suspicion was enough for the young Earl of Sutherland to rally his own forces against him. Bloodshed was only averted through the influence of Ludovic Stewart, second Duke of Lennox, now acting as the King's Lieutenant in the North. The Privy Council bound the parties over to keep the peace, the Earl of Caithness finding caution in 20,000 merks and the Earl of Sutherland and Uisdean Dubh MacKay in amounts not specified.

Aggrandisement of Sutherland

John Gordon, twelfth Earl of Sutherland, now slowly strengthened his position in Sutherland by means of skilful diplomacy. Already, Uisdean Dubh MacKay held the lands of Strathnaver under his superiority, as did the Sutherlands of Duffus and the Rosses of Balnagown farther south. His Gordon kinsmen also purchased lands near Golspie and Strathfleet, which they then held under his superiority as well. The Munros of Foulis likewise came under the superiority of the Earl of Sutherland for their lands in Strathokyell and Creich, as did the Gunns for the lands they held in the Strath of Kildonan. Then in 1601, John Gordon, twelfth Earl of Sutherland, married Agnes Elphinstone, eldest daughter of Alexander Elphinstone, Lord High Treasurer of Scotland. Shortly afterwards, he received a charter giving him powers of regality over his earldom, while all his territories were erected into the Sheriffdom of Sutherland over which the Earls of Sutherland were to have hereditable jurisdiction. He also received in regality not only the churchlands of Caithness, which his father had received from Robert Stewart, Bishop of Caithness, but the lands of Strathnaver as well, held by Uisdean Dubh MacKay, so confirming his undoubted superiority over these lands.

Such aggrandisement on the part of the Earl of Sutherland was a bitter blow to George Sinclair, fifth Earl of Caithness. He had already appeared before the Privy Council in Edinburgh to claim precedence over the Earl of Sutherland, and now he prepared to exert his rights to visit Sutherland and Strathnaver as the hereditary Justiciar of the diocese of Caithness, which included these two districts. This he intended to undertake in the guise of a hunting expedition, but so loudly did he proclaim his intention that the Earl of Sutherland had sufficient time to raise his own forces. A confrontation occurred between them in 1601, when the Earl of Caithness encountered a much larger force under the Earl of Sutherland on the slopes of Ben Griam. Faced with defeat, the Earl of Caithness was forced to retreat ignominiously without even engaging his rival's forces. Later in the same year, the Earl of Sutherland visited Orkney alongwith several of his adherents. Among them were his brother Sir Robert Gordon, his brother-in-law Uisdean Dubh MacKay of Strathnaver and Donald MacLeod of Assynt. Together, they detached Patrick Stewart, Earl of Orkney, from his previous allegiance to the Earl of Caithness.

Financial Transactions by Caithness

George Sinclair, fifth Earl of Caithness, now took to purchasing the trappings of power and influence, just as the Earl of Sutherland had done. He first bought all the churchlands that the Earl of Sutherland held within his own earldom of Caithness for the sum of 40,000 merks in 1604. Not long afterwards, he acquired the property held in Caithness by Lawrence, Lord Oliphant, while some years later he bought the barony of Ackergill from the Keiths, Earls Marischal. It was the start of a disastrous policy whereby the Sinclairs, Earls of Caithness, became so burdened with debt that they eventually lost nearly all their estates. Meanwhile, after yet another attempt to enter Sutherland and Strathnaver, again undertaken in the guise of a hunting expedition, the Earl of Caithness was once more forced in 1607 to come to terms with the Earl of Sutherland. Soon afterwards, however, John Gordon, twelfth Earl of Sutherland, was allowed to go abroad for the sake of his health, and thereafter he took little part in public affairs until his early death in 1615.

The Earl of Caithness now became embroiled with the Sutherlands of Berriedale, and the Sinclairs of Dunbeath, while there was trouble between him and Patrick Stewart, Earl of Orkney. Indeed, the disorder was such that James VI in 1611 gave Alexander Forbes, Bishop of Caithness, a commission to do all in his power to restore law and order in the far north, while strengthening his position by appointing him to the Privy Council. Evidently, he hoped that Bishop Forbes would follow the example of Andrew Knox, Bishop of the Isles, who had already brought a measure of good government to the Western Isles, by establishing the king's peace in the far north.

Earldom of Orkney

Only a few years later, George Sinclair, fifth Earl of Caithness, was given a much-needed chance to restore his reputation with the government when he received a commission to reduce the earldom of Orkney to obedience. After his own family had surrendered the earldom of Orkney in 1470, it had remained in the hands of the Crown until 1564. Only then was Lord Robert Stewart, an illegitimate son of James V and thus the half-brother of Mary Stuart, Queen of Scots, granted a lease of the Crown lands in Orkney and Shetland. However, his lease was almost immediately revoked when James Hepburn, Earl of Bothwell, was created Duke of Orkney in 1567, just before he married Mary Stuart, Queen of Scots. However, he forfeited Orkney along with all his other lands and titles in December 1567 following the queen's abdication. Meanwhile, Lord Robert Stewart had managed to keep hold of the Crown lands in the earldom, while he forced Adam Bothwell, Bishop of Orkney, to give up his lands in the bishopric of Orkney as well. Indeed, he was eventually created Earl of Orkney in 1581, soon after the regency of James Douglas, Earl of Morton, came to an end.

When Robert Stewart died in 1593, he was succeeded as the second Earl of Orkney in the Stewart line by his eldest surviving son, Patrick Stewart. Like his father before him, he ruled over Orkney as a despot, involving himself in vast debts to keep up what was virtually a semi-regal state, and treating the native Orcadians iniquitously with an utter disregard for the law. Indeed, as James Law, then Bishop of Orkney, wrote to James VI in 1608:

> Alas, dear and dread Sovereign, truly it is to be pitied that so many of your Majesty's subjects are so manifoldly and grievously oppressed; some by ejection and banishment from their homes and native soil, others by contorting the laws and extorting their goods, the most part being so impoverished that some of them neither dare nor may complain, but in silent and forced patience groan under their grievance.

Summoned before the Privy Council in 1609 to account for his behaviour, Patrick Stewart was warded in Edinburgh Castle and then held captive in Dumbarton Castle. But even while he was held prisoner, the Orcadians continued to be oppressed by his kinsmen. Then in 1614, he sent his natural son Robert Stewart north to Orkney. He promptly occupied Kirkwall Castle and fortified the Cathedral of St Magnus.

Expedition to Orkney

Faced with such defiance of its own authority, the Privy Council now dispatched a well-manned expedition north to Orkney, armed with a battering ram and a large cannon. It was commanded by George Sinclair, fifth Earl of

Caithness. However, he was only given the commission as he happened to be in Edinburgh on quite another matter at the time. On his arrival in Orkney, he first met with strong resistance from the rebels. Kirkwall Castle only fell after a siege of three weeks, when Robert Stewart, natural son of the Earl of Orkney, was forced by his friends to surrender. He was brought to Edinburgh, where he was hanged for treason along with five others in January 1615. Just a month later, his father Patrick Stewart, second Earl of Orkney, was beheaded at the Mercat Cross in Edinburgh, and all his titles forfeited. It is recorded that his execution for high treason was even delayed so that he could be taught the Lord's Prayer.

Changes in the North

Soon afterwards, John Gordon, twelfth Earl of Sutherland, died in September 1615. He left his eldest son John to succeed him while not yet seven years of age. For the next fifteen years, Sir Robert Gordon, uncle to the young Earl of Sutherland, acted as his guardian and tutor. It was under his tutelage that the Gordons, Earls of Sutherland, rose to supreme power as 'Cocks o' the Far North'. Only two years previously, Uisdean Dubh MacKay of Strathnaver had died as well. He was succeeded by his eldest son Donald MacKay, born of his second marriage with Jane Gordon, daughter of Alexander Gordon, eleventh Earl of Sutherland. Donald MacKay of Strathnaver was thus the nephew of Sir Robert Gordon, and the cousin of John Gordon, thirteenth Earl of Sutherland. Knighted in 1616, he was afterwards created the first Lord Reay.

At first, Sir Donald MacKay of Strathnaver maintained the friendly relations that had previously existed between his own father and the late Earl of Sutherland. However, he became increasingly estranged from Sir Robert Gordon, abandoning the role of loyal lieutenant to his feudal superior once played by his father. Indeed, he seemingly declined to be served heir to his own father, since he was not prepared to recognise the superiority of the Gordons, Earls of Sutherland, implied by such an act. Eventually, he came to adhere more closely to George Sinclair, fifth Earl of Caithness, fearful that Sir Robert Gordon was intent upon using him merely as a pawn in his struggle for power and influence with the Earl of Caithness. Yet Donald MacKay of Strathnaver had already played a large part in Sir Robert Gordon's campaigns against the Earl of Caithness which effectively destroyed the family.

Dispute with Sinclair of Dunbeath

After returning from his successful expedition to Orkney, George Sinclair, fifth Earl of Caithness, faced yet another crisis late in 1615. Despite its trivial beginnings in the burning of a corn yard, it finally caused his downfall. The dispute started over the lands of George Sinclair of Dunbeath who had married a sister of Lord Forbes. According to Sir Robert Gordon, even before George Sinclair of Dunbeath had inherited these lands, his grandfather, William Sinclair of Dunbeath, was so badly treated by the Earl of Caithness that he was forced to live in Moray. Quite likely, the Earl of Caithness was even then manoeuvring to gain possession of the barony of Dunbeath, lying as it did between the lands which he had already purchased from Lawrence, Lord Oliphant. However, it then passed to George Sinclair of Dunbeath, along with the lands of Reay and Sandside on the north coast of Caithness, after his grandfather had died. He too faced the hostility of the Earl of Caithness, who apparently plotted against his life. Eventually, he left all his lands in Caithness to his father-in-law Lord Forbes after he had retired south to live with his wife's family in Aberdeenshire, where he died in 1614.

Arson at Sandside

Meanwhile, Lord Forbes had taken possession of his estates in Caithness. His action greatly angered the fifth Earl of Caithness who judged he had a better title to these estates granted to him earlier by their previous proprietor. Indeed, he reacted by inciting some members of Clan Gunn to set fire to the corn yards of Sandside in November 1615, or so it was later alleged. He evidently hoped that Sir Robert Gordon and Donald MacKay of Strathnaver would get the blame as the Gunns were their tenants. However, after rumours had surfaced that the Gunns were indeed responsible, they approached Sir Robert Gordon and Donald MacKay of Strathnaver, hoping for their protection. They revealed that the Earl of Caithness was indeed behind the act of arson at Sandside and offered to reveal everything to the Privy Council should their lives be spared.

Guilty or not, the Earl of Caithness was now at the mercy of Sir Robert Gordon. He pursued his rival through the law courts until it was claimed that the Earl of Caithness was an object of pity to even his bitterest enemies. The Gunns were first summoned to appear for trial before the Privy Council at the request of Lord Forbes, while the Earl of Caithness and his eldest son William Sinclair, Lord Berriedale, were required to bring the accused to Edinburgh for this very purpose. But fearful that they too would be arrested if they appeared in Edinburgh, they both refused to comply with the orders of the Privy Council. They were promptly denounced as rebels and put to the horn. Then, after testimony had been given to the Privy Council that they had instigated the act of arson at Sandside, George Sinclair, fifth Earl of Caithness, and his son Lord Berriedale were both charged with this crime by Lord Forbes.

Downfall of the Earl of Caithness

Meanwhile, Lord Berriedale had already entered into negotiations with Lord Forbes in an attempt to settle the matter out of court. Now further negotiations took place between the two parties who eventually reached an agreement. Its terms were harsh. The Earl of Caithness was forced to pay 20,000 merks each to Lord Forbes and Sir Donald MacKay of Strathnaver. He had to renounce all jurisdictions he had previously claimed within Sutherland and Strathnaver under his hereditary offices of Justiciar and Sheriff to the diocese of Caithness, and to abandon his claim for precedence over the Earl of Sutherland. Their agreement was then was reported to James VI in London. However, the king now demanded, perhaps at the prompting of Sir Robert Gordon who was a favourite at Court, that justice should be done by prosecuting all those guilty of such a flagrant crime, as well as any accessories to the crime.

Lord Berriedale was therefore apprehended for trial on the latter count, but his father declined to appear on the appointed day. He was again denounced a rebel and outlawed. Eventually, after Lord Berriedale had sought the support of Sir Robert Gordon, James VI was persuaded to pardon George Sinclair, fifth Earl of Caithness, but only after he had agreed to resign for ever to the Crown his hereditary offices of Sheriff and Justiciar of Caithness, to surrender his possession of lands that had once belonged to the Bishop of Caithness worth 2,000 merks a year, and to satisfy all his creditors who were annoying His Majesty with their pressing demands for justice. After promising to do everything in his power to arrest those guilty of the burning of the corn yards at Sandside, Lord Berriedale was then released from Edinburgh Castle.

Imprisonment of Lord Berriedale

Lord Berriedale had scarcely regained his freedom when he was arrested once again, this time at the insistence of his own kinsman Sir James Home of Cowdenknowes. He evidently feared financial ruin since he had agreed to act as surety for the debts, not only of Lord Berriedale himself, but also those of his father, the fifth Earl of Caithness. Indeed, George Sinclair, fifth Earl of Caithness, only narrowly escaped being imprisoned himself by fleeing north to Caithness. Even so, his creditors had enough influence with the Privy Council to prevent him from gaining any pardon under the terms already agreed with James VI unless they were paid. The Earl of Caithness was now granted a series of safe-conducts to come to Edinburgh so that he might settle his debts, but he always returned to Caithness before they expired without repaying his creditors. He thus allowed his eldest son Lord Berriedale to languish in prison for five long years until he was finally released in 1621 through the good offices of Lord Gordon, Earl of Enzie and afterwards the seventh Earl of Huntly.

Conspiracy against Clan Gunn

Nearly two years after Lord Berriedale was imprisoned for debt in 1616, Sir Donald MacKay of Strathnaver broke briefly with Sir Robert Gordon, Tutor of Sutherland. He allayed himself with George Sinclair, fifth Earl of Caithness, now at the nadir of his fortunes. His motives for abandoning the Gordons, Earls of Sutherland, remain obscure. Perhaps he had thought better of an offer to grant lands in Strathnaver to the Gunns, judging it prejudicial to his own financial interests. Indeed, Sir Donald MacKay now visited the fifth Earl of Caithness. They met together in secret near Dounreay at the dead of night, accompanied by only three other men on each side. Together, they agreed to destroy Clan Gunn, whose loyalty they may well have doubted given their indebtedness to Sir Robert Gordon for his protection in the aftermath of their attack at Sandside.

Soon afterwards, however, their secret agreement became public knowledge and the matter of much discussion. Sir Donald MacKay of Strathnaver attempted to appease Sir Robert Gordon by assuring him that his actions were directed solely against the Gunns, only to receive a stunning reproof from his uncle concerning the meaning of honour. Since the Gunns had never been judged guilty of any crime, Sir Robert Gordon affirmed that he was not prepared to abandon them until they were so convicted. Even so, Sir Donald MacKay afterwards crossed into Sutherland in an unsuccessful attempt to capture those responsible for the act of arson at Sandside. His impetuous actions so threatened him that he decided to seek a reconciliation with Sir Robert Gordon in 1619, although differences still remained between them.

Commission against the Earl of Caithness

George Sinclair, fifth Earl of Caithness was now living as an outlaw in the far north of Scotland. Then, one of his servants killed Thomas Lindsay who occupied lands that he had earlier resigned into the hands of the Bishop of Caithness. The affair came to the notice of James VI in London, who demanded of the Privy Council in 1621 that they should give a commission to Sir Robert Gordon to apprehend the Earl of Caithness or to force him into exile and to occupy all his castles. Furthermore, he was to compel all the landed proprietors in Caithness to find sureties, not only for keeping the king's peace, but also for attending the Privy Council in Edinburgh at twice-yearly intervals to answer any complaints.

Sir Robert Gordon declined this commission at first, but he eventually agreed on condition that he was given enough ships and munitions to reduce the Earl of Caithness to obedience. He then managed to convince Lord Berriedale that he should accept the commission instead against his own father, but his creditors refused to accept his release from prison. Only after Lord Gordon, Earl of Enzie, eldest son of George Gordon, sixth Earl of Huntly, had found surety for all his debts was Lord Berriedale finally released from prison, despite the objection of his creditors. Lord Berriedale now returned to Caithness where he failed to apprehend his father. It was not until 1623 that the commission against George Sinclair, fifth Earl of Caithness, was finally put into effect by Sir Robert Gordon. Even so, he only took action after insisting that the names of Sir Donald MacKay of Strathnaver, Sir Alexander Gordon, who was his brother, and James Sinclair of Murkle should all be added to the document.

Expedition against the Earl of Caithness

Sir Robert Gordon evidently had the full cooperation of Lord Berriedale in proceeding with his commission against his father, George Sinclair, fifth Earl of Caithness. Indeed, Lord Berriedale was first sent north to Caithness where he found his father preparing to make a final stand in Ackergill Castle which he had fortified with men, munitions and food. Sir Robert Gordon now prepared to advance into Caithness with his own forces, but no sooner had he reached Berriedale than he received a message that George Sinclair, fifth Earl of Caithness, had fled north to take refuge in Orkney, hoping eventually to reach Norway or Denmark.

Sir Robert Gordon now proceeded to march through Caithness, accepting the submission of various gentlemen and the surrender first of Girnigoe Castle, then of Ackergill Castle and finally of Keiss Castle, without a shot being fired. After accepting the keys to all these castles, he gave them to Lord Berriedale, who held them for the Crown. Afterwards, Lord Berriedale was allowed to administer his father's estates. He died before his father, and was succeeded by his son John Sinclair, Master of Berriedale. However, he died of a fever in 1639 while his grandfather was still alive. Indeed, George Sinclair, fifth Earl of Caithness, only died in 1643 at the age of seventy-eight, leaving his great-grandson George Sinclair to succeed him as the sixth Earl of Caithness. By then, the Gordons, Earls of Sutherland, were supreme in the north, especially after they had espoused the cause of the National Covenant in the years after 1638.

Chapter Eleven

PERSECUTION OF CLAN GREGOR

Soon after James VI had started to rule in his own right after reaching the age of twenty-one in 1587, Parliament passed an Act requiring all landlords, bailies and clan chieftains to enter into a 'General Band'. This required them to find sureties, proportional to their wealth and the size of their estates, for the peaceable and orderly behaviour of their tenants and other adherents. Such a policy may well have been intended to fill the power vacuum that evidently existed in the Highlands during these years, but it eventually forced many of the Highland chieftans into debt and bankruptcy. The Act listed by name more than a hundred landlords and bailies in the Highlands and Islands where 'broken men have dwelt, or presently dwell', and the names of more than thirty clans who lived on the lands of various proprietors but followed their own 'captains' or chieftains, often 'against the will of their landlords'.

Chief among these 'broken men' were the MacGregors, originally of Glenorchy. They mostly lived upon the lands granted out by feudal charter to the Stewarts, Menzies, Murrays, Robertsons and Campbells, while scorning to give any allegiance to these alien chiefs. It is not certain that they were among the 'great thieves, outlaws, robbers, common sorners upon the lieges, cut-throats, murderers, [and] slayers of men's wives and their children', as the accomplices of the MacFarlanes were described in 1544 after a raid upon Luss. But they certainly disturbed the king's peace greatly during the late sixteenth century. They occupied a strategic position on the very fringes of the Highlands. It gave them easy access to the rich lands of the Lowlands, where 'all men take their prey', while allowing them to seek refuge when harried in their remote sanctuaries around the head of Loch Katrine or even farther north in Glenlyon and Rannoch. However, they were partly forced into such lawless activities by the feudal processes which had deprived them of their ancestral lands in favour of the Campbells of Glenorchy.

Early History of Clan Gregor

The early history of the MacGregors is very obscure, although it is hoped that a recent study yet to be published will clarify their origins. They had once occupied the 'three glens', usually identified as Glenorchy, Glenstrae and Glenlochy, lying to the north and east of Dalmally at the head of Loch Awe, perhaps as early as the thirteenth century. Indeed, an ancestor may well be recognised in John of Glenorchy. His lands were listed as lying within the sheriffdom of Argyll, erected by John Balliol in 1292, and he later signed the Ragman Rolls of allegiance to Edward I of England in 1296. According to *The Book of the Dean of Lismore*, John of Glenorchy was descended from Hugh of Glenorchy, whose son Giolla Faolain, or 'Servant of St Fillan', evidently had some connection with the Celtic monastry of St Fillan in Glendochart.

Misfortune later struck the family in the fourteenth century when the senior branch of the family died out in the male line, leaving only an heiress Mariota. She was married to John Campbell, identified by *The Scots Peerage* as a younger son of Sir Colin Campbell of Lochawe. They received a royal grant of the lands of Glenorchy in 1357, so perhaps even then Glenorchy was held by the Campbells as part of their barony of Lochawe granted to them by King Robert the Bruce in 1315. Seemingly, Mariota and her husband left no children to succeed them at their deaths, since Glenorchy came to be held by another branch of the MacGregors. It was most likely founded by Gregor, younger brother of Mariota's grandfather Malcolm, and himself the great-grandson of John of Glenorchy. Living in Glenorchy around the middle of the fourteenth century, it seems Gregor was the eponymous founder of Clan Gregor.

Loss of Glenorchy

Gregor's descendants did not hold Glenorchy for very long since his direct line had died out by 1432. Sir Duncan Campbell of Lochawe, grandfather of the first Earl of Argyll, then granted out these lands to his younger son Sir Colin Campbell of Glenorchy, ancestor of the Earls of Breadalbane. Their strategic importance was recognised not long afterwards in 1440 when Colin Campbell built Kilchurn Castle at the head of Loch Awe to safeguard his territories. It was the start of a steady expansion to the east, which eventually saw his family holding much of Breadalbane around Loch Tay. Meanwhile, the lands of Glenstrae to the west of Glenorchy were still held by Gregor's younger grandson Iain Dubh MacGregor and his descendants. Now recognised as the chiefs of Clan Gregor, they continued to make defiant claims to their ancient possessions in Glenorchy, now bolstered by their belief that they were descended from the ancient kings of Scotland.

The loss of Glenorchy meant that the clan now became widely scattered as it grew in size. Just as the Campbells of Glenorchy expanded east into Breadalbane, especially during the early years of the sixteenth century, so did the MacGregors infiltrate the more remote districts lying farther north to the east of Glenstrae. They gained holdings in Glenlyon and Rannoch as well as farther south around Loch Tay and Fortingall. It was also perhaps around this time that another branch of the family settled farther south around Balquhidder. They came to occupy the upper reaches of the remote glens lying between Ben More and Ben Lomond to the east of Loch Lomond and Glen Falloch beyond Loch Voil, Loch Katrine and Loch Ard. But if they held these lands under alien landlords who received their rents, they still owed their allegiance to their own chief, MacGregor of Glenstrae.

Disorder among the MacGregors

Meanwhile, the senior line of Iain Dubh MacGregor died out in 1519 when another Iain MacGregor was recognised as the laird of Glenstrae by Colin Campbell, third Earl of Argyll, acting as his feudal superior. He was no doubt favoured by the Campbells since he was married to Helen, younger daughter of Sir Colin Campbell of Glenorchy. Descended from the younger son of Iain Dubh MacGregor, he was not accepted by all of Clan Gregor. Indeed, he had a rival in the person of Duncan Ladasach MacGregor, meaning 'Lordly', who was perhaps descended from yet another grandson of the eponymous founder of Clan Gregor. He embarked on a lawless career from the safety of Rannoch, keeping all of Perthshire in fear of his exploits. It reached a climax in 1545 when he abducted Robertson of Struan from his house at Trochry in Strath Braan, which he then put to the flames. At his side was Iain Mac-Gregor's son Alasdair, now recognised as the laird of Glenstrae after his father's death in 1528. Alasdair MacGregor of Glenstrae fought against the English at the Battle of Pinkie in 1547 but died soon afterwards. Duncan Ladasach then became Tutor to Gregor Roy MacGregor, Alasdair's younger brother, who was still a minor.

Meanwhile, Colin Campbell, after succeeding as the great-grandson of Sir Colin Campbell of Glenorchy in 1550, began to take bonds of manrent from his MacGregor tenants in Breadalbane, hoping to weaken their allegiance to their own chief of Glenstrae. After Duncan Ladasach MacGregor had murdered one such tenant for threatening the independence of Clan Gregor, he was caught and executed in 1552. After this show of strength, several other MacGregor tenants entered into bonds of manrent with Colin Campbell of Glenorchy. He became convinced that it was only the presence of their chief in Glenstrae that prevent him from receiving the full allegiance of his MacGregor tenants.

Eviction from Glenstrae

Accordingly, he purchased in 1554 the superiority of Glenstrae from Archibald Campbell, Master of Argyll and afterwards fifth Earl of Argyll. Then, when Gregor Roy MacGregor came of age in 1560, Colin Campbell of Glenorchy refused to recognise him as his tenant. It may well be that Gregor Roy MacGregor, resenting the change in superiority, neglected to take the legal formalities necessary to register his tenancy or disdained to pay the feudal duties due to his superior so long as he remained in undisputed possession of Glenstrae. The next ten years saw Gregor Roy MacGregor waging what was a private war against Colin Campbell of Glenorchy. Almost immediately, the MacGregor tenants in Breadalbane renounced their bonds of manrent with their Campbell superior in favour of their own chief. Then, when Gregor Roy MacGregor himself murdered a Campbell in 1563, he was outlawed. He thus became the mere leader of other outlaws and 'broken men', without any land. Eventually, Gregor Roy MacGregor was captured and beheaded at Kenmore in 1570 after he had joined the surviving sons of Duncan Ladasach in murdering two Stewart brothers at Balquhidder. His widow Marion mourned his death: 'They poured his blood upon the ground; oh, had I a cup, I would drink of it my fill', and his clansmen laid waste to Glenorchy in revenge.

Meanwhile, Colin Campbell of Glenorchy was active in Rannoch, after receiving a commission to oust the MacGregor tenants of Sir James Menzies in favour of the Camerons of Locheil and the MacDonalds of Keppoch. Indeed, Glenorchy obviously hoped to hold these lands in place of Sir James Menzies, who could only complain to Mary Stuart, Queen of Scots, that Colin Campbell of Glenorchy was exceeding his powers. By now, other members of the Campbell family had joined him in acting against the MacGregors, and their high-handed conduct was drawing protests from other proprietors who felt themselves threatened as well.

Effect of the 1587 Act

Gregor Roy MacGregor was succeeded in 1570 by his young son Alasdair who was still a minor. Until he came of age, his uncle Hugh MacGregor acted as Tutor to the clan under the patronage of Sir John Campbell of Cawdor, so gaining some respite for Clan Gregor. However, when he came of age in 1588, Alasdair MacGregor failed to secure his possession of Glenstrae after Duncan Dubh Campbell, now the chief of Glenorchy, had blocked his attempts at legal action to gain his tenancy. Indeed, there was every incentive for landed proprietors to evict any tenants who did not accept their own authority under the Act passed the previous year in 1587, since it made such landowners responsible for the actions of their tenants.

Legal steps were now taken by Duncan Campbell of Glenorchy to evict Alasdair MacGregor from his lands of Glenstrae. Other landlords acted in just the same way against their MacGregor tenants elsewhere in the Highlands. The act itself thus had almost the opposite effect than intended, since it created even more bands of outlaws and 'broken men' who had no other recourse than robbery to support themselves. Many were sheltered by neighbouring landowners in what became known in Scots law as 'resetting'. They acted not just from a sense of humanity but for other reasons as well. Indeed, they often found it convenient to employ these outlaws in prosecuting their own feuds against their neighbours, since such actions could easily be disowned if they were discovered.

Murder of the King's Forester

Thus cheated of what he considered his rightful inheritance, and bitterly resentful, Alasdair MacGregor after coming of age was almost immediately faced by a serious crisis in the affairs of Clan Gregor. It arose from the murder in 1589 of John Drummond, the king's under-forester in Glen Artney. He had apparently ill-treated if not hanged some MacGregors whom he had caught poaching, so it was obviously an act of revenge. The crime itself was committed by the descendants of Duncan Ladasach, known simply as MacEagh, or 'Children of the Mist'. Matters were made far worse when the murderers cut off their victim's head, and brought it to their chief at Balquhidder. There, Alasdair MacGregor in the presence of all his clansmen took upon himself the blood-guilt of the murderers by laying his hand upon the dead man's head, as did all his followers.

Commission against Clan Gregor

A commission was now issued to George Gordon, sixth Earl of Huntly, and Archibald Campbell, seventh Earl of Argyll, among others. They were to arrest 139 persons of the name of MacGregor, using whatever means were necessary. They were given legal powers to confiscate all the lands and property of those named, and to divide the proceeds. The king was to receive half, while the other half went to reward the person making the arrest. Even so, it was left to Duncan Dubh Campbell of Glenorchy, assisted by the Drummonds, to seek out the fugitives.

Their efforts were greatly thwarted by their neighbours, who naturally enough objected to their territories being entered by bands of armed men whether or not they had a Commission of Fire and Sword against the rebels. Furthermore, the MacGregor outlaws were sheltered by the Earl of Atholl and Sir James Menzies, while some even found refuge in Argyll under the protection of Sir John Campbell of Cawdor. Indeed, Cawdor eventually obtained a remission for Alasdair MacGregor and his clansmen, pardoning them for all their crimes, just a month before he was himself murdered in 1592 as already recounted.

Alasdair MacGregor now held his clan together for the next ten years without offending against the king's peace, but in the end his efforts came to nothing. Already, landlords had started to evict any MacGregor tenants from their lands in order to rid themselves of any liability under the General Band of 1587. Indeed, even Alasdair MacGregor was threatened with losing his lands in Rannoch. Equally, he was required to find lowlanders to stand surety, not just for his own good conduct, but for the good behaviour of his clansmen as well. But it was almost impossible to get anyone of substance to take the financial risk. Lacking such sureties, he was required in 1596 to surrender hostages from the three principal MacGregor families to be relieved at stated intervals.

When he failed to do so, perhaps suspecting the good faith of the government, another commission was given in 1601 to Archibald Campbell, seventh Earl of Argyll. He was entrusted with very wide powers to deal with 'the wicked and unhappy race of the Clan Gregor, who so long have continued in blood, theft, reiving and oppression'. Now solely responsible for administering justice over all the MacGregors, Archibald Campbell received within a month a bond of good conduct from Alasdair MacGregor. Yet, little more than a year later, the Earl of Argyll was ordered by the Privy Council to forfeit the surety of 20,000 merks that he had previously surrendered for the good behaviour of Clan Gregor following a complaint from Alexander Colquhoun of Luss. Indeed, the government now apparently suspected Archibald Campbell, seventh Earl of Argyll, of using Clan Gregor as pawns in pursuing his own private feuds.

Raid against Colquhoun of Luss

Indeed, after he had come of age, and survived the plot against him, Archibald Campbell, seventh Earl of Argyll, was involved in a bitter dispute with Ludovic Stewart, second Duke of Lennox, over their powers of jurisdiction. Ranged against the Earl of Argyll in supporting the Duke of Lennox were the MacAulays of Ardincaple and Colquhouns of Luss, as well as the Buchanans and the Galbraiths. They had evidently decided upon a united front, despite their own private quarrels with one another. Alasdair

MacGregor was later to charge that the seventh Earl of Argyll had persuaded Alasdair's own brother Iain Dubh and two of his cousins, sons of the late Tutor of Glenstrae, to mount a raid against the lands of Alexander Colquhoun of Luss after he had himself refused to do so.

Plundering forty-five houses in Glenfinlas, they carried off 300 cows, 100 horses and mares, 800 sheep and goats and many household goods, while two men were slain and many more wounded. Colquhoun of Luss was tired of such raids which had steadily been growing more formidable. Indeed, his father had been killed by MacGregors in 1592, while his family had lost cattle, horses, oxen, sheep and goats valued at £155,501 0s 8d. in the five years from 1590 to 1594. Colquhoun of Luss was therefore easily persuaded by friends to appear before James VI at Stirling, backed up by as many women as there were men wounded or killed, each carrying a blood-stained shirt. James VI, notoriously averse to the sight of blood, promptly gave him a sweeping Commission of Fire and Sword against the MacGregors.

Battle of Glen Fruin

What now persuaded Alasdair MacGregor to mount yet another raid against Colquhoun of Luss, which ended at the Battle of Glen Fruin in February 1603, remains a mystery. However, it is possible that the Earl of Argyll secretly encouraged him, offended that Colquhoun of Luss had infringed his own monopoly of power in accepting the Commission of Fire and Sword against Clan Gregor. Even so, Alasdair MacGregor may well have hoped to mount a pre-emptive strike before any action could be taken against him. In any event, he swept south from Rannoch, gathering 300 men on the way, including some Camerons of Lochiel and MacDonalds of Glencoe. Colquhoun of Luss had the support of his own tenants as well as the burgesses of Dumbarton and the Buchanans, but he was defeated with severe losses, said to amount to eighty dead and many more wounded, despite the numerical superiority of his own forces. Indeed, the MacGregors seemingly lost only Alasdair's brother Iain Dubh from among their principal kinsmen and otherwise suffered few casualties. Evidently, the advantage of surprise lay with the MacGregors, but whether they gained their victory by strategy or subterfuge does not emerge from the conflicting accounts of the battle. But it was a fatal victory, which brought about the final downfall of Clan Gregor.

Proscription of the Name

The MacGregors had displayed such a powerful contempt for authority after all the attempts made to reduce them to obedience that the government was forced to take drastic action. Indeed, James VI regarded it as an intolerable insult that such an affray should occur within twelve miles of Dumbarton only a few weeks before he succeeded to the throne of Elizabeth I of England. He seemed quite unable to govern Scotland, let alone England, while the pretensions of Clan Gregor to be descended from Kenneth macAlpin, King of the Picts and the Scots, may well have fomented the king's own insecurities. Whatever the reason, he decreed that: 'God cannot be appeased, nor the country relieved of the slander which it sustains by that barbarity, unless that unhappy and detestable race be extirpated and rooted out.'

Rewards of up to 1,000 pounds, according to rank, were immediately offered for the capture of Alasdair MacGregor and all his followers, dead or alive. Only a few weeks later, the very name of MacGregor was proscribed. Every member of Clan Gregor was forced under penalty of death to take another surname, most likely that of the landowners who still sheltered them. No signature of a MacGregor and no agreement bearing such a signature was to have any legal force. No minister was to baptise a male child with the name of MacGregor. Ten years later, it was forbidden in 1613 for more than four members of the clan to meet together, again under the penalty of death. In 1621 they were likewise forbidden the possession of any weapon except a knife to cut their meat, provided it had no point. Anyone slaying a MacGregor was to be rewarded with a nineteen-year lease of the dead man's lands.

Execution of Alasdair MacGregor

As for Alasdair MacGregor of Glenstrae, he managed to evade capture for nearly a year after the Battle of Glen Fruin before he was eventually caught. After managing to escape from a boat carrying him to Inveraray, he then surrendered in person to Archibald Campbell, seventh Earl of Argyll, acting it is said on the advice of Campbell of Auchinbreck. The Earl of Argyll agreed to give him a safe-conduct to England, where he hoped to plead his case with James VI. However, he was only taken as far as Berwick, technically on English soil, before he was brought back to Edinburgh to face trial for high treason. The outcome was hardly in doubt despite the suggestion that he should be allowed to emigrate to the colonies with his clansmen.

However, Alasdair MacGregor now sought to implicate the Earl of Argyll in all his actions, charging him with 'falsity and invention'. Indeed, if we are to believe his confession, the Earl of Argyll was behind nearly all the serious misdemeanours he had committed, except perhaps the raid that ended at Glen Fruin. Yet as the Earl of Argyll was Justice-General of Scotland, it is hardly surprising that Alasdair MacGregor was found guilty of treason and hanged at the Mercat Cross in Edinburgh in January 1604 along with four of his followers. A special gallows was erected in the form of a cross, and 'himself being chief, he was hanged his own height above the rest of his friends'. Much less creditable was the summary execution of six or seven hostages that Alasdair MacGregor had earlier surrendered to the government as pledges for his own good conduct. They were hanged at the same time as their chief 'without the knowledge of the assize', even if they were 'reputed honest for their own parts'. Another twenty-five or thirty MacGregors had been brought to trial by May 1604, since it seems few were taken alive. Nearly all of them were also condemned to death.

Commission to 'Lay Mercy Aside'

The years after 1604 saw a lull in the persecution of Clan Gregor which lasted until early in 1611, when James VI ordered a renewed assault against its leading members who still remained at liberty. Then, every able-bodied man between sixteen and sixty in Lennox and the surrounding districts was ordered to assemble so that boats could be carried from Loch Lomond to capture these 'wolves and thieves . . . within their own den and hole' on Eilean Mharnoch in Loch Katrine. Even so, a large number of outlawed MacGregors managed to escape from the island during a blizzard. Breaking out from their refuge and no doubt recruiting as they went, they laid waste to the country as far east as Comrie and Fortingall and as far west as Loch Awe. Eventually they were driven north beyond Rannoch and scattered by Campbell forces.

James VI now renewed his commission to the Earl of Argyll. He was 'to lay mercy aside, and by justice and the sword to root out and extirpate all of that race'. To defray the expenses of his new commission, while rewarding him for all the trouble involved, the Earl of Argyll was granted the life-rents of all the lands confiscated to the Crown which had previously been held by the MacGregors, along with all the other profits of justice. No doubt it provided him with a useful source of income, since his earlier services against the MacDonalds in Kintyre had been undertaken at his own expense and he was now faced with serious debts.

Already, James VI 'in his customary disposition to clemency and mercy', had decreed a free pardon to any MacGregor who would betray his own kinsmen. They were required to bring in the head of another clansman of the same name, equal in rank to his own, or 'two, three, or four [heads] of them which in comparison may be equal to him, and assuredly known to be his deed'. Rewarded with the dead man's possessions or by the payment of blood-money, he then had to change his name and find surety for his future obedience to the Crown. By such means, it seems that nearly all the

MacGregors of any consequence had been captured or killed by 1613, when it was reported to the Privy Council that only around twenty of the principal clansmen remained at liberty, the rest being 'but unworthy, poor, miserable bodies [persons]'.

But while it was intended to encourage the loyalty and obedience of those MacGregors otherwise liable to be coerced into rebellion by their own chieftains, it was a policy open to abuse. It often resulted in the pardon of well-known malefactors such as Robert Abrach, grandson of Duncan Ladasach, who was deemed worthy of a pardon if he brought in half a dozen heads, and who even visited James VI in London to offer his services against his own clansmen. Duncan Dubh Campbell of Glenorchy protested that Robert Abrach had lately raided his lands and murdered several of his tenants and their wives and children, while leaving others to die of cold after burning down their houses. Nevertheless, he received a pardon from James VI. Changing his name to Ramsay and finding surety for his own good conduct, Robert Abrach afterwards sought refuge with Clan Chattan. He resumed a lawless life when he was used by MacIntosh to attack Lord Gordon. Eventually, after taking to a life of banditry in the Lennox, he was so hard-pressed that he was forced to surrender at Perth. There, he 'fell down upon his knees, having a tow about his neck, and offered his sword by the point to the Chancellor of Scotland'. Placed in ward, he afterwards served James VI in fighting his wars overseas, along with many other MacGregors.

Treatment of Women and Children

While the declared purpose of the government to destroy Clan Gregor was largely achieved in the years after 1603, it still had to deal with the clan's women and children. The proposal was even made that the wives of any MacGregors evicted from their homes should be branded on the face and transported overseas, while any sons over the age of fourteen should be sent to Ireland as herdsboys, there to remain under penalty of death. Apparently, since daughters were thought less capable of mischief, it did not matter to the government what happened to them. However, wiser counsels prevailed since it was thought unfair to treat children with such severity, being innocent of any crime owing to their youth and especially if their parents had submitted to the king's peace by changing their names and finding caution for their own good behaviour.

Indeed, the persons who had given sureties for the MacGregors protested that they could not be held responsible for the parents' behaviour if their children were not treated leniently. Eventually, it was decided that any sons of dispossessed MacGregors should be distributed among the local landowners until they reached the age of eighteen, when they were to be exhibited before the Privy Council. Any boy who escaped over the age of fourteen was to be hanged. However, he would only be branded and scourged if he were under this age, unless he escaped for a second time when he too would be hanged.

Survival of the MacGregors

Despite such persecution, however, the MacGregors were broken but not utterly destroyed like the MacLeods of Lewis or the MacDonalds of Dunivaig and the Glens. They survived largely by 'resetting' or taking refuge with other landlords and clan chiefs. Given the penalties decreed by the Privy Council, it may seem surprising that many proprietors were prepared to take the serious risk of sheltering such outlaws, but there were powerful motives at work. Often, it offered them better protection from the lawless activities of Clan Gregor than the government could ever provide. Equally, 'resetting' often proved profitable to such landlords, who doubtless turned a blind eye to any raids launched from their own territories. Indeed, they may well have incited such raids in the first place, especially if they were directed against their own enemies. They were able to demand a share from the spoil of these raids, or they could even let their farms at exhorbitant rents which could only be afforded by those MacGregors who had such spoils to hand. Indeed, Sir Duncan Campbell of Glenorchy even entered into bonds of manrent with the more favoured of the MacGregor chieftains, who were required in return to make extortionate payments to this self-confessed 'blackest laird in all the land'.

But just as important to these landed proprietors was the convenience of having a ready supply of desperate men as their adherents, willing to engage in hazardous enterprises on their behalf or able to defend them from their enemies given the disturbed state of the country. Yet arguably among their various motives in harbouring the MacGregors 'the most widespread of all and most creditable were the promptings of common humanity, which make the records of the large sums collected from resetters of all classes throughout all the Highland counties the brightest page in the MacGregor history', to quote the words of Audrey Cunningham in *The Loyal Clans*. Even Sir Duncan Campbell of Glenorchy subsequently paid out more than £14,000 in compensation to leading members of Clan Gregor whom he had deprived of their lands in Lorne and Breadalbane.

The Final Reckoning

Indeed, when the final reckoning came to be made in 1624, several years after the Earl of Argyll had gone into exile, the enormous sum of 115,068 pounds had been raised in fines against those who had sheltered the MacGregors. The list was headed by the Laird of Grant, who had to pay a staggering 27,000 pounds, while Ruairi MacKenzie, Tutor of Kintail, was fined 4,000 pounds. However, not all the money could be collected and remissions against others reduced the amount to 77,271 pounds. The expenses of collection were also very substantial, while rewards for 'heads' had to be paid. The sums of 1,000 pounds were each paid to Campbell of Lawers, MacDonald of Clan Ranald and Cameron of Locheil. There were also other expenses such as the sum of 100 pounds paid out to Archibald Armstrong for attending His Majesty's service against the MacGregors with 'large dogs' used to hunt them down. All these outgoings reduced the final sum to 44,665 pounds, of which James VI received just over 10,000 pounds.

Subsequent Fortunes of Clan Gregor

Alasdair MacGregor left no sons at his execution in 1604 to succeed him as clan chief, while the government had custody of his three nephews, sons of his brother Iain Dubh who had been killed at the Battle of Glen Fruin. They took the name of Murray after they had found surety from Murray of Tullibardine. Duncan Dubh Campbell of Glenorchy was then allowed to enter the eldest boy as his tenant in Glenstrae in 1620, but only so that he could buy out his rights to Glenstrae for the sum of 10,000 pounds with the agreement of his two other brothers. Thus, Glenorchy gained a legal title to the lands of Glenstrae, while the MacGregors were at least compensated for their loss. When Patrick Roy Murray succeeded his elder brother as head of the family, he took the title of Laird of MacGregor although it was still illegal. By 1641, he was strong enough to demand back from Menzies the ancient lands of his family at the western end of Loch Rannoch. When this was refused, he simply occupied these lands by force of arms, collecting rents and other duties from the tenants.

Indeed, when Montrose first launched his campaign against Archibald Campbell, eighth Earl and first Marquis of Argyll, on behalf of Charles I in 1644, the MacGregors rallied to the Royalist cause. Their support for the Stuart kings during the Civil Wars was sufficient for the penal laws against them to be lifted in 1661 after the restoration of Charles II, even though they did not receive back a legal title to any of their lands. Even so, their support for the Jacobite cause after the 'Glorious Revolution' of 1688 meant that they were penalised again in 1693, and it was only in 1774 that these laws were finally revoked.

Chapter Twelve

SETTLEMENT OF
TERRITORIAL DISPUTES

Even as Clan Gregor was being persecuted and their name proscribed, attempts were made to settle once and forever the territorial disputes in the Highlands and Western Isles of Scotland that had so disturbed the king's peace over the previous half-century. As already recounted, Angus MacDonald of Dunivaig and the Glens first lost his lands in Kintyre to Archibald Campbell, seventh Earl of Argyll. He then mortgaged his Islay estates to Sir John Campbell of Cawdor, who managed to gain possession of these lands after the abortive rebellion of Sir James MacDonald in 1615. The ancient line of the MacDonalds of Dunivaig and the Glens finally became extinct in 1626 when Sir James MacDonald died in London leaving no heirs to succeed him. The MacLeods of Lewis also became extinct around the same time after Sir Kenneth MacKenzie of Kintail had acquired the island of Lewis from the Fife Adventurers in 1610. The extinction of both these families effectively brought the struggle over their lands to an end as they passed into other hands. But there were many other territorial disputes which remained to be settled.

MacLeods of Harris and Dunvegan

Even if Ruairi Mor MacLeod of Harris and Dunvegan had forfeited his lands of Harris, Dunvegan and Glenelg in 1598, he managed to keep hold of his estates against all the odds. He was fortunate that the Fife Adventurers, who first received a charter to his lands in 1598, determined upon Lewis as their first objective. Their ultimate failure to colonise the island was greatly to his benefit. However, he was still threatened by the aggrandisement of Kenneth MacKenzie of Kintail. The MacKenzie chief had not only acquired the island of Lewis from the Fife Adventurers in 1609, but the district of Waternish as well which had originally belonged to the MacLeods of Lewis. However,

Ruairi Mor MacLeod had a legal title to two unciates of land in Trotternish. These he now exchanged for the five unciates of land in Waternish held by Kenneth MacKenzie of Kintail, paying him 9,000 merks to complete the bargain. Even so, he was still faced with a long-standing dispute over Glenelg with the Frasers of Lovat, while he also had a claim to the lands of Trotternish now held by the MacDonalds of Sleat.

Feud with the Frasers over Glenelg

Glenelg originally came into the hands of the MacLeods of Harris and Dunvegan or their distant ancestors when it was still part of the ancient Kingdom of Man. Later, the lands were divided into three parts, and somehow the Frasers of Lovat came to hold a third by the early years of the fifteenth century at the very latest. Although it is said that Leod's son Tormod, progenitor of the MacLeods of Harris and Dunvegan, married Christina Fraser, daughter of the Lord of Lovat, it seems that the two families regarded one another with hostility. Indeed, according to the MacLeods, a battle was fought against the Frasers near Broadford on the Isle of Skye in the years after 1320, while they seemingly raided the Fraser lands of the Aird in the years after 1392. Then, early in the sixteenth century, Alasdair Crotach MacLeod, Chief of Harris and Dunvegan, seized the third of Glenelg belonging to Lord Fraser of Lovat and refused for many years to send him any rents. An attempt was eventually made in 1540 to resolve this dispute by a matrimonial alliance between the two families. However, it did not succeed as only a daughter was born of the marriage between Agnes Fraser, daughter of Lord Fraser of Lovat, and William MacLeod, son and heir of Alasdair Crotach MacLeod of Harris and Dunvegan.

The lack of a male heir to this marriage meant in effect that the MacLeods of Harris and Dunvegan remained in forceful possession of Glenelg until 1611, despite the occasional incursion by the Frasers, weakened as they were by their defeat at Blar-na-Leine in 1544. However, Ruairi Mor MacLeod, Chief of Harris and Dunvegan, had by then placed himself under the protection of Archibald Campbell, seventh Earl of Argyll, alarmed that the Fife Adventurers had been granted yet another charter to his lands of Harris, Dunvegan and Glenelg. We do not know exactly what was agreed between the two men since no documents survive. However, it is certain that Ruairi Mor MacLeod agreed to hold the lands of Glenelg under the superiority of the Earl of Argyll. However, after the signing of the Statutes of Iona, the question of Glenelg was raised by Simon, sixth Lord Fraser of Lovat, and the matter sent to arbitration. It was decided that all of Glenelg belonged to Ruairi Mor MacLeod of Harris and Dunvegan, but that he owed Lord Fraser of Lovat the sum of 12,000 merks for the non-payment of rents and other duties over the last century. Rather surprisingly, he had managed to make a payment of 4,000 merks by 1612.

Ruairi Mor MacLeod of Harris and Dunvegan had already succeeded in gaining a sweeping pardon for all his crimes from James VI in 1610, excepting only treason and witchcraft. By submitting to the king's authority at Iona, and perhaps backed at Court by Archibald Campbell, seventh Earl of Argyll, he then received in 1611 a new charter to the lands of Glenelg to be held under the superiority of the Earl of Argyll, as well as his lands of Harris, Minginish, Bracadale and Lyndale, the Castle of Dunvegan and the district of Waternish. They were all erected into the barony of Dunvegan. It was in effect a renewal of the charter that his forbears had received from James IV in 1498.

Accommodation with MacDonald of Sleat

Thereafter, Ruairi Mor MacLeod of Harris and Dunvegan gained steadily in royal favour, and he was knighted in 1613 after he had surrendered Neil MacLeod of Lewis to the Privy Council. Indeed, he evidently felt strong enough in 1615 to renew his claim to the lands of Sleat, Trotternish and North Uist which had been granted in 1542 to his grandfather, Alasdair Crotach. However, the MacLeods were never able to occupy them against the opposition of the MacDonalds of Sleat. He now used all his diplomatic wiles with masterly effect to ingratiate himself with the king, and indeed had himself served heir to his uncle in the lands under dispute. However, he could finally achieve little more than a face-saving accommodation with Sir Donald Gorm Og MacDonald, now the young chief of the MacDonalds of Sleat after the death of his uncle in 1617.

Sir Ruairi Mor MacLeod of Harris and Dunvegan joined the young chief of Sleat in resigning into the king's hands all their lands of Sleat and North Uist to which they both held charters. Sir Donald Gorm Og MacDonald of Sleat also surrendered the lands of Clan Ranald in South Uist and Benbecula over which he held the superiority. All these lands were now granted to Sir Donald Gorm Og MacDonald of Sleat, so that he gained a legal title to North Uist. He later received a charter to Trotternish as well after he had paid a certain sum of money in compensation to Sir Ruairi Mor MacLeod of Harris and Dunvegan.

MacDonalds of Clan Ranald

The MacDonalds of Clan Ranald had long disturbed the king's peace in the years before 1609. Indeed, they had virtually remained outside the law ever since the time of John Moydertach and the Battle of Blar-na-Leine in 1544. Nevertheless, when he died in 1584 after ruling over Clan Ranald for fifty-three years, John Moydertach had managed to keep his lands intact by sheer strength of arms, aided by the loyalty of his clan who recognised him as their rightful chief. He was followed as Captain of Clan Ranald by his son Alan. He became embroiled in a feud with the MacLeods of Harris and Dunvegan after he had repudiated his marriage with a daughter of Alasdair Crotach MacLeod. If the massacre on Eigg occurred in 1577, as reported to James VI, it must have been as a consequence of this feud. However, as we have already seen, it probably happened much earlier, along with the battle that supposedly took place three years later in Waternish.

After Alan MacDonald died in 1593, he was followed briefly as Captain of Clan Ranald by his eldest son Angus. He, however, was killed the very next year in the continuing feud with the MacLeods of Harris and Dunvegan. The captaincy of Clan Ranald then passed to his younger brother Donald MacDonald. He was soon engaged in a bitter feud with the MacLeans of Duart, acting in support of his father-in-law, Angus MacDonald of Dunivaig and the Glens, whose daughter Mary he had married. Later in 1601, he allied himself briefly with Donald MacDonald of Glengarry in his feud with Kenneth MacKenzie of Kintail over the lands of Wester Ross. He then returned to South Uist. There he put down with much slaughter the territorial ambitions of the MacNeills of Barra, who had encroached on his lands of Boisdale in the south of the island. Finally in 1606 he came to the assistance of Neil MacLeod of Lewis in his struggle against the Fife Adventurers.

By acceding to the Statutes of Iona in 1609, despite such a treasonable record over the previous years, Donald MacDonald of Clan Ranald was received back into royal favour. In 1610, he was granted a royal charter to his lands of Moidart, Arisaig, Morar, Eigg, South Uist and Benbecula which had originally been granted to his grandfather John Moydertach in 1531. North Uist remained in the hands of Donald Gorm Mor MacDonald of Sleat as already noted, while his son and heir was later granted the superiority over the lands of Clan Ranald in South Uist and Benbecula. Even if he now enjoyed a legal title to his vast estates, Donald MacDonald of Clan Ranald was soon involved in several other disputes. The grandson and heir of Ranald Gallda still had a claim on the lands of Clan Ranald, and he managed to obtain a writ from the Sheriff Court of Inverness after he had been ill-treated in some way. Donald MacDonald of Clan Ranald was even declared a rebel after he had failed to satisfy the Court but the matter was apparently soon forgotten, as so often happened. He was then caused further trouble when his sister married Ruairi MacNeill of Barra, who already had a family born of an earlier union with a daughter of MacLean of Duart.

MacNeills of Barra

The MacNeills of Barra were noted pirates and Ruairi MacNeill's eldest son was no exception. He attacked a ship from Bordeaux, presumably laden with wines and brandy, and killed nearly all its crew. Donald MacDonald of Clan Ranald succeeded in capturing him, early in 1610, but his captive died before he could be brought to trial in Edinburgh. The dead man's brothers by their father's first union later took their revenge by seizing their half-brother Neil MacNeill. He was a nephew of Donald MacDonald of Clan Ranald by his sister's marriage with Ruairi MacNeill of Barra. They then besieged the Castle of Kisimul in 1613 and captured their own father Ruairi MacNeill. They kept him imprisoned in irons, thinking that he evidently favoured their half-brother Neil MacNeill to succeed him as the chief of the MacNeills. However, ordered by the Privy Council to bring their prisoner to Edinburgh, they failed to do so. Donald MacDonald of Clan Ranald was given a commission for their capture. He evidently resolved the family quarrel, since his nephew Neil MacNeill not long afterwards became chief of Barra after the death of his father Ruairi MacNeill.

Ancient Feuds in Lochaber

One territorial dispute which was not settled under King James's peace concerned the MacIntosh claim to the lands of Lochaber, then held by the Camerons of Locheil. It dated back nearly two centuries to 1443, if not even earlier, when the MacIntoshes received a royal charter to the lands of Glenloy and Locharkaig. However, they were never able to gain possession of these lands which they claimed had once belonged to their distant ancestors. The MacIntoshes thus became involved in a protracted and very bitter feud with the Camerons of Locheil, despite the occasional attempt to resolve their dispute by allying their two families together by marriage.

Matters were made worse in the sixteenth century when the Campbells, Earls of Argyll, became the feudal superiors of the Camerons of Locheil, while the MacIntoshes allied themselves with the Gordons, Earls of Huntly, who eventually became their feudal superiors. Indeed, William MacIntosh, Captain of Clan Chattan, joined forces with George Gordon, fourth Earl of Huntly, when he invaded Lochaber in 1546 in revenge for the Battle of Blar-na-Leine, pursuing his own private feud with Ewan Cameron of Locheil. As already recounted, he was executed for high treason after he had been captured, along with Ranald MacDonald of Keppoch. However, William MacIntosh then apparently fell foul of the Earl of Huntly who contrived at his death in 1550.

After the execution of Ewen Cameron, the lands of Locheil were forfeited to the Crown and then granted out to George Gordon, fourth Earl of Huntly. However, Huntly died in 1562 at the Battle of Corrichie, rebelling against the authority of Mary Stuart, Queen of Scots. The Camerons of Locheil did not gain greatly from his death since internecine struggles now broke out within the clan. They lasted until 1577, when Allan Cameron, great-grandson of Ewen Cameron, took command of his clan after coming of age. Even if he was an ardent Protestant, he eventually allied himself in 1590 with George Gordon, sixth Earl of Huntly, in his feud with James Stewart, Earl of Moray, whom the MacIntoshes now supported.

Forfeiture of Locheil

Then, after the murder of the 'Bonnie' Earl of Moray in 1592, the Camerons of Locheil fought for the Earl of Huntly at the Battle of Glenlivet in 1594 against Archibald Campbell, seventh Earl of Argyll. Among Argyll's forces were the MacIntoshes. However, although the Earl of Huntly won the battle, he was soon afterwards forced into exile, and Allan Cameron of Locheil was declared a rebel without any protection. Thus, when James VI required the Highland chieftains and other landowners to attend Parliament in 1597 to exhibit their title deeds, he dared not appear even though he had perfectly good charters to his lands.

His failure to appear resulted in the forfeiture of all his estates which came into the hands of Sir Alexander Hay who then sold them off. The greater part around Locheil was acquired by Hector MacLean of Lochbuie, while Knoydart went to Clan Ranald, Lochalsh to MacKenzie of Kintail and his lands in Glengarry to the MacDonalds of Glengarry. Allan Cameron was only left in possession of the disputed lands of Glenloy and Locharkaig, which were still claimed by Lachlan Mor MacIntosh, Captain of Clan Chattan. He then entered into a contract in 1598, agreeing to occupy half of these lands after paying a mortgage of 6,000 merks to Lachlan MacIntosh. Their agreement was only to last for nineteen years before the lands reverted back to their rightful owner. The other half of these lands of Glenloy and Locharkaig he agreed to hold from Lachlan Mor MacIntosh in return for the service of himself and his tenants.

Hector MacLean of Lochbuie later sold his interest in the lands of Locheil to Archibald Campbell, seventh Earl of Argyll. Quite by accident, he had recently discovered an ancient charter at Inveraray that his predecessors had acquired in 1522 to the lands of Locheil. Allan Cameron had little choice but to accept a charter from the Earl of Argyll to his lands of Locheil. They were to be held under Argyll's superiority, and Allan Cameron was required to pay him the same amount of money as the Earl of Argyll had paid MacLean of Lochbuie. Thus, Allan Cameron effectively bought the superiority over his lands of Locheil from MacLean of Lochbuie which the Earl of Argyll now exercised over him.

Dissension within Clan Cameron

Such aggrandisement by the Earl of Argyll so alarmed George Gordon, sixth Earl of Huntly and now the Marquis of Huntly after his restoration to favour by James VI, that he attempted to sow the seeds of dissension among Allan Cameron's kinsmen. The Marquis of Huntly held the superiority over much of Lochaber, and already during the minority of Allan Cameron as the chief of Locheil much blood had been shed between the different branches of the family as they struggled for supremacy. Matters came to a head in 1613, however, when the machinations of the Marquis of Huntly and his allies were defeated by Allan Cameron. He acted 'like an old, subtle fox, perceiving their drift, and being as careful to preserve his head as they were curious to separate him from it'. Indeed, Allan Cameron managed to reassert his own authority over his clan by drawing the defectors into an ambush, killing twenty of their number, after it had seemed likely that his own party would be attacked.

Commission against Locheil

The Marquis of Huntly and his eldest son, Lord Gordon, after making 'hideous representation' at Court, were now granted a Commission of Fire and Sword against Allan Cameron of Locheil. However, it had little effect since no other chieftain was willing to take arms against him. Indeed, even Lachlan MacIntosh, now chief of Clan Chattan after the death of his grandfather in 1606, refused to join forces with the Marquis of Huntly, since any such action was liable to very severe penalties under the terms of the agreement that his grandfather had made with Allan Cameron in 1598 concerning the lands of Glenloy and Locharkaig. He was even imprisoned in Edinburgh Castle for two years after he had forbidden his clansmen to take service against the old enemy of his family.

It seems that Allan Cameron of Locheil remained an outlaw for several years. Indeed, he forcibly prevented Lachlan MacIntosh in 1616 from holding courts at Inverlochy in his capacity of hereditary steward of Lochaber. Lachlan MacIntosh now declared that Allan Cameron had forfeited any benefit of the agreement drawn up between their families in 1598 and indeed the nineteen years was about to lapse. Faced with this threat from his hereditary enemy, Allan Cameron of Locheil was forced in the circumstances to repair his quarrel with George Gordon, Marquis of Huntly. This he did by surrendering the superiority of many of his lands in Lochaber to Huntly's eldest son, Lord Gordon, including the estates held by John Cameron, his eldest son. Even so, he was still threatened by Lachlan MacIntosh, who indeed invaded Lochaber in 1617 with such a large force that he compelled Allan Cameron to come to terms.

Lachlan MacIntosh and Lord Gordon were now given Commissions of Fire and Sword to proceed against Ranald MacDonald of Keppoch and Allan Cameron of Locheil but without much effect. Stalemate then ensued until 1621, when Allan Cameron of Locheil was described as almost the only chieftain remaining defiant in the Highlands, after he had failed to appear before the Privy Council to find security for his own good conduct. Suspecting that Lord Gordon was not prepared to act with any vigour against his own vassal, Sir Lachlan MacIntosh eventually received yet another charter to the disputed lands of Glenloy and Locharkaig in 1621, and then received a commission in 1622 from James VI in London to proceed against Allan Cameron of Locheil. Given the power to call out twenty-two other chiefs and gentlemen of note throughout the Highlands and Islands, he would surely have succeeded had he not suddenly died at Gartenbeg in Strathspey aged only twenty-nine years. Two years later, Allan Cameron of Locheil was pardoned in 1624 for all his previous offences against the Crown, and after finding surety for his own good conduct he was received back into favour under the same terms as agreed by the other Highland chieftains.

Possession of Glenloy and Locharkaig

The immediate threat to Allan Cameron of Locheil was thus averted, since Lachlan MacIntosh was succeeded in 1622 by his son William, then only nine years of age. His affairs were handled by Sir John Grant of Freuchie, who had no special interest in pursuing the ancient feud between the two families and indeed was friendly with Allan Cameron of Locheil. The dispute over the lands of Glenloy and Locharkaig was submitted to the decision of mutual friends for arbitration. They favoured the MacIntoshes, but Allan Cameron of Locheil was to be paid compensation for the loss of his lands. However, it seems that Sir John Grant of Freuchie then granted yet another mortgage to Allan Cameron of Locheil, and indeed, his descendants continued to occupy the disputed lands until 1664, despite repeated attempts by the Crown to evict them.

By then, Lachlan MacIntosh of Torcastle had gained yet another charter to Glenloy and Locharkaig, even if Cameron of Locheil was prepared to buy him out. It was only the threat of force that finally brought the dispute with the MacIntoshes to an end. After arbitration, Sir Ewen Dubh Cameron of Locheil agreed to pay the huge sum of 72,500 merks to gain possession of the lands of Glenloy and Locharkaig that he and his predecessors had occupied 'past memory of man'. But he was forced to accept the feudal superiority of the Earl of Argyll, who paid the purchase money to Lachlan MacIntosh.

MacIains of Ardnamurchan

The last serious rebellion to occur in the Western Highlands during the reign of James VI ended in 1625 when the MacIains of Ardnamurchan failed in their attempt to throw off the superiority of the Campbells, Earls of Argyll. As we have already recorded, after the Lordship of the Isles was forfeited in 1493, John MacIain of Ardnamurchan had supported the Crown in its attempts to suppress the various rebellions of Clan Donald. However, he was killed at the Battle of Creag-an-Airgid in 1518, leaving a mere child as his only surviving son and heir. Colin Campbell, third Earl of Argyll, was then granted the wardship of young MacIain of Ardnamurchan, and after he had died in 1538, Archibald Campbell, fourth Earl of Argyll, received the superiority of his lands of Ardnamurchan from his sister Mariota. Her nephew Alexander now became chief of the MacIains of Ardnamurchan. He was among the allies of John Moydertach of Clanranald, fighting on his behalf at the Battle of Blar-na-Leine in 1544 as well as aiding the second rebellion of Donald Dubh in 1545. Little more is then heard of Alexander MacIain until his death around 1570, when he was succeeded by his eldest son John MacIain of Ardnamurchan.

John MacIain was a close ally of the MacDonalds of Dunivaig and the Glens in their bitter feud with the MacLeans of Duart, who were themselves allied to the Campbell earls of Argyll, and indeed he suffered greatly as a result. After his death in 1591, he was succeeded by his son John Og MacIain. However, he was assassinated in 1596 by his uncle Donald MacIain, who wished to gain the chiefship of the MacIains of Ardnamurchan for himself. However, Donald MacIain did not gain from the murder of his nephew, despite the support of Lachlan Mor MacLean of Duart. He was killed soon afterwards in Morvern at a place in Gleann Dubh called Leac-nan-Saighead, or 'Rock of the Arrows', when the Camerons of Lochiel rallied against the MacLeans of Duart to revenge the death of John Og MacIain who had been promised in marriage to a daughter of their chief.

Aggrandisement of Argyll

After the death of Donald MacIain in 1596, the chiefship of the MacIains passed to his nephew John MacIain, who was himself the son of Donald's younger brother Alexander. Archibald Campbell, seventh Earl of Argyll, now forced John MacIain of Ardnamurchan to enter into a contract in 1602. It required him to surrender his title deeds into the Earl's hands, who agreed for his part to lease out again the lands of Ardnamurchan to John MacIain as his vassal, while promising at the same time to protect him in possessing these lands. However, it seems only John MacIain fulfilled his part of the bargain. His charter of 1499 to the lands of Ardnamurchan fell into the hands of the Earl of Argyll without his ever receiving another charter in return. Whether the Earl of Argyll simply acted in bad faith or whether John MacIain had meanwhile placed himself beyond the bounds of the law by some treasonable action on his part remains unclear. Thereafter, Archibald Campbell had a legal claim to the lands of Ardnamurchan and the MacIains began their long and desperate struggle for survival.

John MacIain died before 1611, leaving only his young son Alexander to succeed him. During his minority, the affairs of the clan were directed by Donald MacIain, uncle of the young chief and known as the Tutor of Ardnamurchan. Up to this time, it seems that the MacIains kept possession of their lands of Ardnamurchan by force. Now, however, Archibald Campbell, seventh Earl of Argyll, taking advantage of the peaceful conditions in the Highlands, gave a commission to Donald Campbell of Barbreck to exercise his own superiority over their lands while young MacIain of Ardnamurchan was still a minor.

Lease of Ardnamurchan

Donald Campbell of Barbreck was himself the natural son of Sir John Campbell of Cawdor who had been murdered in 1592. Although trained to the Church, and appointed Dean of Lismore, his talents evidently lay elsewhere. Described by Edward Cowan in his account of *Clanship and Campbell Expansion in the Time of Gillesbuig Grumach* as a 'sadly vicious and vindictive character', he had first distinguished himself in the eyes of the Earl of Argyll by zealously seeking to bring his father's murderers to justice. He now reduced the district of Ardnamurchan to obedience, garrisoning Mingary Castle with his own forces, and then instituted a harsh regime, fixing and collecting rents and punishing or expelling any recalcitrant tenants. Soon afterwards, he received a lease of Ardnamurchan from the Earl of Argyll, while Donald MacIain, Tutor of Ardnamurchan, declared himself an outlaw by supporting Sir James MacDonald of Dunivaig and the Glens in his ill-fated rebellion of 1615.

Simple error or deliberate deceit then intervened. Archibald Campbell, seventh Earl of Argyll, granted Sir Donald MacDonald of Clan Ranald a lease to the lands of Acharacle and Ardtoe lying to the south of Loch Moidart several years before the lease previously granted to Donald Campbell of Barbreck was due to expire. Then, soon after Sir Donald MacDonald died in 1618, his son John MacDonald, now Captain of Clan Ranald although still a minor, raised a force 200 strong and invaded the lands of Ardnamurchan. He was supported by many MacIain clansmen who now acknowledged him as their chief. Together, they plundered the Campbell tenants of their live-stock, and expelled Donald Campbell and his followers.

The following year, however, John MacDonald of Clan Ranald appeared before the Privy Council to renew his father's acceptance of the Statutes of Iona. His dispute over the lands of Acharacle and Ardtoe was settled legally in favour of Donald Campbell of Barbreck, who regained possession of Ardnamurchan while the MacIains bound themselves to obey him as his tenants. But the settlement greatly offended John MacDonald's uncle Ranald MacDonald of Benbecula, who quite possibly coveted the position of Tutor to his young nephew. He now embarked on a lawless career with disaffected elements of the MacDonalds and the MacIains, threatening to 'draw the young gentleman, their chief, under great trouble and inconvenience, and to shake his whole bounds loose'.

Rebellion of MacIain of Ardnamurchan

Alexander MacIain of Ardnamurchan only came of age in 1622, and he pledged himself to recover his lands by law if possible but by force if need be. Then, two years later, he placed himself at the head of his clansmen in open rebellion against the Crown. Drawn into the insurrection were Sir Ruairi Mor MacLeod of Harris and Dunvegan, John MacDonald of Clan Ranald and Lachlan MacLean of Coll. They had earlier bound themselves to Donald Campbell of Barbreck that they would answer for the peaceful behaviour of his MacIain tenants. Ordered to surrender Alexander MacIain and his chief kinsmen to the Privy Council, these three chieftains were denounced as rebels when they failed to do so. By then, Alexander MacIain and more than a hundred of his followers had taken to a life of piracy after seizing an English ship. The Privy Council learnt that they were terrorising the whole seaboard of the Western Highlands north of Islay, plundering any ships they were able to capture and cruelly and barbarously slaying their crews.

Faced with this threat to shipping, the Privy Council in 1625 dispatched a ship and a pinnace to the Western Isles. Lord Lorne, eldest son of Archibald Campbell, seventh Earl of Argyll, who was now in exile, was given a Commission of Fire and Sword to suppress the rebellion, along with four of his kinsmen. He first pursued the rebels to Skye before they were driven to seek refuge among their kinsmen in Moidart by Sir Ruairi Mor MacLeod of Harris and Dunvegan. Around a hundred settled there with their families under the protection of John MacDonald, Captain of Clan Ranald. It was reported favourably in Edinburgh that Lord Lorne had executed ten of the ringleaders, slain another six and brought another fourteen to the capital for trial.

Exactly how the rebellion ended is not clear but Alexander MacIain evidently survived its aftermath. Indeed, he may well have been compensated for the loss of his lands, given that he paid in 1629 what was then the large sum of 40,000 pounds in a bond with Robert Innes, burgess of the Chanonry of Ross. Donald Campbell of Barbreck had by then become the hereditary proprietor of Ardnamurchan, paying a feu-duty of 2,000 merks for his lands. Knighted, he later became known as Sir Donald Campbell of Ardnamurchan. By then, the MacIains of Ardnamurchan had ceased to exist as a separate clan, and Alexander MacIain himself disappears from the historical record in 1633 leaving no evidence of any descendants.

Chapter Thirteen

THE KING'S PEACE

After the Union of the Crowns in 1603 and the defeat in Ulster of Hugh O'Neill of Tyrone, forced into submission just six days after the death in England of Elizabeth I, the tide had started to turn against Gaeldom. Indeed, James VI now had the resources of England behind him, including its formidable navy. No longer could the Gaelic-speaking chieftains of the Western Isles ally themselves with their compatriots in Ulster. Indeed, it was not long before the Earls of Tyrone and Tyrconnell fled abroad in 1607, leaving their vast estates in Ulster to be forfeited by the Crown. Although the large-scale plantation of Ulster did not occur until later, their Catholic tenants were gradually deprived of their lands which were then granted out to Protestant landlords, often from Lowland Scotland. Much the same policy was pursued in Kintyre.

By then, the political balance had shifted decisively against the chieftains of the Highlands and the Western Isles with their Gaelic language and pro-Catholic sympathies. Ever since the Scottish Reformation of 1560, Scotland and England had shared the same Protestant religion, while more recently the Union of the Crowns and the pro-English policies of James VI prior to 1603 meant that they could no longer rely upon England to support them in their disputes with the Scottish Crown.

As already recounted, the growing strength of the Crown was demonstrated in 1608, after Archibald Campbell, seventh Earl of Argyll, was replaced as King's Lieutenant in the Isles by Alexander Stewart, Lord Ochiltree. He was given a commission to mount a formidable expedition against Angus MacDonald of Dunivaig and the Glens, who evidently still intended to keep hold of his possessions on Islay by force. Lord Ochiltree went armed with detailed instructions from the Privy Council concerning the terms to be demanded from the chieftains of the Western Isles. Faced with such a determined show of armed force, they had little choice but to attend a Parliament held at Aros on the island of Mull, after surrendering their castles into the hands of Lord Ochiltree.

However, it was only by a subterfuge that they were all detained on board His Majesty's ship, the *Moon*, and carried off to Edinburgh, apart from Angus MacDonald of Dunivaig and the Glens, who was released under strict instructions regarding his future behaviour, and Ruairi Mor MacLeod of Harris and Dunvegan, who had not allowed himself to fall into such a trap. Suppressing any mention of how they had been captured, Lord Ochiltree wrote to James VI with the good news that all the chiefs now wanted to pledge their most humble obedience to His Majesty.

Andrew Knox in the Western Isles

The Privy Council had already appointed commissioners to the Isles to advise Lord Ochiltree consisting entirely of Lowlanders and headed by Andrew Knox, Bishop of the Isles. He was now to play an important role in the pacification of the Western Isles. After consulting James VI in London, he proposed to mount another expedition to the Western Isles in the autumn of 1609 armed with a detailed plan drawn up in consultation with the Privy Council. This envisaged their peaceful colonisation, essentially by establishing new towns and seaports which it was thought would encourage trade and industry. Existing landlords were expected to remain in possession of their estates without the need for any sweeping confiscation of their lands. However, if the very size of their estates tempted landlords to act independently of the Crown, they would be deprived of some of their lands which would then be granted out to new settlers. Any landlords resisting these changes would be evicted from their estates, while the common people would be allowed to remain on their own holdings.

Bishop Knox was accompanied in 1609 to the Western Isles by Angus MacDonald of Dunivaig and the Glens and Hector MacLean of Duart who was released from captivity in Edinburgh Castle. All the other chieftains were likewise liberated, but only after they had found very substantial sureties that they would return to Edinburgh as required by the Privy Council. They also agreed to assist the King's Commissioner in making a survey of the Western Isles, noting the extent of the king's properties, the names of his tenants and whether the land was cultivated or waste. Presumably they were forced to cooperate with the government, since they only gained their liberty on such conditions. More to the point, they were now bound financially to others for their own good behaviour, and their cautioners would have a claim against their estates if they did not agree to the proposals of the Privy Council.

There can also be little doubt that they were now thoroughly alarmed by the events that had taken place on the island of Lewis. They too might be dispossessed of their lands in the same way, especially as the estates previously forfeited by Ruairi Mor MacLeod of Harris and Dunvegan and by Donald Gorm Mor MacDonald of Sleat had already been granted out to the Fife Adventurers. They must have realised that James VI had the resources needed to conquer the Western Isles, and indeed an expeditionary force from England was already planned to reduce them to obedience.

Statutes of Iona

There is little doubt that Andrew Knox, Bishop of the Isles, pursued what he thought to be the best interests of his Gaelic-speaking parishioners while sharing the same prejudices as James VI against their language and culture. When he reached the Western Isles, Andrew Knox entered into more detailed negotiations with nine of the principal chieftains whom he summoned to a meeting at Iona. However, they then accepted a policy far less drastic than the scheme originally proposed by the Privy Council for the peaceful colonisation of the Western Isles. There would be no interference with their patriarchal authority as the leaders of their clans, nor with their ancient rights of property. In return, they were prepared to accept his authority in the name of the king, especially as they did not suspect him of profiting from his own position as Commissioner to the Isles.

After these deliberations had concluded, the principal chieftains of the Western Isles signed a Band, pledging themselves to obey the king in all matters of Church and State and to obey the laws of the realm. Indeed, the sentiments expressed by this Band of Loyalty acknowledged the religious sanction for all civil government, while recognising the divine right of James VI to rule over his subjects as they indeed ruled over their own clansmen. There were, however, some more specific regulations to be honoured, nine in number. They came to be known as the Statutes of Icolmkille, as the name of Iona was then rendered from the Gaelic I Chaluim Cille. The provisions of the Statutes were greatly strengthened by the Privy Council in 1616 and 1617, and again in 1622 following the rebellion of Sir James MacDonald of Islay which was joined by several of the chieftains present at Iona.

There can be very little doubt that the Statutes of Iona were deeply humiliating to the chieftains who were forced to accept their provisions. But whether or not they marked a 'watershed' or 'turning-point' in Highland history as sometimes claimed, causing in themselves the way of life in the Western Isles to be utterly altered, remains a moot point. Indeed, they are perhaps more symptomatic of impending change rather than being responsible for such changes as actually occurred in the years ahead. They only arose once central government in the name of the Privy Council could bring its power to bear upon the Western Isles. Certainly, there is nothing to suggest that the Statutes of Iona made the Highland clans susceptible to the later claims of the Stuart kings to rule by divine right. Even so, they provide a fascinating insight into the realities of the clan system and the social conditions which allowed it to flourish.

Strengthening of Religion

The *first statute* implied that the gross ignorance and barbarity typical of the islanders arose from a lack of Protestant clergy and from the contempt in which they were held. Their numbers were to be increased and proper obedience given to them as ministers of the Reformed Church. It was agreed that their stipends should be paid regularly, any ruinous churches should be rebuilt and the Sabbath should be solemnly kept. A separate clause declared illegal the practice of secular marriage whereby liaisons were first contracted for a given number of years before they were either dissolved or the two partners entered into a more permanent union, often on the birth of a male heir. Later, an Act of Parliament in 1622 bound the chieftains to build and repair their parish churches to the satisfaction of the Bishop of the Isles. They promised to meet him at Iona to make what arrangements were need in this matter whenever he required their attendance. But even so, many parishes still wanted a minister by 1638, and few if any kirk sessions had even been established by then. Indeed, the Highlands and especially the Western Isles still remained a haven for Catholicism.

Establishment of Hostelries

The *second statute* ordained that hostelries should be established throughout the Western Isles, not just for the convenience of strangers and travellers but also to relieve their tenants and common labourers of the great burden in providing 'other idle men without any calling or vocation' with meat, drink and entertainment. It was of course a Highland tradition that hospitality was lavished without question on any stranger or fugitive, or even a sworn enemy, who cast themselves upon their protection. The provisions of this statute were augmented by the *fourth statute* which demanded that all persons, whether or not native to the Western Isles, found sorning, or living freely upon the poor inhabitants of the country by exacting hospitality by 'way of conzie', should be tried as thieves and oppressors.

This statute was almost certainly directed against the Irish practice of *buannacht*, as already described, since 'conzie' was an attempt to render the Gaelic term *coinnmheadh* into Lowland Scots. It referred to the custom whereby Highland chieftains quartered their armed retinues upon their tenantry who were compelled to provide them with food and shelter. They were in future to pay for the food and drink they consumed and for their lodgings. Later, the chieftains were required in 1616 to free their estates of all such sorners and other idle men who had no lawful occupation or regular source of income.

Curbs on the Chiefs' Households

The *third statute* sought to diminish the number of idle persons who did no labour, whether they were vagabonds or beggars without any master or indeed high-ranking members of the chief's own household. The expense of supporting such idlers commonly fell upon the tenantry as a further burden in addition to their rents which were thus lost to the Crown. It was therefore enacted that no man should reside within the Isles if he did not have a sufficient income of his own or an adequate trade or craft to support himself. James VI was evidently determined to make redundant the military retainers who constituted the chiefs' households. Indeed, he decreed in February 1609 that these household men or *buannachan* 'might be enforced either to take themselves to industry' or face banishment and transportation to the colonies. In fact, once Charles I came to the throne in 1625, many enrolled to fight in the Thirty-Years War on the continent, joining the British expeditionary forces or acting as mercenary soldiers in the Dutch and Swedish armies.

Furthermore, the chieftains agreed to restrict their private households according to their rank and estate, while each chieftain was to support his household solely by his own means without taxing his tenants. It was decreed that Hector MacLean of Duart should only be allowed to maintain eight gentlemen in his household; Angus MacDonald of Dunivaig and the Glens, Donald Gorm MacDonald of Sleat, Ruairi Mor MacLeod of Harris and Dunvegan and Donald MacDonald of Clan Ranald only six gentlemen; and all the other chieftains only three gentlemen each.

Even so, well over a century later, it seems from Edmund Burt's *Letters from the Highlands* that the great chieftains had households as large as ever, since he writes:

> When a chief goes on a journey in the hills, or makes a formal visit to an equal, he is said to be attended by all or most part of the officers following, viz: the henchman [his chief-servant]; the bard or poet; the bladier or spokesman; the gillemore, bearer of the broadsword; the gillecasflue, to carry the chief when on foot over the fords; the gille constraine, to lead the chief home in dangerous passes; the gille trusha-narnish or baggage-man; the piper, who being a gentleman I should

have named sooner. And lastly, the piper's gillie, who carries the bagpipe. There are likewise some gentlemen near of kin who bear him company; and besides a number of the common sort who have no particular employment, but follow him only to partake of the cheer.

Curbs on Drunkenness

The *fifth statute* argued that the great poverty of the Isles and the great cruelty and inhumane barbarity practised by sundry of their inhabitants upon their natural friends and neighbours was caused by their inordinate love of strong wines and aquavitae, or whisky. As the Privy Council recorded:

> The great and extraordinary excess in drinking of wine, commonly used among the commons and tenants of the Isles, is not only an occasion of the beastly and barbarous cruelties and inhumanities that fall out amongst them, to the offence and displeasure of God, and contempt of law and justice; but with that it draws numbers of them to miserable necessity and poverty, so they are constrained, when they want from their own, to take from their neighbours.

It was therefore forbidden for any merchant living within the Isles to import any wine or aquavitae for sale which could be seized by any person whomsoever without any recompense. Likewise, any native person of the Isles purchasing wine or aquavitae from a merchant on the mainland was liable to heavy fines of 40 pounds and 100 pounds for his first two offences, respectively, while he was liable to forfeit all his possessions and movable goods on committing such an offence for the third time. However, it was lawful for anyone to distil enough aquavitae for his own family, while the barons and other substantial gentlemen were allowed to purchase wine and other liquors from the Lowlands to serve their needs.

Later, the chiefs were prohibited in 1617 from consuming in their own households more than the following quantities of wine: MacDonald of Sleat, MacLean of Duart and MacLeod of Harris and Dunvegan, four tuns each; MacDonald of Clan Ranald, three tuns; and MacLean of Coll, MacLean of Lochbuie and MacKinnon of Strathordle, one tun each. Since each tun of wine was a barrelful consisting of 252 old wine-gallons, such an allowance might still be considered quite liberal. The chieftains themselves were given very strict orders to prevent their tenants from buying or drinking any wine at all, even if they were still allowed to distil their own whisky and to brew their own ale. This suggests that the regulations were more an attack upon the drinking of claret and other imported wines which enhanced the status enjoyed by clan chiefs according to the liberality of their households rather than an attempt to prevent drunkeness among his clansmen. Such consumption was also to be discouraged on financial grounds, since any wine imported from abroad represented an outflow of gold bullion causing a drain upon the Exchequer.

Another Act passed in 1622 prohibited the masters of any vessals from carrying more wine to the Isles than already allowed to the chiefs and other gentlemen. The preamble to this Act explained:

> With the insatiable desire whereof the said Islanders are so far possessed, that, when there arrives any ship or other vessal there with wines, they spend both days and nights in their excess of drinking so long as there is any of the wine left; so that, being overcome with drink, there fall out many inconveniences [feuds] amongst them, to the break of his Majesty's peace.

Matters had not greatly changed over a century later when it was said that Highland chieftains were each attended at their feasts by two servants with a wheelbarrow, whose sole task it was to cart them off to bed when they could drink no more.

Suppression of Gaelic

The *sixth statute* was perhaps the most destructive of the old ways since it was capable of being enforced. Attributing the 'ignorance and incivility' of the islanders to the lack of a good education, it required that each gentleman or yeoman possessed of more than sixty cattle should send his eldest son, or his eldest daughter if he had no sons, to school in the Lowlands or the 'incountry', which consisted of the English-speaking parts of the north of Scotland, chiefly around the shores of the Moray Firth. It was an attempt to bring the chieftains of the Western Isles to follow the practice of other landed proprietors in the Highlands who for generations had sent their children to be educated in the coastal towns of the eastern seaboard. Later, the principal chieftains were ordered in 1616 to send all their children over nine years of age to be educated in the Lowlands, where they were to be maintained until they had learnt to speak, read and write the English language. Furthermore, no child was to be served heir to his father or to become a tenant of the Crown unless he had received such an education.

Again in the words of the Privy Council:

> The chief and principal cause which had procured and procures the continuance of barbarity, impiety, and incivility within the Isles of this kingdom, has proceeded from the small care that the chiefs and principal clansmen of the Isles have had of the education and upbringing of their

children in virtue and learning; who, being careless of their duties in that point, and keeping their children still at home, where they see nothing in their tender years but the barbarous and incivil forms of the country, they are thereby made to apprehend that there are no other forms of duty and civility kept in any other part of the country; so that, when they come to the years of maturity, hardly can they be reclaimed from these barbarous, rude and incivil forms, which, for lack of instruction, were bred and settled in them in their youth: Whereas, if they had been sent to the inland [Lowlands] in their youth, and trained in virtue, learning and the English tongue, they would have been the better prepared to reform their countries, and to reduce the same to godliness, obedience, and civility.

Highland chieftains would thus be transformed by education into Lowland lairds, able to bring 'civility' to their own country.

Evidently, the Privy Council considered the speaking of Gaelic as 'one of the chief and principal causes of the continuance of barbarity and incivility among the inhabitants of the Isles'. Grammar schools were already well-established in the Lowland burghs, and afterwards scholars often attended the universities of Aberdeen, St Andrews, Glasgow and Edinburgh. Parish schools were now to be established throughout the Highlands so that the Gaelic language might be abolished in favour of the 'vulgar English tongue'. Such an education had its effects within one or two generations. When the leading men of Clan Chattan signed a Bond in 1609, half of the twenty-six signatures were made by 'hands led at the pen', but in a similar bond in 1664 there was only one signatory out of twenty-eight who could not sign his name with his own hand. Since the landed proprietors were also made responsible for establishing schools in each parish, it was only very much later that Gaelic was abolished as the language of instruction in the Highlands under the influence of the Scottish Society for the Propagation of Christian Knowledge.

Prohibition of Firearms

The *seventh statute* forbade the bearing of firearms by the islanders, 'owing to their monstrous deadly feuds', and this prohibition even extended to the shooting of deer, hares or fowls. This merely enforced an Act of Parliament which already prohibited the carrying of any firearms whatsoever throughout the kingdom under the most severe penalties. Already in 1608, the Privy Council had agreed to prohibit the use of guns, bows and two-handed swords, allowing only the use of single-handed swords and targes. Later in 1616, the principal chieftains were again prohibited from carrying pistols and hackbuts unless they were employed in the exclusive service of the

Crown. Indeed, only these chieftains and the gentlemen in their households were allowed to wear swords and armour or to carry any other weapon. However, the ban on firearms was relaxed somewhat later in the same year when James VI agreed that the chiefs and their near kinsmen might use firearms for their own sport within a mile of their dwellings. Thus, the privilege to bear arms was still enjoyed by the clan chiefs and their households, so preserving their status in the eyes of their followers.

Proscription of Gaelic Bards

The *eighth statute* was directed against the Gaelic bards and 'other idlers of that class'. The chieftains and other gentry were forbidden to patronise them, and the bards themselves were threatened, first with the stocks, and then with banishment. Their greatest offence in the eyes of the Privy Council was evidently that the Gaelic bards 'flattered' their patrons. Indeed, among their greatest achievements were the panegyric poems or eulogies, composed in praise of their patrons as the chiefs of their clan, often in the form of elegies lamenting their deaths. As John MacInnes has written in discussing *The Panegyric Code in Gaelic Poetry and Its Historical Background*: 'A subject is eulogised; he is addressed by traditional title and patronymic; his generosity and the magnificence of his household are praised; his prowess as a warrior and hunter are celebrated.' But the panegyric code in vernacular Gaelic poetry went much further than simply eulogising individuals in life and death, however worthy they were of praise. As John MacInnes has argued, the prime function of such poetry was to reinforce a sense of Gaelic identity. Indeed, in discussing two such poems from the early seventeenth century, he comments that their authors seem more concerned to express their own feelings, not so much for the dead who had fallen in battle, but for the social order to which they had all belonged. Moreover, the poems appear not so much a lament for the passing of such an aristocratic way of life as an attempt to prolong its very existence by simply reciting its virtues. It is perhaps hardly surprising that the Privy Council was determined on the proscription of such inflammatory propaganda.

But just as the necessity laid upon the chieftains to educate their children in the English language struck at the very heart of the Gaelic language and its culture of bardic poetry, so did this statute. Even so, it is doubtful if more than four bardic schools of any professional standing still flourished under the patronage of particular chiefs at this time. Indeed, it seems the regulation was directed more against the bands of itinerant players and vagabonds, whose activities had been proscribed for more than a century as little more than able-bodied vagrancy.

Appearance before the Privy Council

The *ninth statute* made provision for enforcing all the previous Statutes of Iona. Now known as the Gentlemen of the Isles, the chieftains were each made answerable for the good conduct of all their followers with powers to punish them if they contravened the Statutes. Moreover, they had to appear each year in Edinburgh before the Privy Council to report upon their own conduct and the exercise of their obligations, including the all-important collection of the Crown rents. The chieftains were each made responsible under heavy cautions not only for their own good conduct but for the behaviour of all the other chieftains as well, so that they were expected to police each other's actions. If they failed to do so, they could be put to the horn with all the penalties that entailed.

However, these provisions evidently proved inadequate since the Privy Council took further measures in 1616. By then, the principal chieftains were required to appear every year before the Privy Council on 10 July. They had then to exhibit a certain number of their principal kinsmen, chosen from a list given to the Privy Council. Required to account as well for their clan being 'reduced to civility', their kinsmen could be held as hostages in Edinburgh if the Privy Council was not satisfied until matters were remedied. Several chieftains bound themselves together under heavy penalties to observe these various provisions rather than seek sureties from elsewhere.

Already in 1614, MacLean of Duart, MacDonald of Sleat and MacLeod of Harris and Dunvegan had each to find 10,000 merks in security that they would keep the peace and 5,000 merks caution that they would appear before the Privy Council each year, while MacKinnon of Strathordle and MacLean of Lochbuie had each to find 5,000 merks and 3,000 merks for the same purposes. It was evidently intended that they would make regular payments of feu-duties and other dues that they owed the Crown for their lands. After 1616, the stipulation that the Gentlemen of the Isles attend the Privy Council in Edinburgh was strictly enforced, with only an occasional remission for special circumstances, until the outbreak of the Covenanting Movement in 1638.

'Civil and Comely' Residences

Further civilising influences were proposed in 1616. The chieftains were each to reside at a fixed place as agreed with the Privy Council. If there was no dwelling-house appropriate to their rank at these places, they were to build without delay 'civil and comely' houses or repair any suitable for the purpose if they were ruinous. Moreover, they were to plant policies around their residences, as well as taking mains or home-farms into their own hands. They were then to cultivate these farms, so that 'they might thereby be exercised and eschew idleness'. MacDonald of Clan Ranald, who had no land suitable for a home-farm near his Castle of Eilean Tioram, chose instead the lands of Hobeg on the island of Uist. The chiefs were then to let out the rest of their lands to tenants at a fixed rent, without any other exactions.

Taking of Calps Made Illegal

The taking of *calps* was made illegal in 1617, even if the practice continued for long afterwards. It was a payment made in kind to a chieftain or landlord on the death of a clansman, consisting of his best cow, ox or horse. It marked the repayment of a debt for the protection that the chieftain had offered him during his lifetime. However, since more than one chief or landlord often made conflicting claims upon such a bereaved family, it was a cause of great injustice since four or five animals might have to be surrendered on the occasion of a single death.

Finally, it was decreed that no single chief should keep more than one birlinn, lymphad or galley of sixteen or eighteen oars, given the supremacy of the English navy, and that they should not oppress the common people in their voyages throughout the Isles. Indeed, it had already been established in 1608 that the proper use for such vessals was to carry His Majesty's rents in kind to the mainland.

State of the Highlands after 1625

The political aims of James VI in promulgating the Statutes of Iona, along with the subsequent regulations of the Privy Council in 1616, were largely achieved by the time he had died in 1625. By then, or soon after the accession of Charles I, nearly all the major feuds had been settled in the Highlands and the Western Isles, often to the advantage of the Campbells, Earls of Argyll, or the cadet branches of their family. Only the disputes between the MacIntoshes of Clan Chattan, the Camerons of Locheil and the MacDonalds of Keppoch continued to disturb the peace in Lochaber for much of the seventeenth century, while the aggrandisement of the Campbells against the MacLeans of Duart had yet to erupt in the second half of the century.

Indeed, the years after 1625 were peaceful at first, except that John MacDonald, now Captain of Clan Ranald after the death of his father in 1618, was charged by the Privy Council with allowing a ship from Leith to be plundered of her cargo. Then in 1630, the feud between the Crichtons of Frendraught and the Gordons of Rothiemay culminated in the burning of

Frendraught Castle, when Huntly's son John Gordon, Lord Aboyne, lost his life along with five others. The Gordons were convinced that James Crichton of Frendraught was responsible for burning down his own castle where he had entertained the victims of the fire on the previous evening. But he was not brought to justice, and indeed another was charged with the crime, so the Gordons took the law into their own hands. They raided Frendraught's lands and threatened his servants and tenants to such an extent that he was forced to seek the protection of the Privy Council in 1633.

Although there was apparently serious disorder in the Highlands before the burning of Frendraught, it afterwards became very much worse. Indeed, it was reported to the Privy Council in 1633:

> Disorders are growing to that height that almost nowhere in the north country can any of his Majesty's subjects promise safety to their persons or men, the break of his Majesty's peace in these parts being so universal and fearful as the very burghs and towns themselves are in continual danger and fear of some sudden surprise by fire or otherways from their broken men.

Among these outlaws were members of 'Clan Gregor, Clan Lachlan, Clan Ranald, and other broken clans in Lochaber, Strathdon, Glencoe, Braemar, and other parts of the Highlands, as also divers of the name of Gordon and their dependants and followers'. Earlier, the Privy Council had learnt in 1631 that 'numbers of broken and lawless lymmars [outlaws] of the Clan Gregor and other broken clans, who by the force of his Majesty's authority were some few years bygone reduced to the obedience of law and justice' had broken loose in Menteith and Strathearn.

The government first reacted to this state of anarchy by putting into effect the Act of 1594, requiring all landlords and baillies in the Highlands to find caution for the good behaviour of all the persons in their 'obedience'. Then, after the visit of Charles I to Scotland in 1633, the Privy Council charged all those interested in maintaining law and order to report to the Lord Chancellor the names of all those outlaws known to them and the crimes with which they were charged. Two years later, the measure that had been so successful in the Western Isles was also applied to the Highlands whereby all landlords were required to appear before the Privy Council to give a pledge for the lawful behaviour of their dependants. However, the Highland landlords proved more refractory than the Gentlemen of the Isles, since several were denounced as rebels and outlaws when they failed to appear before the Privy Council despite repeated summonses.

Whether these measures were enough to restore the king's peace to the Highlands will never be known since they were overtaken by more momentous events which culminated in the signing of the National Covenant in February 1638. Nine months later, Archibald Campbell, eighth Earl and afterwards first Marquis of Argyll, had placed himself at the head of the Presbyterian party as the foremost supporter of the Covenant. Thus, when James Graham, Earl of Montrose, belatedly raised his standard on behalf of Charles I in 1644, it was almost inevitable that the Highland clans who had so suffered from the territorial aggrandisement of the Campbells, Earls of Argyll, should rally to the royalist cause. Chief among them were the MacDonalds of Antrim and all the other branches of Clan Donald still in existence, along with nearly all the clans that had once owed allegiance to the MacDonalds, Lords of the Isles.

Indeed, the Marquis of Hamilton advised the king in June 1638 that the clans of the western seaboard would join the Royalist cause 'not say for any great affection they carry to your Majesty, but because of their spleen to Lorne [afterwards eigthth Earl of Argyll] and will do if they durst just contrary to what his men do.' Given the espousal of the Protestant religion by Archibald Campbell, eighth Earl of Argyll, and his descendants, and the adherence of James VII of Scotland to the Catholic religion, it would be a bitter division that persisted until the final defeat of the Jacobite clans at the Battle of Culloden in 1746.

GENEALOGICAL TABLES

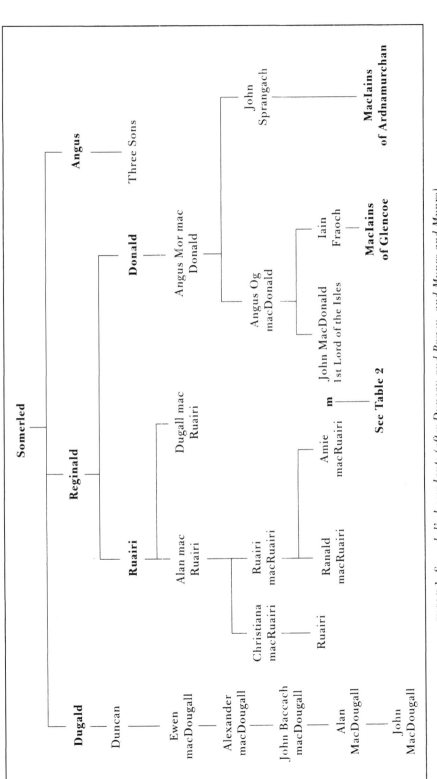

TABLE 1 *Somerled's descendants (after Duncan and Brown, and Munro and Munro).*

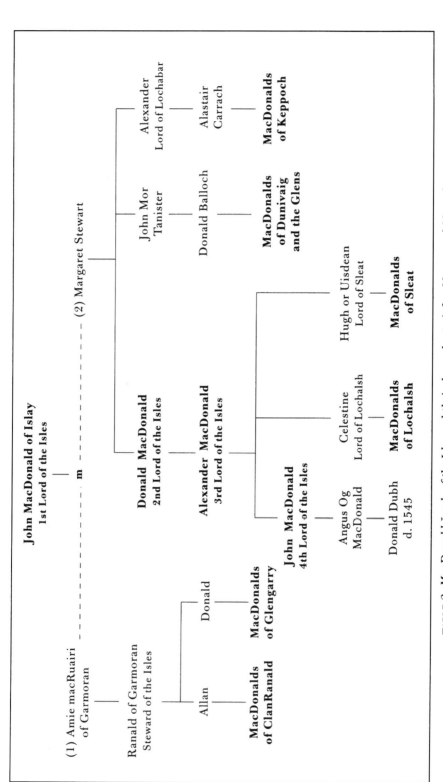

TABLE 2 *MacDonald Lords of the Isles and their descendants (after Munro and Munro)*

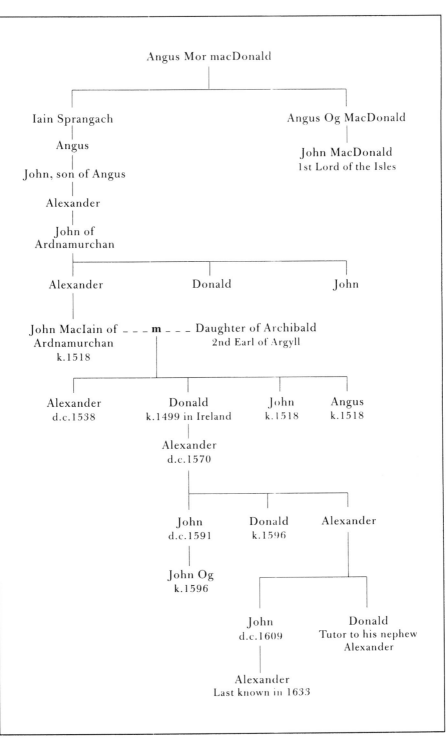

TABLE 3 *MacIains of Ardnamurchan (after MacDonald of Castleton, and Steer and Bannerman).*

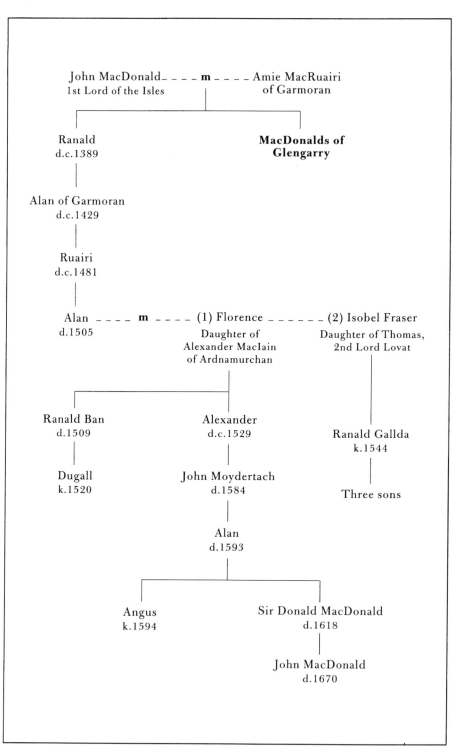

TABLE 4 *MacDonalds of ClanRanald (after MacDonald of Castleton, and Munro and Munro).*

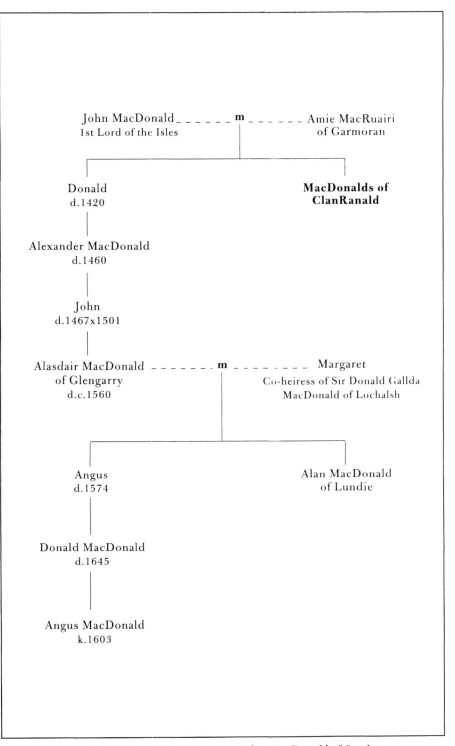

TABLE 5 *MacDonalds of Glengarry (after MacDonald of Castleton, and Munro and Munro).*

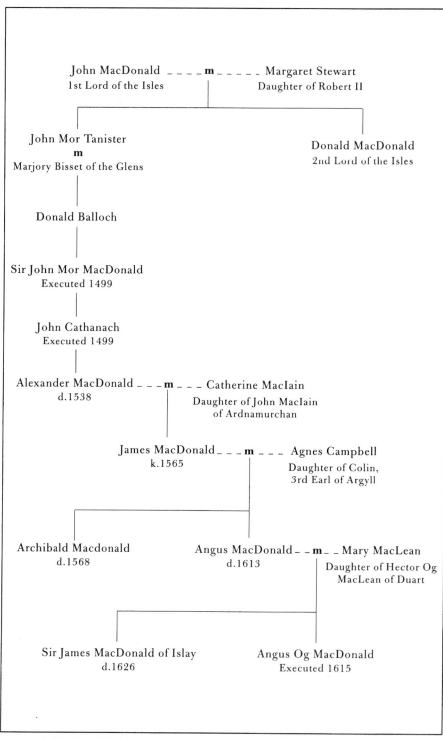

TABLE 6 *MacDonalds of Dunivaig and the Glens (after MacDonald of Castleton, and Munro and Munro).*

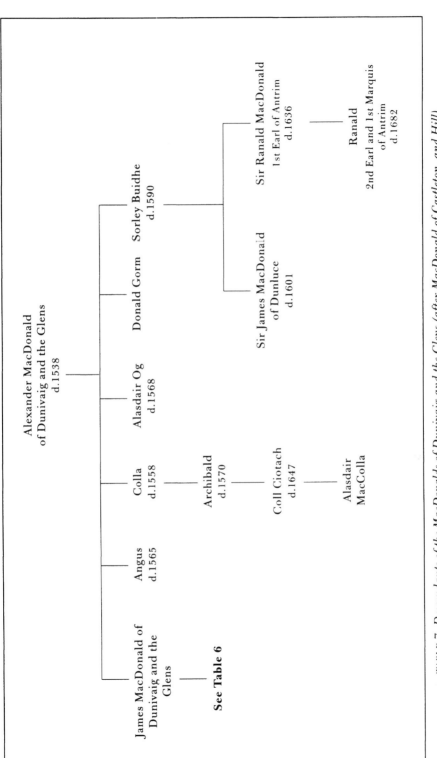

TABLE 7 *Descendants of the MacDonalds of Dunivaig and the Glens (after MacDonald of Castleton, and Hill).*

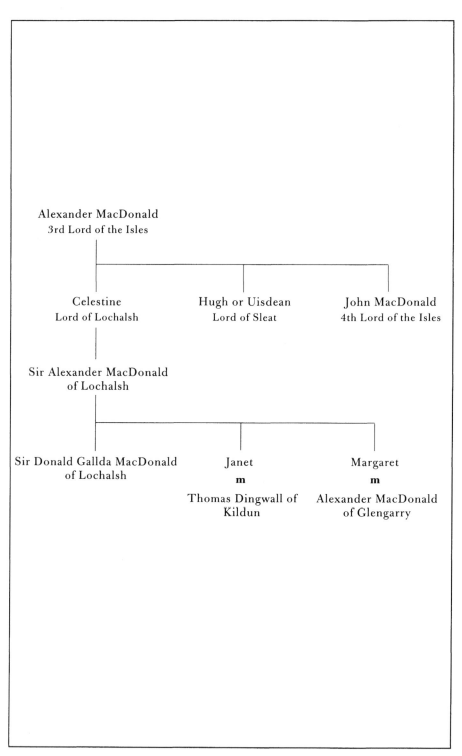

Alexander MacDonald
3rd Lord of the Isles

Celestine
Lord of Lochalsh

Hugh or Uisdean
Lord of Sleat

John MacDonald
4th Lord of the Isles

Sir Alexander MacDonald
of Lochalsh

Sir Donald Gallda MacDonald
of Lochalsh

Janet
m

Thomas Dingwall of
Kildun

Margaret
m

Alexander MacDonald
of Glengarry

TABLE 8 *MacDonalds of Lochalsh (after MacDonald of Castleton,
and Munro and Munro).*

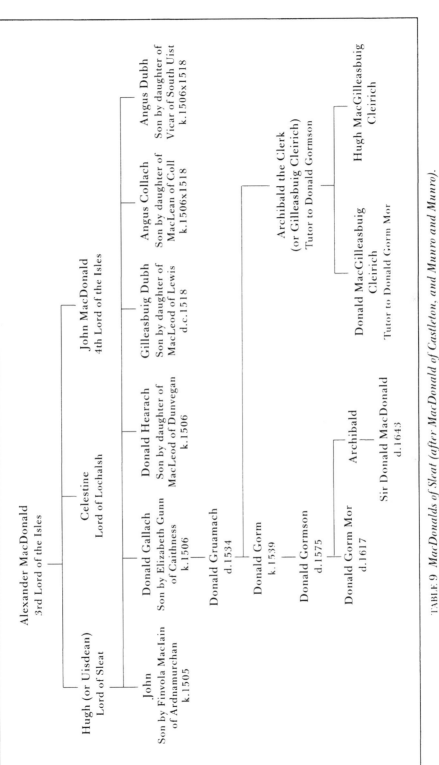

TABLE 9 *MacDonalds of Sleat (after MacDonald of Castleton, and Munro and Munro).*

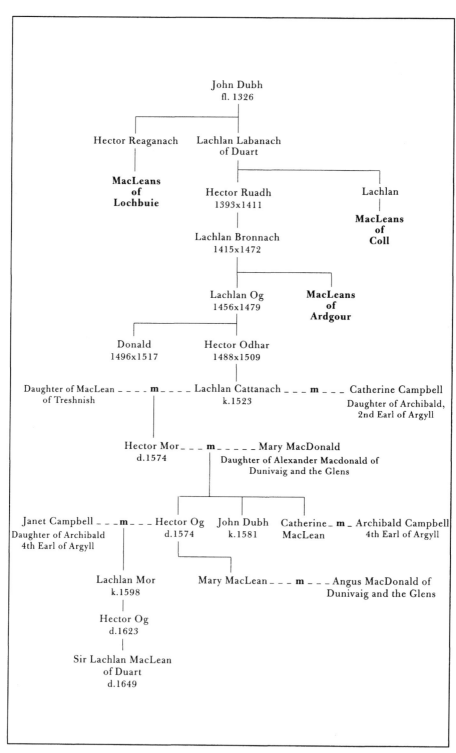

TABLE 10 *MacLeans of Duart (after Maclean-Bristol).*

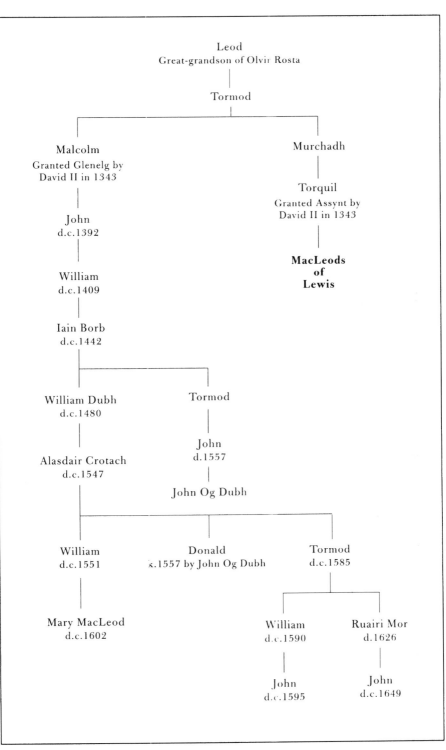

TABLE 11 *MacLeods of Harris and Dunvegan (after MacKinnon and Morrison, Steer and Bannerman, and Matheson).*

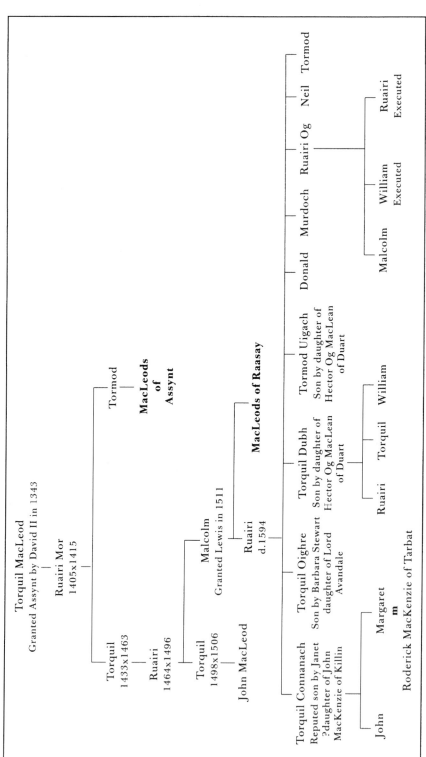

TABLE 12 *MacLeods of Lewis (after MacKinnon and Morrison, and Matheson).*

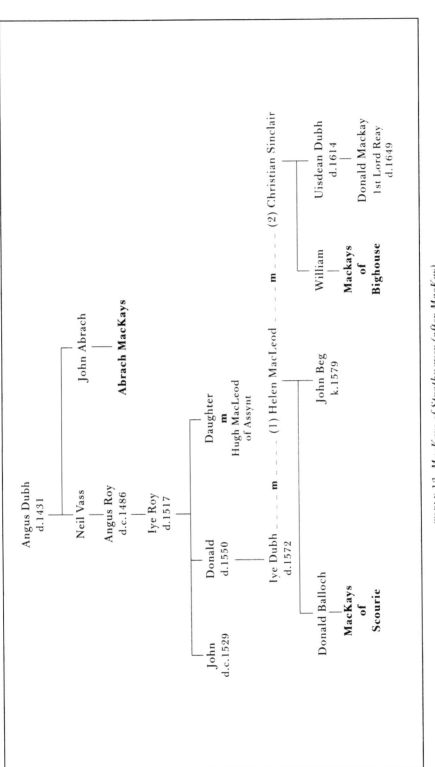

TABLE 13 *MacKays of Strathnaver (after MacKay).*

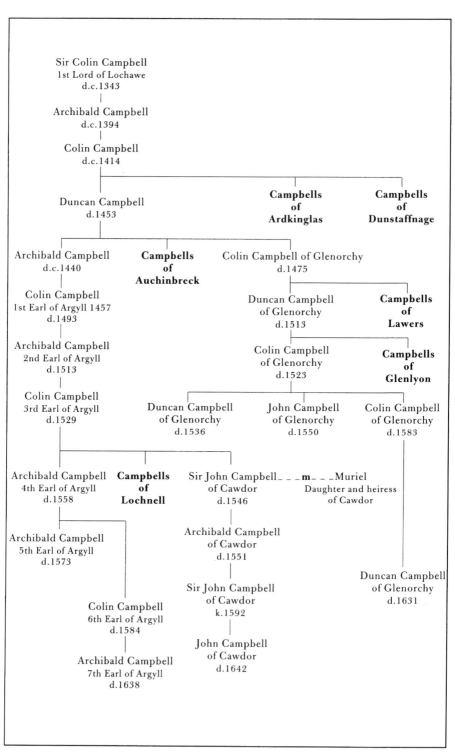

TABLE 14 *Campbells, Earls of Argyll (after* The Scots Peerage*).*

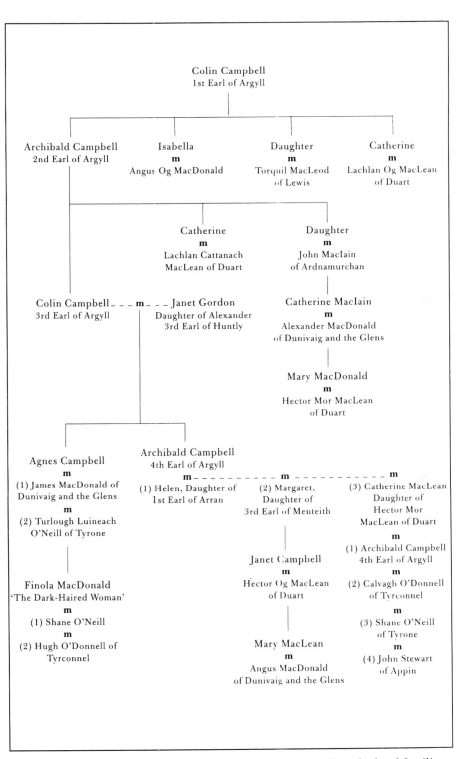

TABLE 15 *Marriage alliances of the Campbells, Earls of Argyll, and related families (after* The Scots Peerage*).*

BIBLIOGRAPHY

There are few modern works which deal as a whole with the period of Highland history covered by the present book. Although virtually unchanged from the first edition of 1836, the best source still remains D. Gregory, *History of the Western Highlands and Isles* (Edinburgh, 2nd edn, 1881, reprinted 1975), augmented by D. Mitchell, *History of the Highlands and Gaelic Scotland* (Paisley, 1900). W. C. MacKenzie, *The Highlands and Isles of Scotland: A Historical Survey* (Edinburgh, 2nd edn, 1949), in dealing with the events of the sixteenth century, has recently been superseded with regard to the history of Clan Donald in Ulster by the meticulous account of J. M. Hill, *Fire and Sword: Sorley Boy MacDonnell and the Rise of Clan Iain Mor, 1538–1590* (London, 1993). W. R. Kermack, *The Scottish Highlands: a Short History, c.300–1746* (Edinburgh, 1957), although admirable, is all too concise. The detailed interpretation by A. Cunningham, *The Loyal Clans* (Cambridge, 1932), discusses Highland history in terms of a simplistic distinction between feudalism and clanship which cannot be sustained. More popular treatments of Highland history are provided by R. W. Munro, *Highland Clans and Tartans* (London, 1977), and Fitzroy MacLean, *Highlanders: A History of the Highland Clans* (London, 1995), among others. J. L. Roberts, *Lost Kingdoms: Celtic Scotland and the Middle Ages* (Edinburgh, 1997), provides a wide-ranging introduction to the political history of Gaeldom prior to the forfeiture of the Lordship of the Isles in 1493, but his book did not take account of two recent articles by S. Boardman and M. Brown on the Badenoch Stewarts (see below under *Military History*).

Biography and Family History

An invaluable guide to the bibliography of Scottish family history is provided by M. Stuart, *Scottish Family History* (Edinburgh, 1930), supplemented by J. P. S. Ferguson, *Scottish Family Histories* (Edinburgh, 2nd edn, 1986).

Biographical details of the Scottish nobility and their antecedents are given by J. Balfour Paul, *The Scottish Peerage* (Edinburgh, 1904-14, 9 vols), augmented by the Royal Historical Society's *Handbook of British Chronology* (1986, 3rd edn by E. B. Fryde).

The standard history of Clan Donald is given in three volumes by A. MacDonald and A. MacDonald, *The Clan Donald* (Inverness, 1896-1904), but D. J. MacDonald of Castleton, *Clan Donald* (Loanhead, 1978) provides a more accessible account if used with caution. See also J. Munro and R. W.Munro, *Acts of the Lords of the Isles* (Scottish History Society, 1986), for biographical details of the various septs of Clan Donald. The excellent account of the MacLeods by I. F. Grant, *The MacLeods: The History of a Clan 1200-1956* (London, 1959), may be augmented by D. MacKinnon and A. Morrison, *The MacLeods: The Genealogy of a Clan* (Edinburgh, 1969-77, 5 vols). W. Matheson, 'The Ancestry of the MacLeods', and 'The MacLeods of Lewis', *Transactions of the Gaelic Society of Inverness*, **51**, 1981, discusses their origins. Two earlier accounts of the MacLeans, namely J. P. MacLean, *A History of Clan MacLean* (Cincinnati, Ohio, 1899), and A. MacLean-Sinclair, *The Clan Gillean* (Charlottetown, Nova Scotia, 1899), have recently been superseded by N. Maclean-Bristol. *Warriors and Priests: The History of Clan MacLean 1300-1570* (East Linton, Scotland, 1995). See also J. P. MacLean, *History of the Island of Mull* (Greenville, Ohio, 1923-5, 2 vols), and N. Maclean-Bristol, 'The MacLeans from 1560-1707: A Reappraisal', in L. MacLean (ed.), *The Seventeenth Century in the Highlands* (Inverness, 1986). The history of the MacKenzies is well documented by A. MacKenzie, *History of the MacKenzies* (Inverness, 2nd edn, 1894), while A. MacKay, *The Book of MacKay* (Edinburgh, 1906), deals with the MacKays. Apart from the detailed account by A. G. M. MacGregor, *History of the Clan Gregor: Volume One, AD 878-1628* (Edinburgh, 1898), W. R. Kermack, *The Clan MacGregor* (Edinburgh and London, 1953), gives a brief account of the MacGregors which may be supplemented by A. Cunningham, *The Loyal Clans* (Cambridge, 1932). No adequate account exists for the Campbells, Earls of Argyll, apart from the articles by J. E. A. Dawson, 'The Fifth Earl of Argyll, Gaelic Lordship and Political Power in Sixteenth-century Scotland', *Scottish Historical Review*, **67**, 1988, and E. J. Cowan, 'Fishers in Drumlie Waters: Clanship and Campbell Expansion in the Time of Gillesbuig Grumach', *Transactions of the Gaelic Society of Inverness*, **54**, 1986, and 'Clanship, Kinship and the Campbell Acquisition of Islay', *Scottish Historical Review*, **58**, 1979. See also the important paper by W. Gillies, 'Some Aspects of Campbell History', *Transactions of the Gaelic Society of Inverness*, **50**, 1978, stressing their position within the Gaelic-speaking world.

Aspects of Military History

The origins of the Highland galloglasses in Ireland is discussed by A. MacKerral, 'West Highland Mercenaries in Ireland', *Scottish Historical Review*, **30**, 1951, but see also G. A. Hayes-McCoy, *Scots Mercenary Forces in Ireland 1565–1603* (London, 1937), and K. Simms, 'Gaelic Warfare in the Middle Ages', in T. Bartlett and K. Jeffrey (eds), *A Military History of Ireland* (Cambridge, 1996), and *From Kings to Warlords: The Changing Political Structures of Gaelic Ireland in the Later Middle Ages* (Woodbridge, 1987). The military basis of lordship as exercised in the central Highlands during the late fourteenth century by Alexander Stewart, 'Wolf of Badenoch', and his son Alexander Stewart, Earl of Mar, is discussed by S. Boardman, 'Lordship in the North-East: The Badenoch Stewarts I; Alexander Stewart, Earl of Buchan, Lord of Badenoch', *Northern Scotland*, **16**, 1996, and M. Brown, 'Regional Lordship in the North-East: The Badenoch Stewarts II; Alexander Stewart, Earl of Mar', *Northern Scotland*, **16**, 1996, whose accounts form the basis of Chapter 1 of the present book.

Clanship and Society

The nature and economic basis of the clan system is described by several authors such as I. F. Grant, *The Social and Economic Development of Scotland before 1603* (Edinburgh, 1930), A. I. MacInnes, *Clanship, Commerce, and the House of Stuart, 1603–1788* (East Linton, Scotland, 1996), and R. A. Dodgshon, *From Chiefs to Landlords: Social and Economic Change in the Western Highlands and Islands, c.1493–1820* (Edinburgh, 1998), while the introductory chapters in T. C. Smout, *A History of the Scottish People, 1560–1830* (Glasgow, 1969), D. Stevenson, *Alasdair MacColla and the Highland Problem in the Seventeenth Century* (Edinburgh, 1980), P. Hopkins, *Glencoe and the End of the Highland War* (Edinburgh, 1986), and T. Devine, *Clanship to Crofter's War* (Manchester, 1994), all consider the nature of the clan system as it existed towards the end of our period. The marriage customs in Gaelic society are discussed in an important paper by W. D. H. Sellar, 'Marriage, Divorce and Concubinage in Gaelic Scotland', *Transactions of the Gaelic Society of Inverness*, **51**, 1981, while J. MacInnes, 'The Panegyric Code in Gaelic Poetry and its Historical Background', *Transactions of the Gaelic Society of Inverness*, **50**, 1978, discusses the mores underlying the clan system.

Local History

Apart from Gregory (1836), there are only a few local histories which usefully augment the family and clan histories already mentioned. Among them are W. D. Lamont, *The Early History of Islay* (Dundee, 1966), and A. MacKay, *The History of the Province of Cat* (Wick, 1914), dealing with Caithness and Sutherland, and W. C. MacKenzie, *History of the Outer Hebrides* (Paisley, 1903), and A. Nicholson, *The History of Skye* (Glasgow, 1930).

Articles and Monographs

This period of Highland history has attracted little attention from Scottish historians. K. Brown, *Bloodfeud in Scotland 1573–1625* (Edinburgh, 1986), although mostly concerned with Lowland Scotland, has a chapter dealing with the feud between the Earls of Huntly and Moray, while J. Wormald, *Lords and Men in Scotland* (Edinburgh, 1985), lists the bonds of manrent made between various Highland chiefs, among others. The political background to the activities of the MacDonalds of Dunivaig and the Glens in Ulster is reviewed by J. E. A. Dawson, 'Two Kingdoms or Three? Ireland in Anglo-Scottish Relations in the Middle of the Sixteenth Century', in R. A. Mason (ed.), *Scotland and England 1286–1815* (Edinburgh, 1987), who stresses the role played by Archibald Campbell, fifth Earl of Argyll, and by H. Morgan, 'The End of Gaelic Ulster: A Thematic Interpretation of Events between 1534 and 1610', *Irish Historical Studies*, **26**, 1988.

Additional References

Bannerman, J. W. M. (1977). 'The Lordship of the Isles: Historical Background, in K. A. Steer and J. W. M. Bannerman (eds), *Late Medieval Sculpture in the Western Highlands* (Edinburgh).

Barrow, G. W. S. (1973). 'The Highlands during the Lifetime of Robert the Bruce', in G. W. S. Barrow (ed.), *The Kingdom of the Scots* (London).

Munro, J. M. (1981). 'The Lordship of the Isles', in L. MacLean (ed.), *The Middle Ages in the Highlands* (Inverness).

Sellar, W. D. H. (1973). *The Earliest Campbells – Normans, Britons or Gaels*. Scottish Studies, 17, 109–25.

INDEX

Printed in the USA/Agawam, MA
January 25, 2011

556313.015